Investment
Guarantees

Founded in 1807, John Wiley & Sons is the oldest independent publishing company in the United States. With offices in North America, Europe, Australia, and Asia, Wiley is globally committed to developing and marketing print and electronic products and services for our customers' professional and personal knowledge and understanding.

The Wiley Finance series contains books written specifically for finance and investment professionals as well as sophisticated individual investors and their financial advisors. Book topics range from portfolio management to e-commerce, risk management, financial engineering, valuation and financial instrument analysis, as well as much more.

For a list of available titles, visit our Web site at www.WileyFinance.com.

Investment
Guarantees

Modeling and Risk Management for Equity-Linked Life Insurance

MARY HARDY

WILEY

John Wiley & Sons, Inc.

This book is printed on acid-free paper. ⊗

Copyright © 2003 by Mary Hardy. All rights reserved.

Published by John Wiley & Sons, Inc., Hoboken, New Jersey.
Published simultaneously in Canada.

No part of this publication may be reproduced, stored in a retrieval system, or transmitted in any form or by any means, electronic, mechanical, photocopying, recording, scanning, or otherwise, except as permitted under Section 107 or 108 of the 1976 United States Copyright Act, without either the prior written permission of the Publisher, or authorization through payment of the appropriate per-copy fee to the Copyright Clearance Center, Inc., 222 Rosewood Drive, Danvers, MA 01928, 978-750-8400, fax 978-750-4470, or on the web at www.copyright.com. Requests to the Publisher for permission should be addressed to the Permissions Department, John Wiley & Sons, Inc., 111 River Street, Hoboken, NJ 07030, 201-748-6011, fax 201-748-6008, e-mail: permcoordinator@wiley.com.

Limit of Liability/Disclaimer of Warranty: While the publisher and author have used their best efforts in preparing this book, they make no representations or warranties with respect to the accuracy or completeness of the contents of this book and specifically disclaim any implied warranties of merchantability or fitness for a particular purpose. No warranty may be created or extended by sales representatives or written sales materials. The advice and strategies contained herein may not be suitable for your situation. You should consult with a professional where appropriate. Neither the publisher nor author shall be liable for any loss of profit or any other commercial damages, including but not limited to special, incidental, consequential, or other damages.

For general information on our other products and services, or technical support, please contact our Customer Care Department within the United States at 800-762-2974, outside the United States at 317-572-3993 or fax 317-572-4002.

Wiley also publishes its books in a variety of electronic formats. Some content that appears in print may not be available in electronic books.

For more information about Wiley products, visit our web site at www.wiley.com.

Library of Congress Cataloging-in-Publication Data:

Hardy, Mary, 1958-
      Investment guarantees : modeling and risk management for equity-linked life insurance / Mary Hardy.
           p. cm. – (Wiley finance series)
      Includes bibliographical references and index.
      ISBN 0-471-39290-1 (cloth : alk. paper)
        1. Insurance, Life-mathematical models. 2. Risk management–Mathematical models.
      1. title. II. Series.

      HG8781.H313 2003
      368.32'0068'1–dc21   2002034200

10 9 8 7 6 5 4 3 2 1

Acknowledgments

This work has been supported by the National Science and Engineering Research Council of Canada, and by the Actuarial Education and Research Fund. I would also like to thank the members of the Department of Statistics at the London School of Economics and Political Science for their hospitality while the book was being completed, especially Anthony Atkinson, Angelos Dassios, Martin Knott, and Ragnar Norberg.

I would like to thank Taylor and Francis, publishers of the Scandinavian Actuarial Journal, for permission to reproduce material from *Bayesian Risk Management for Equity-Linked Insurance* in Chapter 5.

I learned a great deal from my fellow members of the magnificent Canadian Institute of Actuaries Task Force on Segregated Funds. In particular, I would like to thank Geoffrey Hancock, who has provided invaluable advice and assistance during the preparation of this book. Also, thanks to Martin Le Roux, David Gilliland, and the two Chairs, Simon Curtis and Murray Taylor, who had a lot to put up with, not least from me.

I have been very lucky to work with some wonderful colleagues and students over the years, many of whom have contributed directly or indirectly to this book. In particular, thanks to Andrew Cairns, Julia Wirch, David Wilkie, Judith Chan, Karen Chau, Geoff Thiessen, Yuan Tao, So-Yuen Kim, Anping Wang, Boyang Liu, Harry Panjer, and Sheauwen Yang. Thanks also to Glen Harris, who introduced me to regime-switching models. It is a special privilege to work with Ken Seng Tan at the University of Waterloo and with Howard Waters at Heriot-Watt University.

My brother, Peter Hardy, worked with me to prepare the RSLN software (Hardy and Hardy 2002), which is a useful complement to this work. It was good fun working with him.

Mostly I would like to express my deepest gratitude to my husband, Phelim Boyle, for his unstinting encouragement, support, and patience; culinary contributions; and unwavering readiness to share with me his encyclopedic knowledge of finance.

M. H.

Contents

Introduction

This book is designed for all practitioners working in equity-linked insurance, whether in product design, marketing, pricing and valuation, or risk management. It is written with actuaries in mind, but it should also be interesting to other investment professionals. The material in this book forms the basis of a one-semester graduate course for students of actuarial science, insurance, and finance. The aim is to provide a comprehensive and self-contained introduction to modeling and risk management for equity-linked life insurance. A feature of the book is the combination of econometric analysis of investment models with their application in pricing and risk management.

The focus is on the stochastic modeling of embedded guarantees that depend on equity performance. In the major part of the book the contracts that are used to illustrate the methods are single premium, separate account products. This class includes variable annuities in the United States, segregated fund contracts in Canada, and unit-linked contracts in the United Kingdom. The investment guarantees associated with this type of product are usually payable contingent on the policyholder's death, and in some cases also apply to survival benefits. For these contracts, the insurer's liability at the expiry of the contract is the excess, if any, of the guaranteed minimum payout and the amount of the policyholder's separate account. Generally, the probability of the guarantee actually resulting in a benefit is small. In the language of finance, we say that the guarantees are usually deep out-of-the-money. In the past this has led to a certain complacency, but it is now recognized that the risk management of these contracts represents a major challenge to insurers, particularly where the investment guarantee applies to maturity benefits, and where separate account products have proved popular with policyholders.

This book took shape as a result of my membership in the Canadian Institute of Actuaries Task Force on Segregated Fund contracts. After that Task Force completed its report, there was a clear demand for some educational material to help actuaries understand the methods that were recommended in the report, and that were subsequently mandated by the regulators. Also, many actuaries and regulators in the United States took a great interest in the report, and the demand for relevant educational material began to come also from across the United States. Meanwhile, in the United

Kingdom, it was becoming clear that investment guarantees associated with annuitization were creating a crisis in the industry.

Much of the material in this book is not new; there are many excellent texts available on time series modeling, on financial engineering, and on the principles of stochastic simulation, for example. There are numerous papers available on the pricing of investment guarantees in insurance, from the financial engineering viewpoint. The objective of this work is to put all the relevant models and methods that are useful in the risk management of equity-linked insurance into a single volume, and to focus specifically on the parts of the theory that are most relevant. This also enables us to develop the theory into practical methods for insurance companies, and to illustrate these with specific reference to equity linked contracts.

There are two common approaches to risk management of equity-linked insurance, particularly separate account products such as variable annuities or segregated funds. The "actuarial" approach uses the distribution of the guarantee liabilities discounted at the risk-free rate of interest. The dynamic-hedging approach uses financial engineering, and assumes that a portfolio of bonds and stocks is used to replicate the guarantee payoff. The replicating portfolio must be rebalanced at frequent intervals, as the underlying stock price changes. The actuarial approach is commonly used for risk management of investment guarantees by insurance companies in North America and in the United Kingdom. The dynamic-hedging approach is used by financial engineers in banks and hedge funds, and occasionally in insurance companies. It has been the case since the earliest equity-linked contracts were issued that many practitioners who use one of these methods harbor a deep distrust of the other method, often based on a lack of understanding of the other side's methodology.

In this book both approaches are presented, discussed, and extensively illustrated with examples. This should help practitioners on either side of the fence talk to each other, at the very least. My own view is that both methods have their merits, and that the best approach is to use both, in appropriate combination.

I have included in Chapter 7 an introduction to the concepts of no-arbitrage pricing, replication, and the risk-neutral measure. I am aware that many people who read this book will be very familiar with this material, but I am also aware of a great deal of misunderstanding surrounding these very fundamental issues. For example, there are many actuaries working with investment guarantees who do not fully comprehend the role of the Q-measure. By focusing solely on the important concepts, I hope to facilitate a better understanding of the financial economics approach. In order to keep the book to a manageable project, I have not generally included the complication of stochastic interest rates, except in Chapter 12, where it is necessary to explain the annuitization liability under the guaranteed annuity option (GAO) contract. This is often dealt with in the more technical literature on equity-linked insurance, such as Persson and Aase (1994) and Lin and Tan (2001).

The book is presented in a progressive, linear structure, starting with models, progressing through modeling, and finally moving on to risk management. In more detail, the structure of the book is as follows.

The first chapter introduces the contracts and some of the basic ideas from financial economics that will be utilized in later chapters. The next four chapters cover some of the econometrics of modeling equity processes.

In Chapter 2, we introduce a number of families of models that have been proposed for equity returns.

In Chapter 3, we discuss parameter estimation for some of the models, using maximum likelihood estimation (MLE). We also discuss ways of using the likelihood to rank the appropriateness of the models for the data.

Because MLE tends to fit the center of the distribution, and may not fit the tails particularly well for some processes, in Chapter 4 we discuss how to adjust the maximum likelihood parameters to improve the fit in other parts of the distribution. This may be important where the far tail of the equity return distribution is critical in the distribution of the investment guarantee payout. This chapter, incidentally, explains how to satisfy the calibration requirements of the Canadian Institute of Actuaries task force report on segregated funds (SFTF 2000).

Chapter 5 describes how to use the Markov chain Monte Carlo (MCMC) method for parameter estimation. This is a Bayesian method for parameter estimation that provides a powerful method for assessing parameter uncertainty.

Having decided on a model for equity returns, and estimated appropriate parameters, we can start to model the investment guarantees. In Chapter 6, we explain how to use stochastic simulation to model the distribution of the liability outgo for an equity-linked contract. This is the basis of the actuarial approach to risk management.

We then move on to the dynamic-hedging approach. This needs some elementary results from financial economics, which are presented in Chapter 7.

Then, in Chapter 8, we apply the methods to investment guarantees. This chapter goes beyond the pure pricing information provided by the Black-Scholes-Merton framework. We also assess the liability that is not covered by the Black-Scholes hedge. The three sources of this unhedged liability are

1. Transactions costs from rebalancing the hedge.
2. Hedging errors arising from discrete hedging intervals.
3. Additional hedging costs arising from the use of realistic equity models, under which the Black-Scholes hedge is no longer self-financing.

In Chapter 9, we discuss how to use risk measures to quantify the tail risk from a distribution; risk measures can also be used for pricing. The most common risk measure in finance is value at risk (VaR). This is a quantile risk measure. More recent theory favors the conditional tail expectation risk measure, also known as Tail-VaR. Both are described in Chapter 9, with examples of application to benefits such as variable annuities and segregated funds.

Chapter 10 describes stochastic emerging cost modeling. This allows us to bring together the actuarial and dynamic-hedging approaches and compare them in a systematic way. Emerging cost modeling is a powerful tool for making decisions about policy design, pricing, and risk management.

Because stochastic simulation is the fundamental tool for analyzing the liabilities for equity-linked insurance, it is useful to discuss the error and uncertainty associated with the method and to consider ways to reduce the variability of results. In Chapter 11, we examine three sources of forecast uncertainty. The first is random sampling variation. It is possible to reduce the effect of this using variance reduction techniques, and these are described with examples where they are useful in modeling embedded investment guarantees. The second is uncertainty in parameter estimation; this is where the Bayesian approach of Chapter 5 is particularly useful. We discuss how to apply Bayesian methods to quantify the effect of parameter uncertainty. Finally, we discuss model uncertainty—that is, how to assess the risk from the possibility that stock returns in the future follow a different model than that used in forecasts.

The final two chapters expand the application of the methods to two different types of equity-linked contracts. The first is the U.K. unit-linked contract with guaranteed annuity option (GAO). This has similarities with the guaranteed minimum income benefit associated with some variable annuity contracts. Issued in the early 1980s, at a time of very high long-term interest rates, the problems of stochastic interest rates and lack of diversification of risk associated with investment guarantees are, unfortunately, exemplified in the serious problems experienced by a number of U.K. insurers arising from maturing GAO contracts. Chapter 12 discusses the actuarial and the dynamic-hedging approaches to risk management of GAOs. In Chapter 13, we discuss equity-indexed annuities (EIA). These offer a combination of minimum return guarantee plus participation in stock appreciation for some equity index. The benefits appear quite similar to the variable annuity with maturity guarantee. However, as we shall demonstrate, the structure of the product is quite different. The actuarial approach is not appropriate for EIA contracts, and a common approach to risk management is a static strategy, effectively using options purchased from a third party to reinsure the investment guarantee liability.

Although many models are presented in the early chapters of the book, most of the examples in later chapters use the regime-switching lognormal model (RSLN) with two regimes. Part of the justification for this is given in Chapter 3, where this model is shown to provide a superior fit to monthly stock return data. Also, the model is easy to understand and is mathematically tractable. However, although I am partial to the RSLN model myself, nothing in the later chapters depends on it, so feel free to use your own favorite model, subject to some quantitative assessment (along the lines of Chapters 3 through 5) of how well it models the stock return process. For those interested in exploring the RSLN model further, the Society of Actuaries intends to make available a Microsoft Excel workbook for fitting the two-regime model to stock return data. The workbook calculates the likelihood for given parameters and data; calculates the maximum likelihood for given data; calculates the distribution function; tests the left tail against a left-tail calibration table (see Chapter 4); and generates random paths for the stock index for a given set of parameters (see Hardy and Hardy 2002).

After I had written the major part of the book, one of the extensively used stock return indices changed its name and composition. The TSE 300 index has been repackaged as the S&P/TSX Composite index. It is still the broad-based Canadian total return index, but is no longer restricted to 300 companies.

Although many people have helped with this work at various stages, all remaining errors are my responsibility. I am receptive to hearing of any; feel free to e-mail me at mrhardy@uwaterloo.ca.

Investment
Guarantees

CHAPTER 1

Investment Guarantees

INTRODUCTION

The objective of life insurance is to provide financial security to policy-holders and their families. Traditionally, this security has been provided by means of a lump sum payable contingent on the death or survival of the insured life. The sum insured would be fixed and guaranteed. The policy-holder would pay one or more premiums during the term of the contract for the right to the sum insured. Traditional actuarial techniques have focused on the assessment and management of life-contingent risks: mortality and morbidity. The investment side of insurance generally has not been regarded as a source of major risk. This was (and still is) a reasonable assumption, where guaranteed benefits can be broadly matched or immunized with fixed-interest instruments.

But insurance markets around the world are changing. The public has become more aware of investment opportunities outside the insurance sec-tor, particularly in mutual fund type investment media. Policyholders want to enjoy the benefits of equity investment in conjunction with mortality protection, and insurers around the world have developed equity-linked contracts to meet this challenge. Although some contract types (such as uni-versal life in North America) pass most of the asset risk to the policyholder and involve little or no investment risk for the insurer, it was natural for insurers to incorporate payment guarantees in these new contracts—this is consistent with the traditional insurance philosophy.

In the United Kingdom, unit-linked insurance rose in popularity in the late 1960s through to the late 1970s, typically combining a guaranteed minimum payment on death or maturity with a mutual fund type investment. These contracts also spread to areas such as Australia and South Africa, where U.K. insurance companies were influential. In the United States, variable annuities and equity-indexed annuities offer different forms of equity-linking guarantees. In Canada, segregated fund contracts became popular in the late 1990s, often incorporating complex guaranteed values on death or maturity. Germany recently introduced equity-linked endowment insurance. Similar contracts are also popular in many other jurisdictions. In this book the term *equity-linked insurance* is used to refer to any contract that incorporates guarantees dependent on the performance of a stock market indicator. We also use the term *separate account insurance* to refer to the group of products that includes variable annuities, segregated funds, and unit-linked insurance. For each of these products, some or all of the premium is invested in an equity fund that resembles a mutual fund. That fund is the separate account and forms the major part of the benefit to the policyholder. Separate account products are the source of some of the most important risk management challenges in modern insurance, and most of the examples in this book come from this class of insurance. The nature of the risk to the insurer tends to be low frequency in that the stock performance must be extremely poor for the investment guarantee to bite, and high severity in that, if the guarantee does bite, the potential liability is very large.

The assessment and management of financial risk is a very different proposition to the management of insurance risk. The management of insurance risk relies heavily on diversification. With many thousands of policies in force on lives that are largely independent, it is clear from the central limit theorem that there will be very little uncertainty about the total claims. Traditional actuarial techniques for pricing and reserving utilize deterministic methodology because the uncertainties involved are relatively minor. Deterministic techniques use "best estimate" values for interest rates, claim amounts, and (usually) claim numbers. Some allowance for uncertainty and random variation may be made implicitly, through an adjustment to the best estimate values. For example, we may use an interest rate that is 100 or 200 basis points less than the true best estimate. Using this rate will place a higher value on the liabilities than will using the best estimate as we assume lower investment income.

Investment guarantees require a different approach. There is generally only limited diversification amongst each cohort of policies. When a market indicator becomes unfavorable, it affects many policies at the same time. For the simplest contracts, either all policies in the cohort will generate claims or none will. We can no longer apply the central limit theorem. This kind of risk is referred to as *systematic, systemic,* or *nondiversifiable* risk. These terms are interchangeable.

Contrast a couple of simple examples:

■ An insurer sells 10,000 term insurance contracts to independent lives, each having a probability of claim of 0.05 over the term of the contract. The expected number of claims is 500, and the standard deviation is 22 claims. The probability that more than, say, 600 claims arise is less than 10^{-5}. If the insurer wants to be very cautious not to underprice or underreserve, assuming a mortality rate of 6 percent for each life instead of the best estimate mortality rate of 5 percent for each life will absorb virtually all mortality risk.

■ The insurer also sells 10,000 pure endowment equity-linked insurance contracts. The benefit under the insurance is related to an underlying stock price index. If the index value at the end of the term is greater than the starting value, then no benefit is payable. If the stock price index value at the end of the contract term is less than its starting value, then the insurer must pay a benefit. The probability that the stock price index has a value at the end of the term less than its starting value is 5 percent.

The expected number of claims under the equity-linked insurance is the same as that under the term insurance—that is 500 claims. However, the nature of the risk is that there is a 5 percent chance that all 10,000 contracts will generate claims, and a 95 percent chance that none of them will. It is not possible to capture this risk by adding a margin to the claim probability of 5 percent.

This simple equity-linked example illustrates that, for this kind of risk, the mean value for the number (or amount) of claims is not very useful. We can also see that no simple adjustment to the mean will capture the true risk. We cannot assume that a traditional deterministic valuation with some margin in the assumptions will be adequate. Instead we must utilize a more direct, stochastic approach to the assessment of the risk. This stochastic approach is the subject of this book.

The risks associated with many equity-linked benefits, such as variable-annuity death and maturity guarantees, are inherently associated with fairly extreme stock price movements—that is, we are interested in the tail of the stock price distribution. Traditional deterministic actuarial methodology does not deal with tail risk. We cannot rely on a few deterministic stock return scenarios generally accepted as "feasible." Our subjective assessment of feasibility is not scientific enough to be satisfactory, and experience—from the early 1970s or from October 1987, for example—shows us that those returns we might earlier have regarded as infeasible do, in fact, happen. A stochastic methodology is essential in understanding these contracts and in designing strategies for dealing with them.

In this chapter, we introduce the various types of investment guarantees commonly used in equity-linked insurance and describe some of the contracts that offer investment guarantees as part of the benefit package. We also introduce the two common methods for managing investment guarantees: the actuarial approach and the dynamic-hedging approach. The actuarial approach is commonly used for risk management of investment guarantees by insurance companies in North America and in the United Kingdom. The dynamic-hedging approach is used by financial engineers in banks, in hedge funds, and (occasionally) in insurance companies. In later chapters we will develop both of these methods in relation to some of the major contract types described in the following sections.

MAJOR BENEFIT TYPES

Equity Participation

All equity-linked contracts offer some element of participation in an underlying index or fund or combination of funds, in conjunction with one or more guarantees. Without a guarantee, equity participation involves no risk to the insurer, which merely acts as a steward of the policyholders' funds. It is the combination of equity participation and fixed-sum underpinning that provides the risk for the insurer. These fixed-sum risks generally fall into one of the following major categories.

Guaranteed Minimum Maturity Benefit (GMMB) The guaranteed minimum maturity benefit (GMMB) guarantees the policyholder a specific monetary amount at the maturity of the contract. This guarantee provides downside protection for the policyholder's funds, with the upside being participation in the underlying stock index. A simple GMMB might be a guaranteed return of premium if the stock index falls over the term of the insurance (with an upside return of some proportion of the increase in the index if the index rises over the contract term). The guarantee may be fixed or subject to regular or equity-dependent increases.

Guaranteed Minimum Death Benefit (GMDB) The guaranteed minimum death benefit (GMDB) guarantees the policyholder a specific monetary sum upon death during the term of the contract. Again, the death benefit may simply be the original premium, or may increase at a fixed rate of interest. More complicated or generous death benefit formulae are popular ways of tweaking a policy benefit at relatively low cost.

Guaranteed Minimum Accumulation Benefit (GMAB) With the guaranteed minimum accumulation benefit (GMAB), the policyholder has the option to renew the contract at the end of the original term, at a new guarantee level appropriate to the maturity value of the maturing contract. It is a form of guaranteed lapse and reentry option.

Guaranteed Minimum Surrender Benefit (GMSB) The guaranteed minimum surrender benefit (GMSB) is a variation of the guaranteed minimum maturity benefit. Beyond some fixed date the cash value of the contract, payable on surrender, is guaranteed. A common guaranteed surrender benefit in Canadian segregated fund contracts is a return of the premium.

Guaranteed Minimum Income Benefit (GMIB)   The guaranteed minimum income benefit (GMIB) ensures that the lump sum accumulated under a separate account contract may be converted to an annuity at a guaranteed rate. When the GMIB is connected with an equity-linked separate account, it has derivative features of both equities and bonds. In the United Kingdom, the guaranteed-annuity option is a form of GMIB. A GMIB is also commonly associated with variable-annuity contracts in the United States.

CONTRACT TYPES

Introduction

In this section some generic contract types are described. For each of these types, individual insurers' product designs may differ in detail from the basic contract described below. The descriptions given here, however, give the main benefit details.

The first three are all separate account products, and have very similar risk management and modeling issues. These products form the basis of the analysis of Chapters 6 to 11. However, the techniques described in these chapters can be applied to other type of equity-linked insurance. The guaranteed annuity option is discussed in Chapter 12, and equity-indexed annuities are the topic of Chapter 13.

Segregated Fund Contracts—Canada

The segregated fund contract in Canada has proved an extremely popular alternative to mutual fund investment, with around $60 billion in assets in 1999, according to *Risk* magazine. Similar contracts are now issued by Canadian banks, although the regulatory requirements differ.

The basic segregated fund contract is a single premium policy, under which most of the premium is invested in one or more mutual funds on the policyholder's behalf. Monthly administration fees are deducted from the fund. The contracts all offer a GMMB and a GMDB of at least 75 percent of the premium, and 100 percent of premium is common. Some contracts offer enhanced GMDB of more than the original premium. Many contracts offer a GMAB at 100 percent or 75 percent of the maturing value.

The rate-of-administration fee is commonly known as the *management expense ratio* or *MER*. The MER differs by mutual fund type.

The name "segregated fund" refers to the fact that the premium, after deductions, is invested in a fund separate from the insurer's funds. The management of the segregated funds is often independent of the insurer.

A policyholder may withdraw some or all of his or her segregated fund account at any time, though there may be a penalty on early withdrawals.

The insurer usually offers a range of funds, including fixed interest, balanced (a mixture of fixed interest and equity), broad-based equity, and perhaps a higher-risk or specialized equity fund. For policyholders who invest in several funds, the guarantee may apply to each fund separately (a *fund-by-fund* benefit) or may be based on the overall return (the *family-of-funds* approach).

Variable Annuities—United States

The U.S. variable-annuity (VA) contract is a separate account insurance, very similar to the Canadian segregated fund contract. The VA market is very large, with over $100 billion of annual sales each year in recent times.

Premiums net of any deductions are invested in *subaccounts* similar to the mutual funds offered under the segregated fund contracts. GMDBs are a standard contract feature; GMMBs were not standard a few years ago, but are beginning to become so. They are known as VAGLBs or variable-annuity guaranteed living benefits. Death benefit guarantees may be increased periodically.

Unit-Linked Insurance—United Kingdom

Unit-linked insurance resembles segregated funds, with the premium less deductions invested in a separate fund. In the 1960s and early 1970s, these contracts were typically sold with a GMMB of 100 percent of the premium. This benefit fell into disfavor, partly resulting from the equity crisis of 1973 to 1974, and most contracts currently issued offer only a GMDB.

Some unit-linked contracts associated with pensions policies carry a guaranteed annuity option, under which the fund at maturity may be converted to a life annuity at a guaranteed rate. This is a more complex option, of the GMIB variety. This option is discussed in Chapter 12.

Equity-Indexed Annuities—United States

The U.S. equity-indexed annuity (EIA) offers participation at some specified rate in an underlying index. A participation rate of, say, 80 percent of the specified price index means that if the index rises by 10 percent the interest credited to the policyholder will be 8 percent. The contract will offer a guaranteed minimum payment of the original premium accumulated at a fixed rate; a rate of 3 percent per year is common.

Fixed surrender values are a standard feature, with no equity linking. Other contract features vary widely by company. A form of GMAB may be offered in which the guarantee value is set by annual reset according to the participation rate.

Many features of the EIA are flexible at the insurer's option. The MERs, participation rates, and floors may all be adjusted after an initial guarantee period.

The EIAs are not as popular as VA contracts, with less than $10 billion in sales per year. EIA contracts are discussed in more detail in Chapter 13.

Equity-Linked Insurance—Germany

These contracts resemble the U.S. EIAs, with a guaranteed minimum interest rate applied to the premiums, along with a percentage participation in a specified index performance. An unusual feature of the German product is that, for regulatory reasons, annual premium contracts are standard (Nonnemacher and Russ 1997).

EQUITY-LINKED INSURANCE AND OPTIONS

Call and Put Options

Although the risks associated with equity-linked insurance are new to insurers, at least, relative to life-contingent risks, they are very familiar to practitioners and academics in the field of derivative securities. The payoffs under equity-linked insurance contracts can be expressed in terms of *options*.

There are many books on the theory of option pricing and risk management. In this book we will review the relevant fundamental results, but the development of the theory is not covered. It is crucially important for practitioners in equity-linked insurance to understand the theory underpinning option pricing. The book by Boyle et al. (1998) is specifically written with actuaries and actuarial applications in mind. For a general, readable introduction to derivatives without any technical details, Boyle and Boyle (2001) is highly recommended.

The simplest forms of option contracts are:

- A *European call option* on a stock gives the purchaser the right (but not the obligation) to purchase a specified quantity of the underlying stock at a fixed price, called the *strike price,* at a predetermined date, known as the *expiry* or *maturity date* of the contract.
- A *European put option* on a stock gives the purchaser the right to sell a specified quantity of the underlying stock at a fixed strike price at the expiry date.

American options are defined similarly, except that the option holder has the right to exercise the option at any time before expiry. *Asian options* have a payoff based on an average of the stock price over a period, rather than on the final stock price.

To summarize the benefits under the option contracts, we introduce some notation. Let K be the strike price of the option per unit of stock; let S_t be the price of one unit of the underlying stock at time t; and let T be the expiry date of the option. The payoff at time T under the call option will be:

$$(S_T - K)^+ = \max(S_T - K, 0) \qquad (1.1)$$

and the payoff under the put option will be

$$(K - S_T)^+ = \max(K - S_T, 0) \qquad (1.2)$$

In subsequent chapters we shall see that it is natural to think of the investment guarantee benefits under separate account products as put options on the policyholder's fund. On the other hand, it is more natural to use call options to value the benefits under an equity-indexed annuity.

We often use the terms *in-the-money, at-the-money,* and *out-of-the-money* in relation to options and to equity-linked insurance guarantees. A put option that is in-the-money at time $t < T$ has an underlying stock price $S_t < K$, so that if the stock price at maturity were to be the same as the current stock price, there would be a payment under the guarantee. For a call option, in-the-money means that $S_t > K$, and at-the-money means that the stock and strike prices are roughly equal. Out-of-the-money for a put option means $S_t > K$, and for a call option means $S_t < K$; in either case, if the stock price at maturity is the same as the current stock price, no payment would be required under the guarantee or option contract. We say a contract is deep out-of-the-money or in-the-money if the difference between the stock price and strike price is large, so that it is very likely that a deep out-of-the-money contract will remain out-of-the-money, and similarly for the deep in-the-money contract.

The No-Arbitrage Principle

The *no-arbitrage* principle states that, in well-functioning markets, two assets or portfolios having exactly the same payoffs must have exactly the same price. This concept is also known as the *law of one price*; it is a fundamental assumption of financial economics. The logic is that if prices differ by a fraction, it will be noticed by the market, and traders will move in to buy the cheaper portfolio and sell the more expensive, making an instant risk-free profit or *arbitrage*. This will pressure the price of the cheap portfolio back up, and the price of the expensive portfolio back down, until they return to equality. Therefore, any possible arbitrage opportunity will be eliminated in an instant. Many studies show consistently that the no-arbitrage assumption is empirically indisputable in major stock markets.

This simple and intuitive assumption is actually very powerful, particularly in the valuation of derivative securities. To value a derivative security such as an option, it is sufficient to find a portfolio, with known value, that precisely replicates the payoff of the option. If the option and the replicating portfolio do not have the same price, one could sell the more expensive and buy the cheaper, and make an arbitrage profit. Since this is assumed to be impossible, the value of the option and the value of the replicating portfolio must be identical under the no-arbitrage assumption.

Put-Call Parity

Using the no-arbitrage assumption allows us to derive an important connection between the put option and the call option on a stock.

Let c_t denote the value at t of a European call option on a unit of stock, and p_t the value of a European put option on a unit of the same stock. Both options are assumed to mature at the same date $T > t$ with the same strike price, K. Assume the stock price at t is S_t, then an investor who holds both a unit of stock and a put option on that unit of stock will have a portfolio at time t with value $p_t + S_t$. The payoff at expiry of the portfolio will be

$$p_T + S_T = \max(K, S_T) \tag{1.3}$$

Similarly, consider an investor who holds a call option on a unit of stock together with a pure discount bond maturing at T with face value K. We assume the pure discount bond earns a risk-free rate of interest of r per year, continuously compounded, so that the value at time t of the pure discount bond plus call option is $c_t + Ke^{-r(T-t)}$. The payoff at maturity of the portfolio of the pure discount bond plus call option will be

$$c_T + K = \max(K, S_T) \tag{1.4}$$

In other words, these two portfolios—"put plus stock" and "call plus bond"—have identical payoffs. The no-arbitrage assumption requires that two portfolios offering the same payoffs must have the same price. Hence we find the fundamental relationship between put and call options known as put-call parity, that is,

$$p_t + S_t = c_t + Ke^{-r(T-t)} \tag{1.5}$$

Options and Equity-Linked Insurance

Many benefits under equity-linked insurance contracts can be regarded as put or call options. For example, the liability under the maturity guarantee of a Canadian segregated fund contract can be naturally regarded as an embedded put option. That is, the policyholder who pays a single premium of $1000 with a 100 percent GMMB is guaranteed to receive at least

$K = \$1000$ at maturity, even if the market value of her or his portfolio is less than \$1000 at that time. It is the responsibility of the insurer to pay $(1000 - S_T)^+$, the excess of the guaranteed amount over the market value of the assets, meaning that the insurer pays the payoff under a put option.

Therefore, the total segregated fund policy benefit is made up of the policyholder's fund plus the payoff from a put option on the fund. From put-call parity we know that the same benefit can be provided using a bond plus a call option, but that route is not sensible when the contract is designed in the separate account format. Put-call parity also means that the U.S. EIA could either be regarded as a combination of fixed-interest security (meeting the minimum interest rate guarantee) and a call option on the underlying stock (meeting the equity participation rate benefit), or as a portfolio of the underlying stock (for equity participation) together with a put option (for the minimum benefit). In fact, the first method is a more convenient approach from the design of the contract.

The fundamental difference between the VA-type guarantee, which we value as a put option to add to the separate account proceeds, and the EIA guarantee, which we value as a call option added to the fixed-interest proceeds, arises from the withdrawal benefits. On withdrawal, the VA policyholder takes the proceeds of the separate account, without the put option payment. The EIA policyholder withdraws with their premium accumulated at some fixed rate, without the call-option payment.

American options may be relevant where equity participation and minimum accumulation guarantees are both offered on early surrender. Asian options are relevant for some EIA contracts where the equity participation can be based on an average of the underlying stock price rather than on the final value.

There is a substantial and rich body of theory on the pricing and financial management of options. Black and Scholes (1973) and Merton (1973) showed that it is possible, under certain assumptions, to set up a portfolio that consists of a long position in the underlying stock together with a short position in a pure discount bond and has an identical payoff to the call option. This is called the replicating portfolio. The theory of no-arbitrage means that the replicating portfolio must have the same value as the call option because they have the same payoff at the expiry date. Thus, the famous Black-Scholes option-pricing formula not only provides the price but also provides a risk management strategy for an option seller—hold the replicating portfolio to hedge the option payoff. A feature of the replicating portfolio is that it changes over time, so the theory also requires the balance of stocks and bonds to be rearranged at frequent intervals over the term of the contract.

The stock price, S_t, is the random variable in the payoff equations for the options (we assume that the risk-free rate of interest is fixed). The probability distribution of S_t is know as the *real-world* measure, the *physical* measure, or the *P-measure*. The fundamental result of Black, Scholes, and Merton was that securities may be valued and the replicating portfolio derived by taking the expected value of the payoff, but under a different, artificial distribution known as the *Q-measure* (or *risk-neutral measure*). In Chapter 7 we discuss the relationship between these two measures.

There are some complications in applying this theory to the options embedded in equity-linked insurance. The major problem is the very long-term nature of the equity-linked options. The contract term for standard traded options might be a few weeks—an option with a term of more than six months would be considered long term. In contrast, the options implicit in equity-linked insurance commonly have terms of over 10 years, and some may be in force for 30 years or more. A challenge for actuaries managing equity-linked contracts is to adapt the methods of financial economics to the long time scales in which insurance companies work.

PROVISION FOR EQUITY-LINKED LIABILITIES

Reinsurance

An easy way for the insurer to manage the liability from options embedded in equity-linked contracts is to buy options, equivalent to those they have sold, from third parties. This is equivalent to reinsuring the entire risk; indeed, reinsurers have been involved in selling such options to insurers. As with reinsurance, the insurer is likely to pass on a substantial proportion of the expected profit on the contracts along with the risk. Also, (as with reinsurance) the insurer must be aware of the counterparty risk; that is, the risk that the option provider will not survive to the maturity date, which may be decades away.

For some markets, such as that for segregated fund contracts in Canada, reinsurers and other option providers are increasingly unwilling to provide the options at prices acceptable to the insurers.

Dynamic Hedging

As mentioned in the section on equity-linked insurance and options, the Black-Scholes analysis provides a risk management strategy for option providers; use the Black-Scholes equation to find the replicating portfolio. The portfolio will change continuously, so it is necessary to recalculate and adjust the portfolio frequently. Although the Black-Scholes equation contains some strong assumptions that cannot be realized in practice, the replicating portfolio still manages to provide a powerful method of hedging the liability. This method is explored in detail in Chapters 7 and 8.

Most of the academic literature relating to equity-linked insurance assumes a dynamic-hedging management strategy. See, for example, Boyle and Schwartz (1977), Brennan and Schwartz (1975, 1979), Bacinello and Ortu (1993), Ekern and Persson (1996), and Persson and Aase (1994); these papers appear in actuarial, finance, and business journals. Nevertheless, although the application by actuaries in practice of financial economic theory to the management of embedded options is growing, in many areas it is still not widely accepted.

The Actuarial Approach

In the mid 1970s the ground-breaking work of Black, Scholes, and Merton was relatively unknown in actuarial circles. In the United Kingdom, however, maturity guarantees of 100 percent of premium were a common feature of the unit-linked contracts, which were then proving very popular with consumers. The prolonged low stock market of 1973 to 1974 had awakened the actuaries to the possibility that this benefit, which had been treated as a relatively unimportant policy "tweak" with very little value or risk, constituted a serious potential liability. The then recent theory of Black and Scholes was considered to be too risky and unproven to be used for unit-linked guaranteed maturity benefits by the U.K. actuarial profession.[1]

In 1980, the Maturity Guarantees Working Party (MGWP) suggested, instead, using stochastic simulation to determine an approximate distribution for the guarantee liabilities, and then using quantile reserving to convert the distribution into a usable capital requirement. The quantile reserve had already been used for many years, particularly in non-life insurance. To calculate the quantile reserve, the insurer assesses an appropriate quantile of the loss distribution, for example, 99 percent. The present value of the quantile is held in risk-free bonds, so that the office can be 99 percent certain that the liability will be met. This principle is identical to the *value-at-risk* (VaR) concept of finance, though generally applied over longer time periods by the insurance companies than by the banks.

The underlying principle of this method of calculating the capital requirements is that the capital is assumed to be invested in risk-free bonds. The use of the quantile of the distribution as a risk measure is not actually fundamental to this approach, and other risk measures may be preferable (this is discussed further in Chapter 9).

---

[1]This was a decision that has had unfortunate consequences. If the actuarial profession had taken the opportunity to learn and apply option pricing theory and risk management at that time, then the design and management of embedded options in insurance contracts in the last 20 years would have been very different and actuaries would have been better placed to participate in the derivatives revolution.

This method of using stochastic simulation to project the liabilities, and then using the long-term fixed rate of interest to discount them, is referred to in this book (and elsewhere) as the "actuarial" approach. It is inherently different from the dynamic-hedging approach, in which assets are assumed to be invested in the replicating portfolio, not in the bonds. However, it should not be inferred that dynamic hedging is somehow not actuarial. Nor should it be assumed that the actuarial approach is incompatible with dynamic hedging. A synthesis of the two approaches may lead to better risk management than either provides separately.

The actuarial method is still popular (particularly with actuaries) and offers a valid alternative to the dynamic-hedging approach for some equity-linked contracts. The Canadian Institute of Actuaries' Task Force on Segregated Funds (SFTF 2000) uses the actuarial approach as the underpinning methodology for determining capital requirements, although a combined hedging-actuarial approach is also accommodated. In Chapter 6, the actuarial approach to equity-linked liabilities is investigated.

The Ad Hoc Approach

There is a (diminishing) body of opinion amongst actuaries that the statistical analysis that forms the subject of this book is unnecessary or even irrelevant. Their approach to valuation and management of financial guarantees might be described as guesswork, or "actuarial judgment." This is most common for the very low-frequency type options, where there is very little chance of any liability. An example might be a GMMB, which guarantees that the benefit after a 10-year investment will be no less than the original premium. There is very little chance that the separate account will fall to less than the original investment over the course of 10 years. Rather than model the risk statistically, it was common for actuaries to assume that there would never be a liability under the guarantee, so little or no provision was made. This view is uncommon now and tends to be unpopular with regulators.

For any actuary tempted by this approach, the Equitable Life (U.K.) story provides a clear demonstration of the risks of ignoring statistical methodology. Along with many U.K. insurers in the early 1980s, Equitable Life (U.K.) issued a large number of contracts carrying guaranteed-annuity options, under which the guarantee would move into the money only if interest rates fell below 6.5 percent. At the time the contracts were issued, interest rates were higher than 10 percent, and a cautious long-term view was that they might fall to 8 percent. Many actuaries, relying on their personal judgment, believed that these contracts would never move into the money, and therefore made little or no provision for the potential liability. This conclusion was made despite the fact that interest rates had been below 6.5 percent for decades up to the later 1960s. Of course, in the mid-1990s rates fell, the guarantees moved into the money, and the guarantee liabilities were so large that Equitable Life (U.K.), a large mutual company more than 200 years old, was forced to close to new business. Many other companies were also hit hard and only substantial free surplus kept them trading. Yang (2001) has demonstrated that, had actuaries in the 1980s used the stochastic models and methods then available, it would have been clear that substantial provision would be required for this option.

PRICING AND CAPITAL REQUIREMENTS

There are several issues that are important for actuaries and risk managers involved in any area of policy design, marketing, valuation, or risk management of equity-linked insurance. The following are three main considerations:

1. What price should the policyholder be charged for the guarantee benefit?
2. How much capital should the insurer hold in respect of the benefit through the term of the contract?
3. How should this capital be invested?

Much work in equity-linked insurance has focused on pricing without very much consideration of the capital issues. But the three issues are crucially interrelated. For example, using the option approach for pricing maturity guarantees gives a price, but that price is only appropriate if it is suitably invested (in a dynamic-hedge portfolio, or by purchasing the options externally). Also, as we shall see in later chapters, different risk management strategies require different levels of capital (for the same level of risk), and therefore the implied price for the guarantee would vary.

The approach of this book is that all of these issues are really facets of the same issue. The first requirement for pricing or for determination of capital requirements is a credible estimate of the distribution of the liabilities, and that is the main focus of this book. Once this distribution is determined, it can be used for both pricing and capital requirement decisions. In addition, the liability issue is really an asset-liability issue, so the estimation of the liability distribution depends on the risk management decision.

CHAPTER 2

Modeling Long-Term Stock Returns

INTRODUCTION

I t has been stated firmly in the previous chapter that this book will use stochastic methods to analyze and manage risks from investment guarantees. To model the investment guarantee risks, we need to model the underlying equity process upon which the guarantee depends. There are many stochastic models in common use for equity returns. The objective of this chapter is to introduce some of these and discuss their different characteristics. This should assist in the choice of an appropriate model for a given contract.

First, we discuss briefly the case for stochastic models, and some of the interesting features of stock return data. We also demonstrate how often the guaranteed minimum maturity benefit (GMMB) under a 10-year contract would have ended up greater than the fund using the historical returns.

The rest of this chapter introduces the various models. These include the lognormal model, the autoregressive model, the ARCH-type models, the regime-switching lognormal model, the empirical model (where returns are drawn from historic experience), and the Wilkie model. Where it is sufficiently straightforward, we have derived probability functions for the models, but in many cases this is not possible.

DETERMINISTIC OR STOCHASTIC?

Traditional actuarial techniques assume a deterministic, usually constant path for returns on assets. There has been some effort to adapt this technique for equity-linked liabilities; for example, the Office of the Superintendent of Financial Institutions (OSFI) in Canada mandated a deterministic test for the GMMB under segregated fund contracts. (This mandate has since been superseded by the recommendations of the Task Force on Segregated Funds (SFTF) in 2000.) However, there are problems with this approach:

1. It is likely that any single path used to model the sort of extreme behavior relevant to the GMMB will lack credibility. The Canadian OSFI scenario for a diversified equity mutual fund involved an immediate fall in asset values of 60 percent followed by returns of 5.75 percent per year for 10 years. The worst (monthly) return of this century in the S&P total return index was around −35 percent. Insurers are, not surprisingly, rather sceptical about the need to reserve against such an unlikely outcome.
2. It is difficult to interpret the results; what does it mean to hold enough capital to satisfy that particular path? It will not be enough to pay the guarantee with certainty (unless the full discounted maximum guarantee amount is held in risk-free bonds). How extreme must circumstances be before the required deterministic amount is not enough?
3. A single path may not capture the risk appropriately for all contracts, particularly if the guarantee may be ratcheted upward from time to time. The one-time drop and steady rise may be less damaging than a sharp rise followed by a period of poor returns, for contracts with guarantees that depend on the stock index path rather than just the final value. The guaranteed minimum accumulation benefit (GMAB) is an example of this type of path-dependent benefit.

Deterministic testing is easy but does not provide the essential qualitative or quantitative information. A true understanding of the nature and sources of risk under equity-linked contracts requires a stochastic analysis of the liabilities.

A stochastic analysis of the guarantee liabilities requires a credible long-term model of the underlying stock return process. Actuaries have no general agreement on the form of such a model. Financial engineers traditionally used the lognormal model, although nowadays a wide variety of models are applied to the financial economics theory. The lognormal model is the discrete-time version of the geometric Brownian motion of stock prices, which is an assumption underlying the Black-Scholes theory. The model has the advantage of tractability, but it does not provide a satisfactory fit to the data. In particular, the model fails to capture extreme market movements, such as the October 1987 crash. There are also autocorrelations in the data that make a difference over the longer term but are not incorporated in the lognormal model, under which returns in different (nonoverlapping) time intervals are independent. The difference between the lognormal distribution and the true, fatter-tailed underlying distribution may not have very severe consequences for short-term contracts, but for longer terms the financial implications can be very substantial. Nevertheless, many insurers in the Canadian segregated fund market use the lognormal model to assess their liabilities. The report of the Canadian Institute of Actuaries Task Force on Segregated Funds (SFTF (2000)) gives specific guidance on the use of the lognormal model, on the grounds that this has been a very popular choice in the industry.

A model of stock and bond returns for long-term applications was developed by Wilkie (1986, 1995) in relation to the U.K. market, and subsequently fitted to data from other markets, including both the United States and Canada. The model is described in more detail below. It has been applied to segregated fund liabilities by a number of Canadian companies. A problem with the direct application of the Wilkie model is that it is designed and fitted as an annual model. For some contracts, the monthly nature of the cash flows means that an annual model may be an unsatisfactory approximation. This is important where there are reset opportunities for the policyholder to increase the guarantee mid-policy year. Annual intervals are also too infrequent to use for the exploration of dynamic-hedging strategies for insurers who wish to reduce the risk by holding a replicating portfolio for the embedded option. An early version of the Wilkie model was used in the 1980 Maturity Guarantees Working Party (MGWP) report, which adopted the actuarial approach to maturity guarantee provision.

Both of these models, along with a number of others from the econometric literature, are described in more detail in this chapter. First though, we will look at the features of the data.

ECONOMICAL THEORY OR STATISTICAL METHOD?

Some models are derived from economic theory. For example, the efficient market hypothesis of economics states that if markets are efficient, then all information is equally available to all investors, and it should be impossible to make systematic profits relative to other investors. This is different from the no-arbitrage assumption, which states that it should be impossible to make risk-free profits. The efficient market hypothesis is consistent with the theory that prices follow a random walk, which is consistent with assuming returns on stocks are lognormally distributed. The hypothesis is inconsistent with any process involving, for example, autoregression (a tendency for returns to move toward the mean). In an autoregressive market, it should be possible to make systematic profits by following a countercyclical investment strategy—that is, invest more when recent returns have been poor and disinvest when returns have been high, since the model assumes that returns will eventually move back toward the mean.

The statistical approach to fitting time series data does not consider exogenous theories, but instead finds the model that "best fits" the data, in some statistical sense. In practice, we tend to use an implicit mixture of the economic and statistical approaches. Theories that are contradicted by the historic data are not necessarily adhered to, rather practitioners prefer models that make sense in terms of their market experience and intuition, and that are also tractable to work with.

THE DATA

Description of the Data

For segregated fund and variable-annuity contracts, the relevant data for a diversified equity fund or subaccount are the total returns on a suitable stock index. For the U.S. variable annuity contracts, the S&P 500 total return (that is with dividends reinvested) is often an appropriate basis. For equity-indexed annuities, the usual index is the S&P 500 price index (a price index is one without dividend reinvestment). A common index for Canadian segregated funds is the TSE 300 total return index[1] (the broad-based index of the Toronto Stock Exchange); and the S&P 500 index, in Canadian dollars, is also used. We will analyze the total return data for the TSE 300 and S&P 500 indices. The methodology is easily adapted to the price-only indices, with similar conclusions.

For the TSE 300 index, we have annual data from 1924, from the Report on Canadian Economic Statistics (Panjer and Sharp 1999), although the TSE 300 index was inaugurated in 1956. Observations before 1956 are estimated from various data sources. The annual TSE 300 total returns on stocks are shown in Figure 2.1. We also show the approximate volatility, using a rolling five-year calculation. The volatility is the standard deviation of the log-returns, given as an annual rate. For the S&P 500 index, earlier data are available. The S&P 500 total return index data set, with rolling 12-month volatility estimates, is shown in Figure 2.2.

Monthly data for Canada have been available since the beginning of the TSE 300 index in 1956. These data are plotted in Figure 2.3. We again show the estimated volatility, calculated using a rolling 12-month calculation. In Figure 2.4, the S&P 500 data are shown for the same period as for the TSE data in Figure 2.3.

Estimates for the annualized mean and volatility of the log-return process[2] are given in Table 2.1. The entries for the two long series use annual data for the TSE index, and monthly data for the S&P index. For

---

[1] Now superseded by the S&P/TSX-Composite index.
[2] The log-return for some period is the natural logarithm of the accumulation of a unit investment over the period.

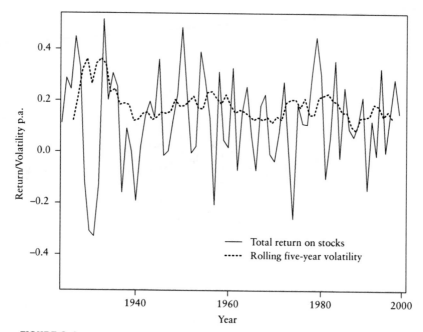

FIGURE 2.1 Annual total returns and annual volatility, TSE 300 long series.

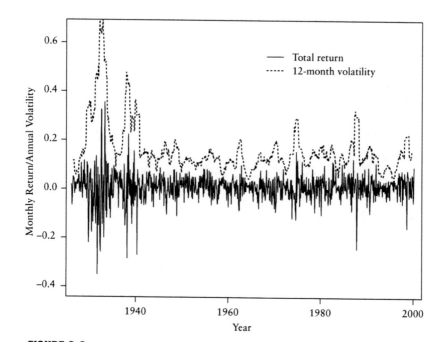

FIGURE 2.2 Monthly total returns and annual volatility, S&P 500 long series.

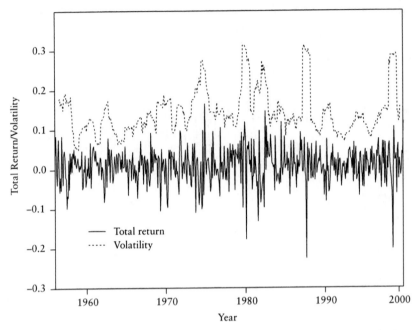

FIGURE 2.3   Monthly total returns and annual volatility, TSE 300 1956–2000.

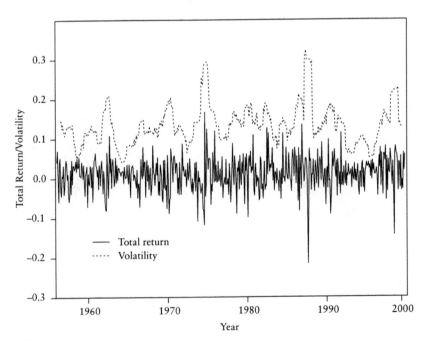

FIGURE 2.4   Monthly total returns and annual volatility, S&P 500 1956–2000.

TABLE 2.1 Means, standard deviations, and autocorrelations of log returns.

Series	$\hat{\mu}(\%)$	$\hat{\sigma}(\%)$
TSE 300 1924–1999	9.90 (5.5, 15.0)	18.65 (15.7, 21.7)
S&P 500 1928–1999	10.61 (6.2, 15.0)	19.44 (18.7, 20.5)
TSE 300 1956–1999	9.77 (5.1, 14.4)	15.63 (14.3, 16.2)
S&P 500 1956–1999	11.61 (7.4, 15.9)	14.38 (13.4, 15.1)

Autocorrelations:

Series	1-Month Lag	6-Month Lag	12-Month Lag
TSE 300 1956–1999	0.082	0.013	−0.024
S&P 500 1956–1999	0.027	−0.057	0.032

the shorter series, corresponding to the data in Figures 2.3 and 2.4, we use monthly data for all estimates. The values in parentheses are approximate 95 percent confidence intervals for the estimators. The correlation coefficient between the 1956 to 1999 log returns for the S&P 500 and the TSE 300 is 0.77.

A glance at Figures 2.3 and 2.4 and Table 2.1 shows that the two series are very similar indeed, with both indices experiencing periods of high volatility in the mid-1970s, around October 1987, and in the late 1990s. The main difference is an extra period of uncertainty in the Canadian index in the early 1980s.

Selecting the Appropriate Data Series for Calibration

There is some evidence, for example in French et al. (1987) and in Pagan and Schwert (1990), of a shift in the stock return distribution at the end of the great depression, in the middle 1930s. Returns may also be distorted by the various fiscal constraints imposed during the 1939–1945 war. Thus, it is attractive to consider only the data from 1956 onward.

On the other hand, for very long term contracts, we may be forecasting distributions of stock returns further forward than we have considered in estimating the model. For segregated fund contracts, with a GMAB, it is common to require stock prices to be projected for 40 years ahead. To use a model fitted using only 40 years of historic data seems a little incautious. However, because of the mitigating influence of mortality, lapsation, and discounting, the cash flows beyond, say, 20 years ahead may not have a very substantial influence on the overall results.

Investors, including actuaries, generally have fairly short memories. We may believe, for example, that another great depression is impossible, and that the estimation should, therefore, not allow the data from the prewar period to persuade us to use very high-volatility assumptions; on the other hand, another great depression is what Japan seems to have experienced in the last decade. How many people would have also said a few years ago that such a thing was impossible? It is also worth noting that the recent implied market volatility levels regularly substantially exceed 20 percent. Nevertheless, the analysis in the main part of this paper will use the post-1956 data sets. But in interpreting the results, we need to remember the implicit assumption that there are no substantial structural changes in the factors influencing equity returns in the projection period.

In Hardy (1999) some results are given for models fitted using a longer 1926 to 1998 data set; these results demonstrate that the higher-volatility assumption has a very substantial effect on the liability.

Current Market Statistics

Perhaps the world is changing so fast that history should not be used at all to predict the future. This appears to be the view of some traders and some actuaries, including Exley and Mehta (2000). They propose that distribution parameters should be derived from current market statistics, such as the volatility. The implied market volatility is calculated from market prices at some instant in time. Knowing the price-volatility relationship in the market allows the volatility implied by market prices to be calculated from the quoted prices. Usually the market volatility differs very substantially from historical estimates of long-term volatility.

Certainly the current implied market volatility is relevant in the valuation of traded instruments. In application to equity-linked insurance, though, we are generally not in the realm of traded securities—the options embedded in equity-linked contracts, especially guaranteed maturity benefits, have effective maturities far longer than traded options. Market volatility varies with term to maturity in general, so in the absence of very long-term traded options, it is not possible to state confidently what would be an appropriate volatility assumption based on current market conditions, for equity-linked insurance options.

Another problem is that the market statistics do not give the whole story. Market valuations are not based on true probability measure, but on the adjusted probability distribution known as the *risk-neutral* measure. In analyzing future cash flows under the equity-linked contracts, it will also be important to have a model of the true unadjusted probability measure.

A third difficulty is the volatility of the implied volatility. A change of 100 basis points in the volatility assumption for, say, a 10-year option may have enormous financial impact, but such movements in implied volatility are common in practice. It is not satisfactory to determine long-term strategies for the actuarial management of equity-linked liabilities on assumptions that may well be deemed utterly incorrect one day later.

GMMB Liability: The Historic Evidence

It is a piece of actuarial folk wisdom, often quoted, that the long-term maturity guarantees of the sort offered with segregated fund benefits would *never* have resulted in a payoff greater than zero. In Figure 2.5 the net proceeds of a 10-year single-premium investment in the S&P 500 index are given. The premium is assumed to be $100, invested at the start date given by the horizontal axis. Management expenses of 2.5 percent per year are assumed. A nonzero liability for the simple 10-year put option arises when the proceeds fall below 100, which is marked on the graph. Clearly, this has not proved impossible, even in the modern era. Figure 2.6 gives the same figures for the TSE 300 index. The accumulations use the annual data up to 1934, and monthly data thereafter.

For both the S&P and TSE indices, periods of nonzero liability for the simple 10-year put option arose during the great depression; the S&P index shows another period arising in respect of some deposits in 1964 to 1965, the problem caused by the 1974 to 1975 oil crisis. Another hypothetical liability arose in respect of deposits in December 1968, for which the

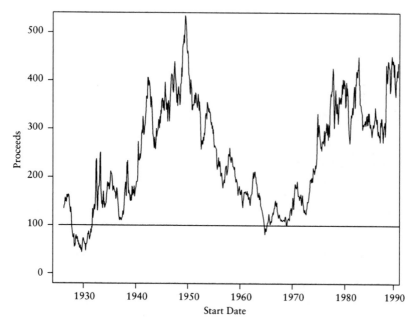

FIGURE 2.5 Proceeds of a 10-year $100 single-premium investment in the S&P 500 index.

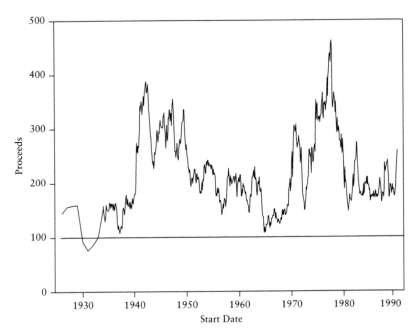

FIGURE 2.6 Proceeds of a 10-year $100 single-premium investment in the TSE 300 index.

proceeds in 1978 were 99.9 percent of deposits.[3] These figures show that, even for a simple maturity guarantee on one of the major indices, substantial payments are possible. In addition, extra volatility from exchange-rate risk, for example for Canadian S&P mutual funds, and the complications of ratchet and reset features of maturity guarantees would lead to even higher liabilities than indicated for the simple contracts used for these figures.

THE LOGNORMAL MODEL

The traditional approach to modeling stock returns in the financial economics literature, including the original Black-Scholes paper, is to assume that in continuous time stock returns follow a geometric Brownian motion. In discrete time, the implications of this are the following:

1. Over any discrete time interval, the stock price accumulation factor is lognormally distributed. Let S_t denote the stock price at time $t > 0$. Then the lognormal assumption means that for some parameters, μ and σ, and for any $w > 0$,

---

[3]We are using monthly intervals. Different starting dates within each month give slightly different results.

$$\frac{S_{t+w}}{S_t} \sim LN(w\mu, \sqrt{w}\sigma) \implies \log \frac{S_{t+w}}{S_t} \sim N(w\mu, w\sigma^2) \qquad (2.1)$$

where LN denotes the lognormal distribution and N denotes the normal distribution. Note that μ is the mean log-return over a unit of time, and σ is the standard deviation for one unit of time. In financial applications, σ is referred to as the volatility, usually in the form of an annual rate.

2. Returns in nonoverlapping intervals are independent. That is, for any t, u, v, w such that $t < u \leq v < w$,

$$\frac{S_u}{S_t} \text{ and } \frac{S_w}{S_v} \text{ are independent} \qquad (2.2)$$

Parameter estimation for the lognormal model is very straightforward. The maximum likelihood estimates of the parameters μ and σ^2 are the mean and variance[4] of the log returns (i.e., the mean and variance of $Y_t = \log \frac{S_{t+1}}{S_t}$). Table 2.1, discussed earlier, shows the estimated parameters for the lognormal model for the various series. In Figure 2.7, we show the

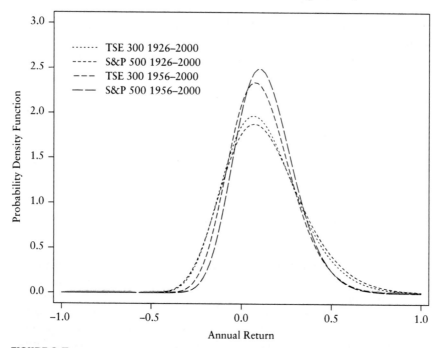

FIGURE 2.7 Lognormal model, density functions of annual stock returns for TSE 300 and S&P 500 indices; maximum likelihood parameters.

---

[4]Actually the maximum likelihood estimation (MLE) for σ^2 is $\frac{n-1}{n}s^2$ where s^2 is the variance of the log-returns. However, we generally use s^2 because it is an unbiased estimator of σ^2.

probability density functions for the four sets of parameters from Table 2.1. This shows the significance of the choice of data to use to fit the distribution. Including the great depression data gives density functions with much fatter tails for both indices, which means a greater probability of very low or very high returns.

The probability density function of a lognormal distribution with parameters $w\mu$, $\sqrt{w}\sigma$ is

$$f(x) = \frac{1}{x\sigma\sqrt{2\pi w}} \exp\left\{-\frac{1}{2}\frac{(\log(x) - w\mu)^2}{w\sigma^2}\right\} \tag{2.3}$$

The model is very attractive to use; probabilities are easily calculated using the standard normal distribution function Φ, since

$$\Pr\left[\frac{S_{t+w}}{S_t} \le x\right] = \Phi\left(\frac{\log(x) - w\mu}{\sqrt{w}\sigma}\right) \tag{2.4}$$

and both option prices and probability distributions for payoffs under standard put options can be derived analytically. The mean and variance of the stock accumulation function under the lognormal model are given by the following expressions.

$$E\left[\frac{S_{t+w}}{S_t}\right] = e^{w\mu + w\sigma^2/2} \tag{2.5}$$

$$V\left[\frac{S_{t+w}}{S_t}\right] = e^{2w\mu + w\sigma^2}(e^{w\sigma^2} - 1) \tag{2.6}$$

Other models we discuss later use conditional lognormal distributions but do not have the serial independence of its independent lognormal model.

The independent lognormal (LN) model is simple and tractable, and provides a reasonable approximation over short time intervals, but it is less appealing for longer-term problems. Empirical studies indicate, in particular, that this model fails to capture more extreme price movements, such as the October 1987 crash. We need a distribution with fatter tails (leptokurtic) to include such values. The LN model also does not allow for autocorrelation in the data. From Table 2.1 the one-month autocorrelation is small but potentially significant in the tail of the distribution of accumulation factors. Also important, the LN model fails to capture volatility bunching—periods of high volatility, often associated with severe downward stock price movements. Bakshi, Cao, and Chen (1999) identify stochastic variation in volatility as the critical omission with respect to the LN model. In the models that follow, various ways of introducing stochastic volatility are proposed.

AUTOREGRESSIVE MODELS

The autoregressive models described here are discrete processes where the deviation of the process from the long-term mean influences the distribution of subsequent values of the process. In all cases, we work with the log-return variable, $Y_t = \log \frac{S_{t+1}}{S_t}$. If we assume a long-term mean for Y_t of μ, then the deviations from the mean used to define the distribution of Y_t are the values of $Y_s - \mu$ for some $s \leq t - 1$.

In each of the cases below, the white noise process, denoted ε_t, is assumed to be a sequence of independent random innovations, each with Normal(0,1) distribution. It is common to assume a normal distribution but not essential, and other distributions may prove more appropriate for some series. The necessary assumptions are that the values of ε_t are uncorrelated, each with zero mean and unit variance.

AR(1)

The LN model implies independent and identically distributed variables, Y_t. This is not true for AR (autoregressive) processes, which incorporate a tendency for the process to move toward the mean. This tendency is effected with a term involving previous values of the deviation of the process from the mean, meaning that, if the long-term mean value for the process is μ, the AR(q) process variable Y_t has terms in $(Y_{t-r} - \mu)$ for $r = 1, 2, \ldots, q$. The parameter q is called the order of the process.

The AR(1) process is the simplest version, and can be defined for a process Y_t as

$$Y_t = \mu + a(Y_{t-1} - \mu) + \sigma \varepsilon_t$$
$$\varepsilon_t \text{ independent and identically distributed (iid)}, \varepsilon_t \sim N(0, 1) \qquad (2.7)$$

The process only makes sense if $|a| < 1$, and so we assume this is true. The process reverts to a LN process when $a = 0$. If a is near 1, then the process moves slowly back to the mean, on average. If a is near zero, then the process tends to return to the mean more quickly. Negative values for a indicate a tendency to bounce beyond the mean with each time step, meaning that if the process is above the mean at $t - 1$, it will tend to fall below the mean at t, and from there it will tend to jump back above the mean at $t + 1$. If a is negative and near zero, these oscillations are very dampened; if a is near -1, the successive oscillations are only a little smaller in severity each time step.

The autocorrelation function for an AR(1) process is $\rho_k = a^k$ where a is the AR parameter. The AR(1) model captures autocorrelation in the data in a simple way. However, it does not, in general, capture the extreme values or the volatility bunching that have been identified as features of the monthly stock return data.

ARCH(1)

It was observed very early in empirical studies that the volatility of stock prices is not constant, as assumed in the LN model. There are many ways of modeling stochastic changes in volatility, and the class of *AR conditionally heteroscedastic (ARCH)* models has been a popular choice in many areas of econometrics, including stock return modeling. Using ARCH models, the volatility is a stochastic process, more than one step ahead. Looking forward a single step the volatility is fixed.

There are many variations of the ARCH process, and we describe two here: ARCH and generalized ARCH (GARCH). The basic ARCH model has a variance process that is a function of the evolving return process as follows:

$$Y_t = \mu + \sigma_t \varepsilon_t \tag{2.8}$$

$$\sigma_t^2 = a_0 + a_1 (Y_{t-1} - \mu)^2 \tag{2.9}$$

The ARCH model was introduced by Engle (1982) who applied the model to quarterly U.K. inflation data. The rationale is that the uncertainty in forecasting from period to period, which is represented by the conditional variance σ_t, depends on the evolving process Y_t. The ARCH approach was designed by Engle to model volatility clustering. A value of Y_{t-1} falling a long way from the mean increases the conditional variance σ_t, leading to a greater probability of the next value, Y_t, also falling a long way from the mean. The variance process, σ_t^2 looks like an AR(1) process, but without the random innovation. This means that, conditional on knowing Y_{t-1}, the variance is not random. Unconditionally, the variance is stochastic through Y_{t-1}. The fact that the variance is fixed conditional on Y_{t-1} significantly improves the tractability of this model compared with conditionally stochastic variance models. Essentially, this means that volatility clustering is modeled, with periods of higher volatility generated by the random, occasional extreme value for Y_t, after which the volatility gradually returns to the longer-term value.

In the original form of equations 2.8 and 2.9, the ARCH model does not allow for autocorrelation, because all covariances are zero. However, we can combine the AR(1) structure with ARCH variance to give a model:

$$Y_t = \mu + a(Y_{t-1} - \mu) + \sigma_t \varepsilon_t$$
$$\varepsilon_t \text{ iid } \sim N(0, 1) \tag{2.10}$$

and

$$\sigma_t^2 = a_0 + \alpha (Y_{t-1} - \mu)^2 \tag{2.11}$$

This version of the model allows for volatility bunching and for autocorrelations in the data.

GARCH(1,1)

The GARCH model, developed by Bollerslev (1986), is an extension of the ARCH model. The GARCH model is more flexible and has been found to provide a significantly better fit for many econometric applications than the ARCH model. The simplest version of the GARCH model for the stock log-return process is

$$Y_t = \mu + \sigma_t \varepsilon_t \tag{2.12}$$

$$\sigma_t^2 = \alpha_0 + \alpha_1 (Y_{t-1} - \mu)^2 + \beta \sigma_{t-1}^2 \tag{2.13}$$

The variance process for the GARCH model looks like an AR moving-average (ARMA) process, except without a random innovation. As in the ARCH model, conditionally, (given Y_{t-1} and σ_{t-1}) the variance is fixed. If $\alpha_1 + \beta < 1$, then the process is wide-sense stationary. This is a necessary condition for a credible model, otherwise it will have a tendency to explode, with ever-increasing variance. For the parameters fitted to the stock returns data summarized in Table 2.1, we have $\alpha_1 + \beta < 1$.

As with the ARCH model, we can capture autocorrelation by combining the AR(1) model with the GARCH variance process, for a model where:

$$Y_t = \mu + a(Y_{t-1} - \mu) + \sigma_t \varepsilon_t \quad \varepsilon_t \text{ iid } \sim N(0, 1) \tag{2.14}$$

and

$$\sigma_t^2 = \alpha_0 + \alpha_1 (Y_{t-1} - \mu)^2 + \beta \sigma_{t-1}^2 \tag{2.15}$$

Using ARCH and GARCH Models

The ARCH and GARCH processes are easily simulated. In Figure 2.8 are shown probability density functions of the proceeds of a unit investment, accumulated for 10 years assuming a three-parameter ARCH process or a four-parameter GARCH process. The ARCH and GARCH density functions are estimated by simulation. The LN distribution is also plotted for comparison. The parameters used are estimated from the TSE 300 data summarized in Table 2.1.

The method of parameter estimation does not automatically match means, and clearly the ARCH and GARCH models estimated have higher means and variances than the LN. However, they are not substantially fatter-tailed on the crucial left side of the distribution.

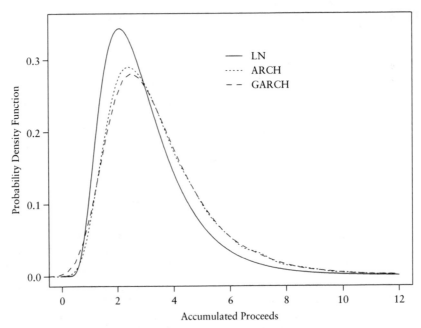

FIGURE 2.8 Distribution of the proceeds of a 10-year $100 single-premium investment, assuming LN, ARCH, and GARCH log return processes

REGIME-SWITCHING LOGNORMAL MODEL (RSLN)

Regime-switching models assume that a discrete process switches between, say, K regimes randomly. Each regime is characterized by a different parameter set. The process describing which regime the price process is in at any time is assumed here to be Markov—that is, the probability of changing regime depends only on the current regime, not on the history of the process.

One of the simplest regime-switching models is the regime-switching LN model (RSLN), where the process switches randomly at each time step between K LN processes. This approach maintains some of the attractive simplicity of the independent LN model, in particular mathematical tractability, but more accurately captures the more extreme observed behavior. This is one of the simplest ways to introduce stochastic volatility; the volatility randomly moves between the K values corresponding to the K regimes.

The rationale behind the regime-switching framework is that the market may switch from time to time between, for example, a stable, low-volatility regime and a more unstable high-volatility regime. Periods of high volatility may arise because of some short-term political or economic uncertainty.

Regime-switching models for economic series were introduced by Hamilton (1989), who described an AR regime-switching process. In Hamilton and Susmel (1994), several regime-switching models are analyzed, varying the number of regimes and the form of the model within regimes. The models within each regime are assumed to follow ARCH and GARCH processes, with the residuals, ε_t, having normal or Student's t distribution. The simpler form using LN models within regimes was used by Bollen (1998), who constructed a lattice for valuing American options. Harris (1999) has developed a vector AR regime-switching model for actuarial use, fitted to quarterly Australian data.

It emerges in Chapter 3 that the two-regime RSLN model provides a very good fit to the stock index data relevant to equity-linked insurance. For that reason, it will be the main model used throughout the rest of the book. We will derive the relevant probability functions in some detail here.

Under the RSLN model we assume that the stock return process lies in one of K regimes or states. We let ρ_t denote the regime applying in the interval $[t, t + 1]$ (in months), $\rho_t = 1, 2, \ldots K$, and let S_t be the total return index value at t, and let Y_t be the log-return process, then if $Y_t = \log(S_{t+1}/S_t)$,

$$Y_t \big| \rho_t \sim N(\mu_{\rho_t}, \sigma^2_{\rho_t})$$

where μ_R, σ^2_R are the mean and variance parameter of the Rth regime.

Users of regime-switching models have found, in general, that two or three regimes are sufficient (that is, $K = 2$ or $K = 3$). Hamilton and Susmel (1994), looking at weekly economic data (from 1962 to 1987), and assuming ARCH models for returns within each state, found some evidence for using three regimes—adding a very low-volatility regime applied for a single period of the early 1960s. Harris (1999), using quarterly economic data, and assuming AR models within each regime, found no evidence for using more than two regimes. In Chapter 3 we will demonstrate the relative merits of using two or three regimes for the total return data. Generally, the two-regime model (RSLN-2) appears to be sufficient. The two-regime process can be illustrated by the diagram in Figure 2.9.

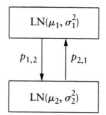

FIGURE 2.9 RSLN, with two regimes.

The transition matrix $\mathbf{P}$ denotes the probabilities of switching regimes. Regime switching is assumed to take place at the end of each time unit, so that, for example, $p_{1,1}$ is the probability that the process stays in regime 1, given that it is in regime 1 for the previous time period, and in general:

$$p_{i,j} = \Pr[\rho_{t+1} = j \,|\, \rho_t = i] \quad i = 1, 2 \quad j = 1, 2 \qquad (2.16)$$

So for a RSLN model with two regimes, we have six parameters to estimate,

$$\Theta_{K=2} = \{\mu_1, \mu_2, \sigma_1, \sigma_2, p_{1,2}, p_{2,1}\} \qquad (2.17)$$

With three regimes we have 12 parameters,

$$\Theta_{K=3} = \{\mu_j, \sigma_j, p_{i,j}\} \quad j = 1, 2, 3, \quad i = 1, 2, 3, \, i \neq j \qquad (2.18)$$

In the following chapter we discuss issues of parsimony. This is the balance of added complexity and improvement of the fit of the model to the data. In other words—do we really need 12 parameters?

Using the RSLN-2 Model

Although the regime-switching model has more parameters than the ARCH and GARCH models, the structure is very simple and analytic results are readily available. In this section, we will derive the distribution function for the accumulated proceeds at some time n of a unit investment at time $t = 0$. Let S_n denote the proceeds, so that

$$S_n = \exp\left(\sum_{j=1}^{n} Y_j\right) \qquad (2.19)$$

The key technique is to condition on the time spent in each regime. Let R denote the number of months spent in regime 1, so that $n - R$ is the number of months spent in regime 2. Then the conditional sum $\sum_{j=1}^{n} Y_j \,|\, R$ is the sum of both the following:

- R independent, normally distributed random variables with mean μ_1 and variance σ_1^2.
- $n - R$ independent, normally distributed random variables with mean μ_2 and variance σ_2^2.

This sum is also (conditionally) normally distributed, with mean $R\mu_1 + (n - R)\mu_2$ and variance $R\sigma_1^2 + (n - R)\sigma_2^2$. This means that the conditional variable $S_n | R$ is lognormally distributed. So, if we can derive a probability function for the total time spent in regime 1, then we can use that function to find the distribution function, density function, and moments of the sum of the log-returns and therefore of S_n.

Probability Function for Total Sojourn in Regime 1

Let R_n be the total number of months spent in regime 1 for a process $\{S_t\}_{t=0}^{n}$, then $R_n \in \{0, 1, \ldots, n\}$. We want to derive the probability function $\Pr[R_n = r] = p_n(r)$. Let $R_n(t)$ be the total sojourn in regime 1 in the interval $[t, n)$, and consider

$$\Pr[R_n(t) = r|\rho_{t-1}]$$

for $r = 0, 1, \ldots, n - t$ and $t = 1, \ldots, n - 1$. Clearly $\Pr[R_n(t) = r|\rho_{t-1}] = 0$ for $r > n - t$ or $r < 0$. For example, $\Pr[R_n(n - 1) = 0|\rho_{t-1} = 1]$ is the probability that the last time unit is not spent in regime 1, given that the process is in regime 1 in the previous period, that is, for $t \in [n - 2, n - 1)$, so that $\Pr[R_n(n - 1) = 0|\rho_{t-1} = 1] = p_{1,2}$. Similarly,

$$\Pr[R_n(n - 1) = 1|\rho_{t-1} = 1] = p_{1,1}$$
$$\Pr[R_n(n - 1) = 0|\rho_{t-1} = 2] = p_{2,2}$$
$$\Pr[R_n(n - 1) = 1|\rho_{t-1} = 2] = p_{2,1}$$

We can work backward from these values to the required probabilities for $R_n = R_n(0)$ using the relationship:

$$\Pr[R_n(t) = r|\rho_{t-1}] = p_{\rho_{t-1},1} \Pr[R_n(t + 1) = r - 1|\rho_t = 1]$$
$$+ p_{\rho_{t-1},2} \Pr[R_n(t + 1) = r|\rho_t = 2] \quad (2.20)$$

The justification for this is that, in the unit of time $t \to t + 1$, one of the following is true:

- The process is in regime 1 ($\rho_t = 1$) with probability $p_{\rho_{t-1},1}$, which leaves $r - 1$ time periods to be spent in regime 1 subsequently.
- The process is in regime 2 ($\rho_t = 2$) with probability $p_{\rho_{t-1},2}$, in which case r time periods must be spent in regime 1 in the interval $[t + 1, n)$.

Ultimately, this recursion will deliver the probability functions for R_0 conditional on regime 1 as the starting point, $\Pr[R_n(0) = r|\rho_{-1} = 1]$, and conditional on regime 2 as a starting point, $\Pr[R_n(0) = r|\rho_{-1} = 2]$. In Chapter 4, an example of the distribution of R for $n = 12$ is given.

For the unconditional probability distribution, use the invariant distribution of the regime-switching Markov chain. The invariant distribution $\pi = (\pi_1, \pi_2)$ is the unconditional probability distribution for the Markov process. This means that at any time, with no information about the process history, the probability that the process is in regime 1 is π_1, and the probability that it is in regime 2 is $\pi_2 = 1 - \pi_1$. Under the invariant distribution, each transition returns the same distribution; that is

$$\pi P = \pi \tag{2.21}$$

$$\implies \pi_1 p_{1,1} + \pi_2 p_{2,1} = \pi_1 \tag{2.22}$$

and

$$\pi_1 p_{1,2} + \pi_2 p_{2,2} = \pi_2 \tag{2.23}$$

and since

$$p_{1,1} + p_{1,2} = 1 \tag{2.24}$$

$$\pi_1 = \frac{p_{2,1}}{p_{1,2} + p_{2,1}} \quad \text{and} \quad \pi_2 = 1 - \pi_1 = \frac{p_{1,2}}{p_{1,2} + p_{2,1}} \tag{2.25}$$

Using the invariant distribution for the regime-switching process, the probability function of $R_n(0)$ is $\Pr[R_n(0) = r] = p_n(r)$ where

$$p_n(r) = \pi_1 \Pr[R_n(0) = r | \rho_{-1} = 1] + \pi_2 \Pr[R_n(0) = r | \rho_{-1} = 2] \tag{2.26}$$

Probability Functions for S_n

Using the probability function for R_n, the distribution of the total return index at time n can be calculated analytically. Let S_n represent the total return index at n, assume $S_0 = 1$, then

$$S_n | R_n \sim \text{LN}(\mu^*(R_n), \sigma^*(R_n)) \quad \text{where} \quad \mu^*(R_n) = R_n \mu_1 + (n - R_n) \mu_2 \tag{2.27}$$

and

$$\sigma^*(R_n) = \sqrt{R_n \sigma_1^2 + (n - R_n)\sigma_2^2} \tag{2.28}$$

Then, if $p_n(r)$ is the probability function for R_n:

$$F_{S_n}(x) = \Pr(S_n \leq x) = \sum_{r=0}^{n} \Pr(S_n \leq x \mid R_n = r)p_n(r) \qquad (2.29)$$

$$= \sum_{r=0}^{n} \Phi\left(\frac{\log x - \mu^*(r)}{\sigma^*(r)}\right)p_n(r) \qquad (2.30)$$

where $\Phi()$ is the standard normal probability distribution function.
Similarly, the probability density function for S_n is:

$$f_{S_n}(x) = \sum_{r=0}^{n} \frac{1}{\sigma^*(r)}\, \phi\left(\frac{\log x - \mu^*(r)}{\sigma^*(r)}\right)p_n(r) \qquad (2.31)$$

where $\phi()$ is the standard normal density function.

Equation 2.31 has been used to calculate the density functions shown in Figure 2.10. This shows the RSLN and LN density functions for the

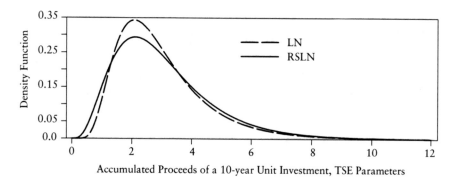

FIGURE 2.10 Probability density curves for independent LN and RSLN models, TSE and S&P data.

stock price at $t = 10$ years, given $S_0 = 1.0$, using both the TSE and S&P parameters. In both cases, over this long term, the left tail is substantially fatter for the RSLN model than for the LN model. This difference has important implications for longer-term actuarial applications.

The probability function for the sojourn times can also be used to find unconditional moments of the stock price at any time n.

$$E[(S_n)^k] = E[E[(S_n)^k \mid R_n]]$$

$$= E\left[\exp(k(R_n\mu_1 + (n - R_n)\mu_2) + \frac{k^2}{2}(R_n\sigma_1^2 + (n - R_n)\sigma_2^2)\right]$$

$$= E\left[\exp\left(R_n\left(k(\mu_1 - \mu_2) + \frac{k^2}{2}(\sigma_1^2 - \sigma_2^2)\right)\right)\right]\exp\left(k\,n\mu_2 + \frac{k^2}{2}\,n\sigma_2^2\right)$$

$$= \exp\left(kn\mu_2 + \frac{k^2}{2}n\sigma_2^2\right)\sum_{r=0}^{n}\exp\left(r\left(k(\mu_1 - \mu_2) + \frac{k^2}{2}(\sigma_1^2 - \sigma_2^2)\right)\right)p_n(r)$$

THE EMPIRICAL MODEL

Under the *empirical* model of stock returns, we use the historic returns as the sample space for future returns, each being equally likely, sampling with replacement. That is, assume we have n observations of the total stock return:

$$\text{Return on stocks in } [t - 1, t) = i_t \quad t = 1, 2, 3, \ldots, n$$

Then we may simulate future values for stock returns for any period $[r - 1, r)$ as I_r where

$$\Pr[I_r = i_t] = \frac{1}{n} \quad \text{for } t = 1, 2, \ldots, n$$

The empirical model assumes returns in successive periods are independent and identically distributed. It provides a simple method for simulation, though, obviously, analytical development is not possible.

This distribution is useful as a simple, quick method to obtain simulated returns. It suffers from the same problems in representing the data as the LN model (which it closely resembles in distribution). Although we are sampling from the historical returns, by assuming independence we lose the autocorrelation in the data. The autocorrelation means that low returns tend to be bunched together, giving a larger probability of very poor returns than we get from random sampling of individual historical returns. The autocorreleation is the source of fatter left tails in the accumulation factor distribution. Similarly, high returns also tend to be bunched together, giving fatter right tails. So the empirical model tends to be too thin-tailed, and the assumption of independence also means that volatility bunching is not modeled. One adaptation that would reintroduce some of the autocorrelation is to sample in blocks of several months at a time.

The empirical method is used by some financial institutions for value-at-risk calculations, but these tend to be quite short-term applications. One particularly useful feature of the method, though, is the ease of constructing multivariate distributions. Suppose we are interested in a bivariate distribution of long-term interest rates and stock returns. These are not independent, but by sampling the pair from the same date using the empirical method, some of the relationship is automatically incorporated. We lose any lagged correlation, however.

THE STABLE DISTRIBUTION FAMILY

Stable distributions appear in some econometrics literature, for example, McCulloch (1996). Panneton (1999) and Finkelstein (1995) both used stable distributions for valuing maturity guarantees. One reason for their popularity is that stable distributions can be very fat-tailed, and are also easy to combine, as the sum of stable distributions is always another stable distribution. Stable distributions are related to *Levy processes*; if $\{Y_t\}_{t>0}$ is a Levy process, then at any fixed time Y_t has a corresponding stable distribution.

A distribution with distribution function F is a stable distribution if for independent, indentically distributed X_1, X_2, X, and for any $a, b > 0$, there exists $c > 0$, d such that:

$$aX_1 + bX_2 \sim cX + d \qquad (2.32)$$

(We use $\sim$ here to mean having the same distribution.) This relationship is clearly true for the normal distribution—the sum of any two normal random variables is also normal, and all normal random variables can be standardized to the same distribution. It is not true of, for example, the Poisson distribution. The sum of two independent, identically distributed Poisson random variables is also Poisson, but cannot be expressed in terms of the same Poisson parameter as the original distribution.

It is not possible, in general, to describe stable distributions in terms of their probability or distribution functions, which require special functions.

It is possible to summarize the family in terms of the characteristic function,

$$\phi(X) = E[e^{iXt}] = \exp\{i\gamma t - c|t|^\alpha(1 - i\beta \operatorname{sign}(t) z(t, \alpha))\} \qquad (2.33)$$

where $c > 0$, $\alpha \in (0, 2]$, $\beta \in [-1, 1]$ and

$$z(t, \alpha) = \begin{cases} \tan\left(\frac{\pi\alpha}{2}\right) & \text{if } \alpha \neq 1 \\ -\frac{2}{\pi} \log|t| & \text{if } \alpha = 1 \end{cases} \qquad (2.34)$$

The γ parameter is a location parameter; the α component is called the *characteristic exponent* and is used to classify distributions within the stable family. We say that a distribution is α-stable if it is stable with characteristic component α. The case $\alpha = 2$ corresponds to the normal distribution and $\alpha = 1$ is the Cauchy distribution. The inverse Gaussian distribution corresponds to $\alpha = 1/2$, $\beta = 1$. For $\alpha < 2$, the distribution is fat-tailed, with infinite variance. If $\beta = 0$, then the distribution is symmetric.

As with the normal distribution, stable distributions can be used to describe stochastic processes. Let $\{Y_t\}$ be a stochastic process, such as the log-return process. If Y_t has independent and stationary increments (for any time unit), then Y_t is a stable or Levy process and Y_t has an α-stable distribution.

Stable processes have been popular for modeling financial processes because they can be very fat-tailed, and because of the obvious attraction of being able to convolute the distribution. However, they are not easy to use; estimation requires advanced techniques and it is not easy to simulate a stable process, although a method is given in Chambers et al. (1976), and software using that method is available from Nolan (2000). The model specifically does not incorporate autocorrelations arising from volatility bunching, and therefore does not, in fact, fit the data sets in the section on data particularly well. An excellent source of explanatory and technical information on the use of stable distributions is given in Nolan (1998); also, on his Web site (2000), Nolan provides software for analyzing stable distributions.

GENERAL STOCHASTIC VOLATILITY MODELS

We can allow volatility to vary stochastically without the regime constraints of the RSLN model. For example, let $y_t = \mu + \sigma_t \varepsilon_t$ and $\sigma_t^2 = \sigma_{t-1}^2 + a(\sigma_{t-1} - \sigma)^2 + \varepsilon_t^\sigma$ where ε_t and ε_t^σ are random innovations. It is convenient to assume ε_t^σ are distributed on $(0, \infty)$. For example, we might use a gamma distribution. These models, and more complex varieties, are highly adaptable. However, in general, it is very difficult to estimate the parameters.

THE WILKIE MODEL

The Wilkie Model Structure

The Wilkie model (Wilkie 1986, 1995) was developed over a number of years, with an early version applied to GMMBs in the MGWP Report (1980) and the full version first applied to insurance company solvency by the Faculty of Actuaries Solvency Working Party (1986). The Wilkie model differs in several fundamental ways from the models covered so far:

- It is a *multivariate* model, meaning that several related economic series are projected together. This is very useful for applications that require consistent projections of, for example, stock prices and inflation rates or fixed interest yields.
- The model is designed for long-term applications. Wilkie (1995) looks at 100-year projections, and suggests that it is ideally suited for applications requiring projections more than 10 years ahead.
- The model is designed to be applied to annual data. Without changing the AR structure of the individual series, it cannot be easily adapted to more frequent data. Attempts to produce a continuous form for the model, by constructing a Brownian bridge between the end-year points (e.g., Chan 1998) add complexity. The annual frequency means that the model is not ideal for assessing hedging strategies, where it is important that stocks are bought and sold at intervals much shorter than the one-year time unit of the Wilkie model.

The Wilkie model makes assumptions about the stochastic processes governing the evolution of a number of key economic variables. It has the cascade structure illustrated in Figure 2.11; this is not supposed to represent

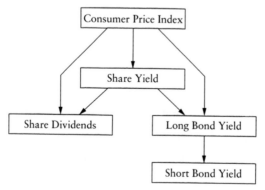

FIGURE 2.11 Structure of the Wilkie investment model.

a causal development, but is related to the chronological processes. Each series incorporates some factor from connected series higher up the cascade, and each also incorporates a random component.

The Wilkie model is widely used in the United Kingdom and elsewhere in actuarial applications by insurance companies, consultants, and academic researchers. It has been fitted to data from a number of different countries, including Canada and the United States. The Canadian data (1923 to 1993) were used for the figures for quantile reserves for segregated fund contracts in Boyle and Hardy (1996).

The integrated structure of the Wilkie model has made it particularly useful for actuarial applications. For the purpose of valuing equity-linked liabilities, this is useful if, for example, we assume liabilities depend on stock prices while reserves are invested in bonds. Also, for managed funds it is possible to project the correlated returns on bonds and stocks.

What is commonly called the Wilkie model is actually a collection of models. We give here the equations of the most commonly used form of the model. However, the interested reader is urged to read Wilkie's excellent 1995 paper for more details and more model options (e.g., for the ARCH model of inflation).

The notation can be confusing because there are many parameters and five integrated processes. The notation used here is derived from (but is not the same as) Wilkie (1995). The subscript q refers to the inflation series, subscript y to the dividend yield, d to the dividend index process, c to the long-term bond yield, and b to the short-term bond yield series. The μ terms all indicate a mean, although it may be a mean of the log process, so μ_q is the mean of the inflation process modeled, which is the force of inflation process. The term a indicates an AR parameter; σ is a (conditional) variance parameter; and w is a weighting applied to the force of inflation within the other processes. For example, the share dividend yield process includes a term $w_y \delta_q(t)$, which is how the current force[5] of inflation $(\delta_q(t))$ influences the current logarithm of the dividend yield (see equation 2.36). The random innovations are denoted by $z(t)$, with a subscript denoting the series. These are all assumed to be independent $N(0,1)$ variables.

The Inflation Model

Let $\delta_q(t)$ be the force of inflation in the year $[t - 1, t)$, then $\delta_q(t)$ follows an AR(1) process:

$$\delta_q(t) = \mu_q + a_q(\delta_q(t - 1) - \mu_q) + \sigma_q z_q(t) \qquad (2.35)$$

---

[5] A *force* of interest or inflation is the continuously compounded annualized rate.

where

$\delta_q(t)$ is the force of inflation in the tth year,

μ_q is the mean force of inflation, assumed constant.

a_q is the parameter controlling the strength of the AR (or rather the weakness, since large a_q implies weak autoregression)—that is, how strong is the pull back to the mean each year.

σ_q is the standard deviation of the white noise term of the inflation model.

$z_q(t)$ is a $N(0,1)$ white noise series.

The ultimate distribution for the force of inflation is $N(\mu_q, \sigma_q^2/(1 - a_q^2))$, so that, if $Q(t)$ is an index of inflation, the ultimate distribution of $Q(t)/Q(t-1)$ is LN. However, unlike the LN model, successive years are correlated through the AR.

Share Prices and Dividends

We model separately the dividend yield on stocks, and the force of dividend inflation. The share dividend yield in year t, $y(t)$ is generated using:

$$y(t) = \exp\{w_y\,\delta_q(t) + \mu_y + yn(t)\} \qquad (2.36)$$

where

$$yn(t) = a_y\,yn(t-1) + \sigma_y\,z_y(t) \qquad (2.37)$$

So $yn(t)$ is an AR(1) process, independent of the inflation process, $z_y(t)$ being a Normal(0,1) white noise series.

Clearly

$$E[y(t)] = e^{\mu_y}\,E[\exp(w_y\,\delta_q(t))]\,E[\exp(yn(t))] \qquad (2.38)$$

because $\delta_q(t)$ and $yn(t)$ are independent. $E[\exp(w_y\,\delta_q(t))]$ is $M_{\delta_q}(w_y)$, where $M_{\delta_q}(u)$ is the moment generating function of $\delta_q(t)$. For large t, the moment generating function of $\delta_q(t)$ is

$$M_{\delta_q}(u) = \exp(u\,\mu_q + u^2\,(\sigma_q)^2/2) \qquad (2.39)$$

So

$$E[y(t)] = e^{\mu_y}\,M_q(w_y)\left[\exp\left(\mu_{yn} + \frac{\sigma_y^2}{2\,(1 - a_y^2)}\right)\right] \qquad (2.40)$$

The force of dividend growth, $\delta_d(t)$, is generated from the following relationship:

$$\delta_d(t) = w_d\,DM(t) + (1 - w_d)\,\delta_q(t) + d_y\,\sigma_y\,z_y(t - 1) + \mu_d + b_d\sigma_d z_d(t - 1) + \sigma_d z_d(t)$$

where

$$DM(t) = d_d\delta_q(t) + (1 - d_d)DM(t - 1) \qquad (2.41)$$

The force of dividend then comprises:

- A weighted average of current and past inflation—the total weight assigned to the current $\delta_q(t)$ being $w_d\,d_d + (1 - w_d)$. The weight attached to past forces of inflation is $w_d\,d_d(1 - d_d)^\tau$ for the force of inflation in the τth year before t.
- A dividend yield effect where a fall in the dividend yield is associated with a rise in the dividend index, and vice versa (i.e., $d_y < 0$).
- An influence from the previous year's white noise term.
- A white noise term where $z_d(t)$ is a Normal(0,1) white noise sequence.

The force of dividend can be used to construct an index of dividends,

$$D(t) = D(t - 1) \times e^{\delta_d(t)}$$

A price index for shares, $P(t)$, can be constructed from the dividend index and the dividend yield, $P(t) = D(t)/y(t)$. The overall return on shares each year $py(t)$ can be summarized in the gross rolled up yield,

$$py(t) = \frac{P(t) + D(t)}{P(t - 1)} - 1.0$$

Long-Term and Short-Term Bond Yields

The yield on long-term bonds, $c(t)$, is split into a *real* part, $cn(t)$, and an inflation-linked part, $cm(t)$, so that

$$c(t) = cm(t) + cn(t)$$

where

$$cm(t) = d_c\,\delta_q(t) + (1 - d_c)cm(t - 1)$$

and

$$cn(t) = \mu_c\exp(a_c\,cn(t - 1) + y_c\,\sigma_y\,z_y(t) + \sigma_c\,z_c(t))$$

The inflation part of the model is a weighted moving-average model. The real part is essentially an autoregressive model of order one (i.e., AR(1)), with a contribution from the dividend yield. The yield on short-term bonds, $b(t)$, is calculated as a multiple of the long-term rate $c(t)$, so that

$$b(t) = c(t) \exp(-bd(t))$$

where

$$bd(t) = \mu_b + a_b(bd(t-1) - \mu_b) + b_c \, \sigma_c \, z_c(t) + \sigma_b \, z_b(t)$$

These equations state that the model for the log of the ratio between the long-term and the short-term rates is AR(1), with an added term allowing for a contribution from the long-term residual term.

Other Series

Wilkie (1995) also describes integrated models for wage inflation, property, bonds linked to an inflation index ("index-linked stocks"), and exchange rates. The paper also presents and investigates alternative models, including ARCH models in place of the AR models used, transfer functions, and a vector autoregression model.

Parameters

The parameters suggested in Wilkie (1995) for Canada and the United States are given in Table 2.2. Note that figures for the short-term interest rate for the United States are not available. These parameters were fitted using 1923 to 1993 data for the Canadian figures, and data from 1926 to 1989 for the United States.

To run the Wilkie model, one can start the simulations at neutral values of the parameters. These are the stationary values we would obtain if all the residuals were zero. Alternatively, we can start the model at the current date and let the past data determine the initial parameter values. For general purposes, it is convenient to start the simulations at the neutral values of the parameters so that the results are not distorted by the particular nature of the current investment conditions. If new contracts are to be written for some time ahead, the figures using neutral Wilkie starting parameters are close to the average figures that would be obtained at different dates using formerly current starting values. However, for strategic decisions that are designed for immediate implementation it is appropriate to use the contemporary data for starting values for the series.

TABLE 2.2 Parameters for Wilkie model, Canada and United States, from Wilkie (1995).

Parameter	Canada	U.S.
Inflation Model		
μ_q	0.034	0.030
a_q	0.64	0.65
σ_q	0.032	0.035
Dividend Yield		
w_y	1.17	0.50
a_y	0.7	0.7
μ_y	0.0375	0.0430
σ_y	0.19	0.21
Dividend Growth		
w_d	0.19	1.00
d_d	0.26	0.38
μ_d	0.0010	0.0155
y_d	−0.11	−0.35
b_d	0.58	0.50
σ_d	0.07	0.09
Long-Term Interest Rates		
d_c	0.040	0.058
a_c	0.95	0.96
μ_c	0.0370	0.0265
y_c	0.10	0.07
σ_c	0.185	0.210
Short-Term Interest Rates		
μ_b	0.26	
a_b	0.38	
c_b	0.73	
σ_b	0.21	

Some Comments on the Wilkie Model

The Wilkie model has been subject to a unique level of scrutiny. Many companies employ their own models, but few issue sufficient detail for independent validation and testing. The most vigorous criticism of the Wilkie model has come from Huber (1997). Huber's work is concerned with:

■ Evidence of a permanent change in the nature of economic time series in Western nations around the second world war is not allowed for. This criticism applies to all stationary time-series models of investment, but nonstationary models can have even more serious problems in generating impossible scenarios with explosive volatility, for example. It is useful to be aware of the limitations of all models—to be aware, for example, that in the event of a major world conflagration the predicted distributions from any stationary model may well be incorrect. On the other hand, in such circumstances this may not be our first worry.

■ The inconsistency of the Wilkie model with some economic theories, such as the efficient market hypothesis. Note, however, that the Wilkie model is very close to a random walk model over short terms, and the random walk model is consistent with the efficient market hypothesis. Huber himself points out that there is significant debate among economists about the applicability of the efficient market hypothesis over long time periods, and the Wilkie approach is not out of line with those of other econometricians.

■ The problem of "data mining," by which Huber means that a statistical time-series approach, which finds a model to match the available data, cannot then use the same data to test the model. Thus, with only one data series available, all non-theory-based time-series modeling is rejected. One way around the problem is to use part of the available data to fit the model, and the rest to test the fit. The problem for a complex model with many parameters is that data are already scarce.

This argument is, as Huber noted, not specifically or even accurately aimed at the Wilkie model. The Wilkie model is substantially theory driven, informed by standard statistical time-series analysis.

Huber's work is not intended to limit actuaries to a deterministic methodology, although it has often been quoted in support of that view. However, it is certainly important that actuaries make themselves aware of the provenance, characteristics, and limitations of the models they use.

VECTOR AUTOREGRESSION

The Wilkie model is an example of a vector AR approach to modeling financial series. The vector represents the various economic series. The cascade structure makes parameter estimation easier and, perhaps, makes the model more transparent. The more general vector AR is to use an AR(q) structure for a vector of relevant financial series, with correlations between the series captured in a variance-covariance matrix.

The vector AR equation is used to generate a vector of economic indicators at each time step. Let $x_t = (x_{1,t}, x_{2,t}, \ldots, x_{m,t})^T$ be the vector, so that, for example, $x_{1,t}$ represents the inflation rate in the period $(t-1, t]$, $x_{2,t}$ represents the total return on shares, $x_{3,t}$ represents the yield on long-term bonds, and so forth. The vector AR equation with order q is then:

$$x_t = \mu + \sum_{j=1}^{q} A_j(x_{t-j} - \mu) + L Z_t \qquad (2.42)$$

where μ is a $(m \times 1)$ vector of conditional mean values for the processes, A_j is a $(m \times m)$ matrix of AR coefficients, for $j = 1, 2, \ldots, q$; Z_t is an independent, identically distributed, standard multivariate normal random variable with mean 0 and variance-covariance matrix 1; and $L.L^T = \Sigma$, the variance-covariance matrix of the series residuals.

An example of a vector AR model for stock returns, inflation, and bond yields is given in Wright (1997). Wright's model is slightly more complex, as inflation is treated as an exogenous variable—that is, it is modeled independently of the other series and then included as an extra term in the vector autoregression equation. The advantage of this model is that much of the correlation between series is explained by correlations with inflation. By removing inflation from the formula, many of the covariance terms in Σ can be set to zero.

CHAPTER 3

Maximum Likelihood Estimation for Stock Return Models

INTRODUCTION

I n order to use any of the models in Chapter 2, we need to determine appropriate parameters. There are two major approaches to parameter estimation in common use. The first is maximum likelihood estimation (MLE), which is the subject of this chapter. The second approach, less common but also with important advantages, is the Bayesian approach, which is described in Chapter 5.

In this chapter, we discuss some of the features of MLE, particularly in the context of time series estimation. We also show how to apply MLE to determine parameters for some of the univariate models discussed in Chapter 2. These include the regime-switching lognormal (RSLN) and the autoregressive conditionally heteroscedastic (ARCH) and generalized-ARCH (GARCH) models.

Likelihood is also commonly used as a basis for model selection. Reading Chapter 2 one might wonder which model is the best for stock returns. The answer is not clear cut, but using some of the model selection criteria in common use, it is possible to rank the models to some extent, and we do this in the section on likelihood-based model selection in this chapter.

Intuitively, the MLE is the parameter value giving the highest probability of observing the data values, represented by $x = (x_1, x_2, \ldots, x_n)$. This is found by maximizing the *likelihood function*, which is just the joint probability function of the data expressed as a function of the parameters. For example, suppose we have a sample of three independent observations, $x = (2.8, 3.2, 3.9)$ and we are interested in fitting a normal distribution with mean μ and variance σ^2 to this data. Since the observations are independent, the likelihood function, which is the joint probability density function (pdf) for the data, is simply the product of the individual density functions. It is unlikely, looking at the three values, that the μ parameter for the model is, for example, 2.0. This is confirmed by calculating the likelihood function for these data, using parameters $\mu = 2.0$ and $\sigma = 1.4$ for the normal distribution, we get a joint pdf equal to 0.0054 (which is the best we can do for this value of μ). If instead we use $\mu = 3.3$ and $\sigma = 0.454606$, the joint pdf increases to 0.15079. So, we say that the second set of parameters is more likely than the first; in fact, no other pair of values for μ and σ will give a higher value for the joint pdf, so these are the maximum likelihood parameters.

The likelihood function can be also be expressed in terms of a sample of random variables $X = (X_1, X_2, \ldots, X_n)$. In this case, it is also a random variable. The maximum likelihood estimators can be found in terms of the sample X and are random variables. It is not usually specified whether we are using the observed likelihood function with the observed data x or the random function with the random sample X; the context determines which is meant.

For an unknown parameter θ (scalar) or $\boldsymbol{\theta} = (\theta_1, \theta_2, \ldots, \theta_n)'$ (a vector of parameters), the likelihood function is the value of the joint probability (density) function of X or x. This function depends on the unknown $\boldsymbol{\theta}$. The maximum likelihood estimate $\hat{\boldsymbol{\theta}}$ of $\boldsymbol{\theta}$ is the value that gives the highest value for the joint probability (density) over all the possible parameters. The parameter $\boldsymbol{\theta}$ here is regarded as fixed but unknown. The estimator $\hat{\boldsymbol{\theta}}$ is a function of the sample X. Like the data, $\hat{\boldsymbol{\theta}}$ is considered as a random variable for random X, or as an *observed* value for observed x. The likelihood function is defined as

$$L(\boldsymbol{\theta}) = f(X_1, X_2, X_2, \ldots, X_n; \boldsymbol{\theta}) \tag{3.1}$$

In the case of discretely distributed random variables, the likelihood function is the joint probability of X, which depends on the parameter $\boldsymbol{\theta}$. For continuous random variables, the likelihood is the pdf for the multivariate random variable X. Again, this joint density is a function of the parameter $\boldsymbol{\theta}$. In both cases, the likelihood must be nonnegative, and therefore finding the maximum of $L(\boldsymbol{\theta})$ is equivalent to finding the maximum of the log-likelihood $l(\boldsymbol{\theta}) = \log L(\boldsymbol{\theta})$: It is almost always simpler to work with the log-likelihood function rather than with the likelihood itself.

If the model being fitted assumes individual observations are independent and identically distributed, then the joint probability (density) function is simply the product of the individual probability functions, so

$$L(\boldsymbol{\theta}) = \prod_{t=1}^{n} f(x_t; \boldsymbol{\theta})$$

and

$$l(\boldsymbol{\theta}) = \sum_{t=1}^{n} \log f(x_t; \boldsymbol{\theta}) \tag{3.2}$$

For models that assume some serial dependence, things are not quite so straightforward. Iteratively, using the fact that a bivariate random variable (X, Y) has probability function $f(x, y) = f(x|y)f(y)$, the joint probability function for the multivariate series $\{x_1, x_2, \ldots, x_n\}$ can be written as

$$L(\boldsymbol{\theta}) = f(x_1; \boldsymbol{\theta})f(x_2; \boldsymbol{\theta}|x_1)f(x_3; \boldsymbol{\theta}|x_1, x_2) \ldots f(x_n; \boldsymbol{\theta}|x_1, \ldots, x_{n-1}) \quad (3.3)$$

so that

$$l(\boldsymbol{\theta}) = \sum_{t=1}^{n} \log f(x_t; \boldsymbol{\theta}|x_1, \ldots, x_{t-1}) \quad (3.4)$$

In some cases, it is possible to determine the parameters that maximize the log-likelihood for a given data set analytically. If this is not possible, maximization of the log-likelihood is generally relatively easily determined using computer software, provided the likelihood function can be calculated. Further details for some individual models are given in the section on using MLE for the TSE and SSP.

The MLE is described in many textbooks covering statistical inference, including Klugman, Panjer, and Willmot (1998). The application to financial time series is covered admirably in Campbell, Lo, and MacKinlay (1996), which is an excellent, comprehensive reference. Subject to some regularity conditions, estimates found using maximum likelihood have many attractive properties. Considered as a function of the random sample X, the estimator $\hat{\boldsymbol{\theta}}$ is a random variable, so we can talk about its distribution and its moments. This enables us to estimate the accuracy associated with a parameter estimate by considering its mean and variance.

PROPERTIES OF MAXIMUM LIKELIHOOD ESTIMATORS

Stationary Distributions

The asymptotic properties for maximum likelihood estimators are generally derived using independent samples. With dependent time series samples it can be shown that the same results hold provided the time series is *strictly stationary*, which we now define.

A series $Y_t = Y_1, Y_2, \ldots$ is strictly stationary if for any sequence $t_1, t_2, \ldots t_r$, the joint distribution of $\left(Y_{t_1}, Y_{t_2}, \ldots, Y_{t_r}\right)$ is identical to that of $\left(Y_{t_1 - k}, Y_{t_2 - k}, \ldots, Y_{t_r - k}\right)$.

A series $Y_t = Y_1, Y_2, \ldots$ is *weakly stationary* or *covariance stationary* if the unconditional mean is constant, and all covariances $\text{Cov}[Y_t, Y_{t-j}]$ depend only on j. In other words, there must exist μ and a covariance function γ_j such that

$$E[Y_t] = \mu \quad \text{for all } t \quad (3.5)$$

and

$$E\left[(Y_t - \mu)(Y_{t-j} - \mu)\right] = \gamma_j \quad \text{for all } t \text{ and } j \quad (3.6)$$

If the joint density of any selection $(Y_{t_1}, Y_{t_2}, \ldots, Y_{t_r})$ is multivariate normal and the process is covariance stationary, then it is also strictly stationary, because the mean and covariances completely determine the multivariate normal distribution. The reason this is important here is that the most attractive properties of maximum likelihood estimators for independent samples also apply to maximum likelihood estimators for any strictly stationary time series.

Asymptotic Unbiasedness

Taken as a function of the random sample X, the *bias* of an estimator $\hat{\theta}$ of a parameter θ is

$$b(\theta) = E[\hat{\theta} - \theta] \tag{3.7}$$

If an estimator is unbiased then it has expected value equal to the unknown parameter.

The maximum likelihood estimator $\hat{\theta}$ is asymptotically unbiased; this means that for large sample sizes, the expected value of the estimate $\hat{\theta}$ tends to the parameter θ. In many cases $\hat{\theta}$ may be an unbiased estimator for all sample sizes.

Asymptotic Minimum Variance

Provided an estimator is unbiased or nearly unbiased, a low variance estimator is preferred. The variance of an estimator measures how much the estimate will change from one sample to the next. A low variance indicates that different samples will give similar values for the parameter estimate.

The asymptotic (or large sample) variance of the maximum likelihood estimator is related to the *expected information*, $I(\theta)$, defined as follows: for scalar θ

$$I(\theta) = E\left[-\frac{d^2}{d\theta^2} l(\theta) \right]$$

For vector $\boldsymbol{\theta}$, with s elements, $I(\boldsymbol{\theta})$ is an $s \times s$ matrix with i, j entry:

$$I(\boldsymbol{\theta})_{i,j} = E\left[-\frac{\partial^2}{\partial \theta_i \partial \theta_j} l(\theta) \right]$$

The expectation is with respect to the random vector X. In the scalar case, the asymptotic variance of the estimator is $I(\theta)^{-1}$. In the vector case, $I(\boldsymbol{\theta})^{-1}$ gives the asymptotic variance-covariance matrix for the estimator.

The inverse information function is the Cramer-Rao lower bound for the variance of an estimator. It doesn't get better than this for large samples, although for small samples other estimation methods may perform better than maximum likelihood for both bias and variance.

The asymptotic variance $I(\theta)^{-1}$ is often used as an approximate variance of an estimator, even where the sample size is not large. A problem in practice is that, in general, $I(\theta)$ is a function of the unknown parameter θ. To put an approximate value on the variance of $\hat{\theta}$, we use the estimator $\hat{\theta}$ in place of θ. Another problem arises if the likelihood function is very complicated, because then the information matrix is difficult to find analytically. In these cases, we can use numerical methods.

Asymptotic Normal Distribution

Estimates are *asymptotically normal* (multivariate normal if θ is a vector), with mean equal to the parameter(s) being estimated, and variance (matrix) $I(\theta)^{-1}$, where $I(\theta)$ is the information function defined above. For large samples, this can be used to set confidence intervals for the parameters.

MLE of $g(\theta)$ — The Delta Method

The maximum likelihood estimate of a function of θ, say $g(\theta)$, is simply $g(\hat{\theta})$. The value of this can be seen with the lognormal model, for example. Given parameters μ and σ^2 (the mean and variance of the associated normal distribution), the mean of the lognormal distribution is

$$g(\mu, \sigma) = e^{\mu + \sigma^2/2}$$

If we use maximum likelihood to determine parameter estimates $\hat{\mu}$ and $\hat{\sigma}$, the maximum likelihood estimate of the mean is

$$g(\hat{\mu}, \hat{\sigma}) = e^{\hat{\mu} + \hat{\sigma}^2/2}$$

The asymptotic variance of the MLE $g(\hat{\theta})$ is

$$V = \partial' \Sigma \partial$$

where

$$\partial' = \left(\frac{\partial g(\theta)}{\partial \theta_1}, \frac{\partial g(\theta)}{\partial \theta_2}, \ldots, \frac{\partial g(\theta)}{\partial \theta_s} \right)$$

and

$$\Sigma = I(\theta)^{-1}$$

The asymptotic distribution of $g(\hat{\theta})$ is $N(g(\theta), V)$. An approximate 95 percent confidence interval for $g(\theta)$ is, therefore,

$$g(\hat{\theta}) \pm 1.96 \sqrt{V} \tag{3.8}$$

SOME LIMITATIONS OF MAXIMUM LIKELIHOOD ESTIMATION

Although MLE is the first method that most statisticians would use for parameter estimation, and despite the fact that the estimates have all the attractive properties listed above, there are some disadvantages. The first problem is that the asymptotic results do not apply for models that are not strictly stationary. For nonstationary models, other methods may be preferable. The time series that we use in this book are stationary (subject to some parameter constraints).

The asymptotic results cannot be relied on if a parameter is estimated near the boundaries of the parameter space. For example, in the stable distribution described in the section on the stable distribution family in chapter 2, the β parameter must lie in $[-1, 1]$. Using the S&P 500 data, and using MLE, the value estimated is $\hat{\beta} = -1$. Therefore, the asymptotic MLE properties do not apply for this estimator. This problem has also arisen for GARCH and three-regime RSLN models for some stock index data, and the problem should be considered carefully when estimating parameters, especially for more complex models.

The asymptotic properties are only useful if we have a reasonably large sample. For small samples, other estimation methods may have better performance in terms of bias and variance than the MLE. Also, the information available on association between parameter estimates is an asymptotic result—for smaller samples or nonstationary distributions we may have no information about the relationships between the parameter estimates.

Maximum likelihood will find parameters that fit the data for a given model; it will not tell you how close the fit is. For example, we may fit a lognormal model to data and have a very small standard error for the parameters. It should not be assumed however, that a small standard error means the model is a good fit; it just means that, given the lognormal model, there is little uncertainty about the parameters. The model may still provide a worse fit than another model with larger standard errors. However, we can use likelihood as a basis for comparing different models, and we do so in the section on likelihood-based model selection, in this chapter.

USING MLE FOR TSE AND S&P DATA

The Lognormal (LN) Model

Under the lognormal (LN) assumption, the log returns Y_t are assumed to be normally distributed with parameters μ and σ. (The maximum likelihood estimators of the parameters of the normal distribution for Y_t are the same as the maximum likelihood parameters of the LN distribution for the monthly stock returns.) The returns are assumed to be independent, so the version of the log-likelihood given in equation 3.2 can be used; that is, for a sample of n observations, $y_1, y_2, \ldots, y_n$ with mean $\bar{y}$ and sample standard deviation s_y:

$$l(\mu, \sigma) = \sum_{t=1}^{n} \log\left(\frac{1}{\sqrt{2\pi}\,\sigma} \exp\left\{-\frac{1}{2}\left(\frac{y_t - \mu}{\sigma}\right)^2\right\}\right) \tag{3.9}$$

$$= \frac{-n}{2}\log 2\pi - n\log\sigma - \frac{1}{2}\sum_{t=1}^{n}\left(\frac{y_t - \mu}{\sigma}\right)^2 \tag{3.10}$$

So

$$\frac{\partial l(\mu, \sigma)}{\partial \mu} = \frac{1}{\sigma}\left(\sum_{t=1}^{n} y_t - n\mu\right) \tag{3.11}$$

$$\frac{\partial l(\mu, \sigma)}{\partial \sigma} = -\frac{n}{\sigma} + \frac{1}{\sigma^3}\sum_{t=1}^{n}(y_t - \mu)^2 \tag{3.12}$$

The maximum likelihood estimates for μ and σ are found by setting the partial derivatives equal to 0 for parameter estimates, signified by $\hat{\ }$. This gives

$$\hat{\mu} = \bar{y} \tag{3.13}$$

and

$$\hat{\sigma} = \sqrt{\frac{\sum_{t=1}^{n}(y_t - \hat{\mu})^2}{n}} \tag{3.14}$$

So the MLE for the mean of the log-returns is the mean of the log-data. The MLE for the variance is $\frac{n}{n-1}s_y^2$.

The estimator for μ is unbiased for all sample sizes. The estimator for σ is asymptotically unbiased but *is* biased for finite samples. The standard deviation of the log-data, s_y, is an unbiased estimator for σ for any sample size. The sample standard deviation is, therefore, often used in preference to the MLE discussed previously. However, MLE software routines will output the biased estimator.

To find the approximate standard errors for these estimates, first take the second partial derivatives for the likelihood using the random sample $Y_1, \ldots Y_n$:

$$\frac{\partial^2 l(\mu, \sigma)}{\partial \mu^2} = -\frac{n}{\sigma} \tag{3.15}$$

$$\frac{\partial^2 l(\mu, \sigma)}{\partial \mu \partial \sigma} = -\frac{1}{\sigma^2} \left(\sum_{t=1}^{n} Y_t - n\mu \right) \tag{3.16}$$

$$\frac{\partial^2 l(\mu, \sigma)}{\partial \sigma^2} = -\frac{3}{\sigma^4} \sum_{t=1}^{n} (Y_t - \mu)^2 + \frac{n}{\sigma^2} \tag{3.17}$$

Next, take expectations with respect to the variables Y_t, which are independent and identically distributed by assumption, with common distribution $N(\mu, \sigma)$; that is, $E[Y_t] = \mu$ and $E[(Y_t - \mu)^2] = \sigma^2$. The elements of the information matrix then are:

$$E\left[-\frac{\partial^2 l(\mu, \sigma)}{\partial \mu^2} \right] = \frac{n}{\sigma} \tag{3.18}$$

$$E\left[-\frac{\partial^2 l(\mu, \sigma)}{\partial \mu \partial \sigma} \right] = 0 \tag{3.19}$$

$$E\left[-\frac{\partial^2 l(\mu, \sigma)}{\partial \sigma^2} \right] = \frac{2n}{\sigma^2} \tag{3.20}$$

So

$$I(\mu, \sigma) = \begin{pmatrix} n/\sigma^2 & 0 \\ 0 & 2n/\sigma^2 \end{pmatrix} \tag{3.21}$$

and the asymptotic covariance matrix for the estimators $\hat{\mu}$ and $\hat{\sigma}$ is the inverse:

$$\Sigma = \begin{pmatrix} \sigma^2/n & 0 \\ 0 & \sigma^2/2n \end{pmatrix} \tag{3.22}$$

Since we do not know the parameter σ, we approximate with the estimated value $\hat{\sigma}$ for an approximate asymptotic covariance matrix:

$$\Sigma \approx \begin{pmatrix} \hat{\sigma}^2/n & 0 \\ 0 & \hat{\sigma}^2/2n \end{pmatrix} \tag{3.23}$$

TABLE 3.1 LN model parameter estimates, per month, with approximate standard errors.

Series	$\hat{\mu}$	$\hat{\sigma}$
TSE 300 1956–2001	0.00767 (0.002)	0.04591% (0.0014)
S&P 500 1956–2001	0.00947 (0.001)	0.04167% (0.0013)

Using the fact that the estimators are approximately normally distributed allows us to construct approximate confidence intervals for the estimators.

The results for the United States and Canadian total return indices are given in Table 3.1; approximate standard errors are given in parentheses.

Maximum Likelihood for the AR(1) Model for Log-Returns

Under the AR(1) model with $N(0, 1)$ error terms, successive returns are assumed to be dependent. Given the return in the tth time interval, the next return has a normal distribution such that

$$Y_t | Y_{t-1} \sim N(\mu(1 - a) + aY_{t-1}, \sigma^2) \quad t = 2, 3, \ldots, n. \tag{3.24}$$

So, in the likelihood calculation,

$$f(Y_k; \theta | Y_1, Y_2, \ldots, Y_{k-1}) = \frac{1}{\sigma} \phi \left(\frac{Y_t - ((1 - a)\mu + a\, Y_{t-1})}{\sigma} \right)$$

This leaves just the first term in the likelihood, $f(Y_1; \theta)$. Unconditionally, (i.e., if we have no information on earlier returns) the return distribution is

$$Y_t \sim N \left(\mu, \frac{\sigma^2}{1 - a^2} \right)$$

For the initial value Y_1, we use this unconditional distribution. So, the log-likelihood function for the three parameters is

$$
\begin{aligned}
l(\mu, \sigma, a) = {}& \log \left(\sqrt{\frac{1 - a^2}{2\pi\sigma^2}} \exp \left\{ -\frac{1}{2} \left(\frac{(Y_1 - \mu)^2(1 - a^2)}{\sigma^2} \right) \right\} \right) \\
& + \sum_{t=2}^{n} \log \left(\sqrt{\frac{1}{2\pi\sigma^2}} \exp \left\{ -\frac{1}{2} \left(\frac{(Y_t - (1 - a)\mu - aY_{t-1})^2}{\sigma^2} \right) \right\} \right) \quad (3.25) \\
= {}& -\frac{n}{2} \log(2\pi) + \frac{1}{2} \log(1 - a^2) - n \log \sigma \\
& - \frac{1}{2} \left\{ \left(\frac{(Y_1 - \mu)^2(1 - a^2)}{\sigma^2} \right) + \sum_{t=2}^{n} \left(\frac{(Y_t - (1 - a)\mu - aY_{t-1})^2}{\sigma^2} \right) \right\} \quad (3.26)
\end{aligned}
$$

TABLE 3.2   AR(1) model parameter estimates per month, with approximate standard errors.

Series	$\hat{\mu}$	$\hat{a}$	$\hat{\sigma}$
TSE 300 1956–2001	0.0077 (0.22)	0.0918 (0.043)	0.0457 (0.14)
S&P 500 1956–2001	0.0090 (0.19)	0.0250 (0.044)	0.0421 (0.13)

The equations $\partial l(\theta)/\partial\theta_i = 0$, where $\theta = (\mu, a, \sigma)'$, form a system of nonlinear equations in μ, a, σ. However, it is quite straightforward to maximize the likelihood with standard computer routines. The "solver" tool in Microsoft Excel works well.[1]

For large samples, the variances of the estimators are approximately:

$$V[\hat{\mu}] \approx \frac{\sigma^2}{n(1-a^2)} \qquad V[\hat{\sigma}] \approx \frac{\sigma^2}{2n} \qquad V[\hat{a}] \approx \frac{1-a^2}{n} \qquad (3.27)$$

The asymptotic covariances of the estimators are all zero, using the expected information matrix.

The maximum likelihood estimators for the United States and Canadian total return indices are given in Table 3.2. Again, approximate standard errors are given in parentheses.

Maximum Likelihood Estimation of ARCH and GARCH Models

For the ARCH(1) and GARCH(1,1) models, we adopt a similar approach to that used for the AR(1) estimation. Conditional on the previous value or values of the series, each value is normally distributed with fixed volatility, leaving only the first term of the series, for the probability density for Y_1, to be determined.

That is, for the ARCH(1) model where

$$Y_t = \mu + \sigma_t \varepsilon_t \qquad (3.28)$$

$$\sigma_t^2 = a_0 + a_1(Y_{t-1} - \mu)^2 \qquad (3.29)$$

we have:

$$Y_t|Y_{t-1} \sim N\left(\mu, a_0 + a_1(Y_{t-1} - \mu)^2\right) \quad t = 2, 3, \ldots, n \qquad (3.30)$$

---

[1]All the likelihoods in this chapter were maximized using solver in Excel. As with all optimization routines, it is necessary to find reasonable starting values to avoid finding local maxima. We found no great difficulty getting good results.

TABLE 3.3 ARCH model parameter estimates (per month).

Series	$\hat{\mu}$	$\hat{a}_0$	$\hat{a}_1$
TSE 300 1956–2001	0.00925 (0.00193)	0.0018 (0.0001)	0.1607 (0.063)
S&P 500 1956–2001	0.01000 (0.00178)	0.0016 (0.0001)	0.0790 (0.039)

TABLE 3.4 GARCH model parameter estimates (per month).

Series	$\hat{\mu}$	$\hat{a}_0$	$\hat{a}_1$	$\hat{\beta}$
TSE 300	0.0087 (0.0018)	0.0004 (0.00004)	0.1395 (0.030)	0.7033 (0.024)
S&P 500	0.0088 (0.0017)	0.0000 (0.00001)	0.0765 (0.009)	0.8708 (0.008)

and for the GARCH(1,1) model, where

$$Y_t = \mu + \sigma_t \varepsilon_t \tag{3.31}$$

$$\sigma_t^2 = \alpha_0 + \alpha_1 (Y_{t-1} - \mu)^2 + \beta \sigma_{t-1}^2 \tag{3.32}$$

we have:

$$Y_t | Y_{t-1} \sim N(\mu, \sigma_t^2) \quad t = 2, 3, \ldots, n \tag{3.33}$$

In both cases, the only problem is with the initial value for the variance process, σ_1^2. One simple approach is to treat this as an extra parameter. The effect of this "parameter" on the final likelihood will be small if the data series is a reasonable size.

The ARCH and GARCH models are stationary, and approximate large sample variances for the estimators can be found. Parameter estimates and approximate standard errors are given in Tables 3.3 and 3.4.

Maximum Likelihood Estimation for the RSLN-2 Model

The RSLN-2 model is the two-regime LN model, introduced in the section on the RSLN model in Chapter 2. The log-returns Y_t are assumed to depend on an underlying two-state Markov process, where the state in the interval t to $t + 1$ is denoted by $\rho_t = 1, 2$, and within each regime the log-returns are normally distributed, with parameters specific to the regime.

The six parameters of the RSLN-2 distribution are the values of μ and σ for either regime, denoted $\mu_1, \sigma_1, \mu_2, \sigma_2$, and the two transition probabilities

$p_{1,2}$ and $p_{2,1}$. Then $Y_t|\rho_t = \mu_{\rho_t} + \sigma_{\rho_t}\varepsilon_t$ where the ε_t are independent, identically distributed, $N(0, 1)$ random innovations. The contribution to the log-likelihood of the tth observation is

$$\log f(y_t|y_{t-1}, y_{t-2}, \ldots, y_1, \boldsymbol{\theta})$$

We can calculate this recursively, following Hamilton and Susmel (1994), for example, by calculating for each t:

$$f(\rho_t, \rho_{t-1}, y_t \mid y_{t-1}, \ldots, y_1, \boldsymbol{\theta}) =$$
$$p(\rho_{t-1}|y_{t-1}, \ldots, y_1, \boldsymbol{\theta})\, p(\rho_t|\rho_{t-1}, \boldsymbol{\theta})\, f(y_t|\rho_t, \boldsymbol{\theta}) \qquad (3.34)$$

On the right-hand side of this equation:

- $p(\rho_t = j|\rho_{t-1} = i, \boldsymbol{\theta})$, for $i, j = 1, 2$ is the transition probability between the regimes, which we have denoted $p_{i,j}$.
- If we know the regime the process is in, then the return has a straightforward normal distribution with the parameters of that regime. So, given ρ_t there is no dependence on earlier values of y_r, and

$$f(y_t|\rho_t, \boldsymbol{\theta}) = \frac{1}{\sigma_{\rho_t}}\, \phi((y_t - \mu_{\rho_t})/\sigma_{\rho_t})$$

  where ϕ is the standard normal probability density function.
- The probability function $p(\rho_{t-1}|y_{t-1}, y_{t-2}, \ldots, y_1, \boldsymbol{\theta})$ is found from the previous recursion; it is equal to

$$\sum_{\rho_{t-2}=1}^{2} \frac{f(\rho_{t-1}, \rho_{t-2}, y_{t-1}|y_{t-2}, \ldots, y_2, y_1, \boldsymbol{\theta})}{f(y_{t-1}|y_{t-2}, \ldots, y_2, y_1, \boldsymbol{\theta})}$$

Now, if we sum over the four values of equation 3.34, with $\rho_t = 1, 2$ and $\rho_{t-1} = 1, 2$, the sum is $f(y_t|y_{t-1}, y_{t-2}, \ldots, y_1, \boldsymbol{\theta})$, which is the contribution of the tth value in the series to the likelihood function. To start the recursion, we need a value (given $\boldsymbol{\theta}$) for $p(\rho_0)$, which we can find from the invariant distribution of the regime-switching Markov chain. The invariant distribution $\pi = (\pi_1, \pi_2)$ is the unconditional probability distribution for the process.

Under the invariant distribution π, each transition returns the same distribution; that is $\pi\mathbf{P} = \pi$, giving

$$\pi_1 p_{1,1} + \pi_2 p_{2,1} = \pi_1$$

and

$$\pi_1 p_{1,2} + \pi_2 p_{2,2} = \pi_2$$

Clearly

$$p_{1,1} + p_{1,2} = 1.0$$

so that

$$\pi_1 = \frac{p_{2,1}}{p_{1,2} + p_{2,1}}$$

and similarly

$$\pi_2 = 1 - \pi_1 = \frac{p_{1,2}}{p_{1,2} + p_{2,1}}$$

Hence, we can start the recursion by calculating for a given parameter set $\boldsymbol{\theta}$:

$$f(\rho_1 = 1, y_1 | \boldsymbol{\theta}) = (\pi_1) \frac{1}{\sigma_1} \phi\left(\frac{y_1 - \mu_1}{\sigma_1}\right)$$

$$f(\rho_1 = 2, y_1 | \boldsymbol{\theta}) = (\pi_2) \frac{1}{\sigma_2} \phi\left(\frac{y_1 - \mu_2}{\sigma_2}\right)$$

$$f(y_1 | \boldsymbol{\theta}) = f(\rho_1 = 1, y_1 | \boldsymbol{\theta}) + f(\rho_1 = 2, y_1 | \boldsymbol{\theta})$$

and we calculate for use in the next recursion the two values of

$$p(\rho_1 | y_1, \boldsymbol{\theta}) = \frac{f(\rho_1, y_1 | \boldsymbol{\theta})}{f(y_1 | \boldsymbol{\theta})}$$

Results for the S&P and TSE data are given in Table 3.5. Relatively minor adaptations of this method will yield the likelihood for a three-regime RSLN model, or a two-regime AR(1) model.

We have also fitted the model to the U.K. FTSE[2] All-Share total return index for the guaranteed annuity option contract discussed in Chapter 12. The parameters indicate a thinner tail here than for the TSE 300 results, and a fatter tail than for the S&P 500. The maximum likelihood parameters indicate higher volatility in both regimes than the North American data, with a smaller probability of transition from regime 1 to regime 2.

---

[2] Financial Times Stock Exchange.

TABLE 3.5   Maximum likelihood parameters for RSLN-2 model, with estimated standard errors.

TSE 300 (1956–2001)

$\hat{\mu}_1 = 0.0127$ (0.002)	$\hat{\sigma}_1 = 0.0348$ (0.001)	$\hat{p}_{1,2} = 0.0398$ (0.013)
$\hat{\mu}_2 = -0.0161$ (0.010)	$\hat{\sigma}_2 = 0.0748$ (0.007)	$\hat{p}_{2,1} = 0.1896$ (0.064)

S&P 500 (1956–2001)

$\hat{\mu}_1 = 0.0127$ (0.002)	$\hat{\sigma}_1 = 0.0351$ (0.001)	$\hat{p}_{1,2} = 0.0468$ (0.014)
$\hat{\mu}_2 = -0.0162$ (0.015)	$\hat{\sigma}_2 = 0.0691$ (0.010)	$\hat{p}_{2,1} = 0.3232$ (0.125)

LIKELIHOOD-BASED MODEL SELECTION

Introduction

The principle of parsimony indicates that more complex models require significant improvement in fit to be worthwhile. More complex, here, means using more parameters. The tests described in this section use the maximum values of the likelihood functions attained by each of the models, that is the value of the likelihood function evaluated using the MLE parameter estimates. In all cases listed in Table 3.6, except the Stable distribution, the maximum likelihood has been found using the "solver" tool from Excel.

For models with an equal number of parameters, it is appropriate to choose the model with the higher log-likelihood. For models with different numbers of parameters, common selection criteria are the likelihood ratio test, the Akaike information criterion (AIC) (Akaike 1974), and the Schwartz-Bayes criterion (SBC) (Schwartz 1978). This comparison uses models fitted to the TSE 300 and S&P 500 data between 1956 and 1999, which is two fewer years than used in Tables 3.3, 3.4, and 3.5.

The Likelihood Ratio Test

The likelihood ratio test (see, for example, Klugman, Panjer, and Willmot 1998) compares embedded models, where a model with k_1 parameters is a special case of a more complex model with $k_2 > k_1$ parameters. Let l_1 be the log-likelihood of the simpler model, and l_2 be the log-likelihood of the more complex model. The test statistic is $2(l_2 - l_1)$. The null hypothesis is

H_0: No significant improvement in Model 2

Under the null hypothesis, the test statistic has a χ^2 distribution, with degrees of freedom equal to the difference between the number of parameters in the two models.

TABLE 3.6 Comparison of selection information for lognormal, autoregressive, and regime-switching models.

TSE 300 (1956–1999 Monthly Total Returns)					
Model j	Parameters k_j	logL l_j	SBC $l_j - \frac{1}{2}k_j \log n$	AIC $l_j - k_j$	LRT p
LN	2	885.7	879.4	883.7	$< 10^{-8}$
AR(1)	3	887.4	878.0	884.4	$< 10^{-8}$
ARCH	3	889.4	880.0	886.4	$< 10^{-8}$
AR-ARCH	4	889.4	876.9	885.4	$< 10^{-8}$
STABLE	4	912.2	899.7	908.2	$< 10^{-4}$
GARCH	4	896.2	883.7	892.2	$< 10^{-8}$
AR-GARCH	5	900.2	884.5	895.2	$< 10^{-8}$
RSLN-2	6	922.7	903.9	916.7	
RSAR-2	8	923.0	898.7	915.0	0.82
RSLN-3	12	925.9	888.3	913.9	0.38

S&P 500 (1956–1999 Monthly Total Returns)					
Model j	Parameters k_j	logL l_j	SBC $l_j - \frac{1}{2}k_j \log n$	AIC $l_j - k_j$	LRT p
LN	2	929.8	923.5	927.8	$< 10^{-8}$
AR(1)	3	930.0	920.6	927.0	$< 10^{-8}$
ARCH	3	933.8	924.4	930.8	$< 10^{-8}$
AR-ARCH	4	935.0	922.5	931.0	$< 10^{-8}$
STABLE	4	945.2	932.7	941.2	0.0003
GARCH	4	939.1	926.6	935.1	$< 10^{-6}$
AR-GARCH	5	939.1	923.4	934.1	$< 10^{-6}$
RSLN-2	6	953.4	934.6	947.4	
RSAR-2	8	953.8	928.7	945.8	0.98
RSLN-3	12	962.7	925.1	950.7	0.01

We use likelihood ratio test to compare the models discussed above, and a few that are not dealt with in detail above. The following models are compared with this test:

- LN—the independent lognormal model.
- AR(1)—the first-order autoregressive model.
- ARCH—the first-order autoregressive conditionally heteroscedastic model.
- AR-ARCH—the ARCH model with an additional autoregressive component for the mean, described in the section on ARCH in Chapter 2.
- STABLE—the stable distribution described in the section on the stable distribution family in Chapter 2.

- GARCH—the first-order generalized autoregressive conditionally heteroscedastic model.
- AR-GARCH—the GARCH model with an additional autoregressive component for the mean, described in the section on GARCH(1,1) in chapter 2.
- RSLN-2—the regime-switching lognormal model with two regimes.
- RSAR-2—a regime-switching, first-order autoregressive model with two regimes.
- RSLN-3—the regime-switching lognormal model with three regimes.

Not all of the models we consider are embedded; if we denote embeddedness by $\subset$, we have LN $\subset$ RSLN-2 $\subset$ RSLN-3 and RSLN-2 $\subset$ RSAR(1). However, even where models are not embedded, the likelihood ratio test may be used for model selection, although the χ^2 distribution is, in this case, only an approximation. Even where models are embedded, there may be theoretical problems with the likelihood ratio test. In particular, Hamilton (1994) points out that the likelihood ratio test is not a valid test for the number of regimes in a regime-switching model. The results of the likelihood ratio tests, then, should be viewed with caution.

In Table 3.6, the final column gives the p-value for a likelihood ratio test of the RSLN model against each of the other models listed. For models with fewer than six parameters, the null hypothesis is that the simpler model is a "better" fit than the RSLN. Low p-values indicate rejection of the null hypothesis. Comparing the two-regime RSLN-2 model with models that have more than six parameters, acceptance of the null hypothesis (high p-value) implies acceptance of the RSLN-2 model.

The Akaike Information Criterion (AIC)

The Akaike information criterion (AIC) uses the model that maximizes $l_j - k_j$, where l_j is the log-likelihood under the jth model, and k_j is the number of parameters. Using this criterion, each extra parameter must improve the log-likelihood by at least one.

The Schwartz-Bayes Criterion

The Schwartz-Bayes criterion uses the model that maximizes $l_j - \frac{1}{2}k_j \log n$, where n is the sample size. For a sample of 527 (corresponding to the monthly data from 1956 to 1999), each additional parameter must increase the log-likelihood by at least 3.1.

Results—TSE and S&P Data

Table 3.6 shows that the RSLN-2 model provides a significant improvement over all other models for the TSE data, using each of the three selection criteria. For the S&P data, the ranking is not quite so definite. According

TABLE 3.7 Maximum likelihood parameters for RSLN-3 model, 1956 to 2001 data.

S&P 500			
$\hat{\mu}_1 = 0.0106$	$\hat{\sigma}_1 = 0.0353$	$\hat{p}_{1,2} = 0.0291$	$\hat{p}_{1,3} = 0.0000$
$\hat{\mu}_2 = -0.0238$	$\hat{\sigma}_2 = 0.0695$	$\hat{p}_{2,1} = 0.0000$	$\hat{p}_{2,3} = 0.2318$
$\hat{\mu}_3 = 0.0504$	$\hat{\sigma}_3 = 0.0150$	$\hat{p}_{3,1} = 0.4643$	$\hat{p}_{3,2} = 0.0000$

to the likelihood ratio test and the AIC, there is a marginal improvement in fit for RSLN-3 compared with RSLN-2. The third regime is an ultra-low volatility regime that is always visited between the high-volatility regime and the low-volatility regime. Maximum likelihood parameters are given in Table 3.7. The Schwartz-Bayes criterion still favors the two-regime model. This illustrates the useful message that model selection is usually not very clear cut. The results of the comparisons of this section inform the decision process, but there is room for judgment too. The evidence in favor of the three-regime model may not outweigh the added complexity.

MOMENT MATCHING

A quick method of fitting parameters is to match the mean, variance, covariances, and (if necessary) higher moments of the data to the mean, variance, covariance, and so forth, of the distribution. For the LN distribution, working with the log-returns and a normal distribution assumption, set

$$\tilde{\mu} = \bar{y} \qquad \tilde{\sigma} = s_y \qquad (3.35)$$

where $\bar{y}$ and s_y^2 are the mean and variance of the data.

It is interesting to note that if we match moments of the observed one-month accumulation factors, $x_t = S_{t+1}/S_t$ (so $x_i = \exp(y_i)$), we would match the LN mean and variance to the moments of x_i giving

$$\bar{x} = \exp(\tilde{\mu} + \tilde{\sigma}^2/2)$$

$$s_x^2 = (\exp(2\tilde{\mu} + \tilde{\sigma}^2))(\exp(\tilde{\sigma}^2) - 1)$$

These two ways of matching moments for the same distributional assumption would give quite different results. For the monthly S&P data set we have been using in this chapter, the first formulation, using the log-returns and the normal distribution, would give

$$\tilde{\mu} = 0.987 \text{ percent} \qquad \tilde{\sigma} = 4.145 \text{ percent} \qquad (3.36)$$

and using the accumulation factors and the LN distribution we find

$$\tilde{\mu} = 0.977 \text{ percent} \qquad \tilde{\sigma} = 4.096 \text{ percent} \qquad (3.37)$$

The first version is very close to the maximum likelihood estimates and will have smaller variance than the second.

In general, matching moments is an unreliable method of fitting parameters. The overall fit may not be very satisfactory, and the standard errors can be large. For a satisfactory overall fit it is better to employ more of the distribution than the first two moments. A common use for the matched moments estimators is as starting values for an iterative optimization procedure.

Both MLE and moment matching emphasize the fit in the center of the distribution. In the next chapter, we see how to adapt the estimates if we are interested in other parts of the distribution.

CHAPTER 4

The Left-Tail Calibration Method

INTRODUCTION

Maximum likelihood has many advantages for large samples, but there are circumstances where other methods may be preferable. Maximum likelihood estimation (MLE) provides a fit of the whole distribution, with an emphasis on the center of the distribution, which contributes more to the likelihood than the tails. For separate account products though, we may be more interested in the probability that the stock returns over a period are very poor. That probability depends on the left tail of the stock return distribution. In this chapter, we discuss a method of matching the left tail by matching quantiles. This is the method recommended in the Task Force on Segregated Funds (SFTF 2000) to be required of actuaries assessing segregated fund guarantee risk. In other jurisdictions, similar calibration requirements are being discussed; and even where it is not required, it is highly recommended that some detailed examination of the tail of the returns model should be undertaken where the guarantee liability depends on that part of the distribution.

Although the left-tail matching illustrated in this chapter is important for the guaranteed minimum maturity benefits (GMMBs) associated with separate account insurance, for other applications other parts of the distribution are more critical. It may be appropriate to examine the fit in the center or right tail, or in both tails, for other applications.

In this chapter, we first look at the method of the Canadian Institute of Actuaries (CIA) report (SFTF 2000), and consider some of the empirical evidence. We then demonstrate the method using distributions introduced in the previous chapters. In some cases the calibration can be calculated analytically. For less tractable distributions, the calibration requires stochastic simulation. Both methods are discussed in the following sections.

QUANTILE MATCHING

A p-quantile of a distribution with distribution function $F(y)$ is the value z_p such that:

$$F(z_p) = p \tag{4.1}$$

We can determine parameters for a model by matching the model and empirical quantiles. For example, to fit the lognormal distribution we need any two quantiles of the empirical distribution. Say we decide to use the 10th and 25th percentiles of the empirical and lognormal distributions. The 10th percentile of the log-return for the TSE 300 monthly data from 1956 to 2001 is -0.04682 and the 25th percentile is -0.01667.

We equate these empirical percentiles with the model percentiles. The model 25th percentile is $z_{0.25}$ where

$$\Phi\left(\frac{z_{0.25} - \mu}{\sigma}\right) = .25 \tag{4.2}$$

$$\implies \left(\frac{z_{0.25} - \mu}{\sigma}\right) = -0.6745 \tag{4.3}$$

$$\implies z_{0.25} = -0.6745\sigma + \mu \tag{4.4}$$

Similarly, $z_{0.1} = -1.2816\sigma + \mu$. We equate these with the empirical percentiles to get:

$$\implies \mu = 0.0168 \quad \text{and} \quad \sigma = 0.0497 \tag{4.5}$$

Now these are quite different values to those found by using maximum likelihood ($\mu = 0.0081$ and $\sigma = 0.0451$), or by matching moments. The reason is that by choosing to match the 10th and 25th percentiles, we have chosen to fit the left side of the distribution rather than the center. It should be noted, though, that the precise choice of quantiles to match will have a substantial effect on the resulting calibrated parameters.

We have seen in Chapter 3 that the lognormal distribution does not actually give a very good fit to the observed data. In Figure 2.10, the density functions of the 10-year accumulation functions are plotted, using MLE parameters. It is clear that the left tail of the lognormal distribution is very thin compared with the regime-switching lognormal (RSLN) model, which provides a far superior overall fit. The lognormal distribution is also far too thin-tailed compared with the empirical evidence; that is, we see far more examples of very poor returns in the historical data than we would expect to, using the lognormal model with MLE parameters. Using quantile matching, we can get a better fit in the tail if we want to use the lognormal distribution despite the poor overall fit.

THE CANADIAN CALIBRATION TABLE

Quantile matching is the basis of the CIA Task Force on Segregated Funds calibration requirement (SFTF 2000). The Task Force does not mandate a specific distribution because they do not want to constrain companies unnecessarily, or to discourage the development of new models. However, some restriction was thought necessary to avoid the overly optimistic assessment of the guarantee liabilities that would emerge from, for example, a lognormal model fitted using maximum likelihood. The recommended approach is to allow any model to be used, provided it can be adjusted to give an adequate fit in the left tail of the distribution, since that is the critical area for segregated fund guarantees. The calibration method details how the left-tail adjustment should be effected.

The Task Force calibration does not work with the distribution of the log-returns, but with the associated accumulation factors using one-year, five-year, and 10-year time periods. The accumulation factor is the amount that a unit investment accumulates to over some period.

If $Y_1, Y_2, \ldots$ are the random monthly log-returns on equities, then the n-month accumulation factor random variable is

$$S_n = \exp(Y_1 + Y_2 + \cdots + Y_n) \qquad (4.6)$$

The calibration table used by the Task Force relates to TSE 300 total monthly returns data, from 1956 to 1999. The table is reproduced here as Table 4.1.

TABLE 4.1 Calibration table of maximum acceptable quantiles from the CIA SFTF report (2000).

Accumulation Period	2.5th Percentile	5th Percentile	10th Percentile
1-year	0.76	0.82	0.90
5-year	0.75	0.85	1.05
10-year	0.85	1.05	1.35

In SFTF (2000) it is recommended that any model used by an insurer, when fitted to the TSE 300 (1956–1999) data, must generate accumulation factors with at least as much left-tail probability as those in the table. For example, the one-year accumulation factor must have a probability of at least 2.5 percent of falling below 0.76, a probability of at least 5 percent of falling below 0.82, and a probability of at least 10 percent of falling below 0.90. Similarly, for a 10-year accumulation factor, the probability of falling below 0.85 must be at least 2.5 percent. Setting calibration standards for different durations allows for duration dependent models, where successive values of stock returns are not independent.

In addition, the calibration requirements state that the mean one-year accumulation factor should lie in the range 1.10 to 1.12, and the standard deviation of the one-year accumulation factor should be at least 0.175. The report suggests that maximum likelihood, or some other suitable method should be used first to estimate parameters, and that the quantile matching should be used to adjust parameters to get an adequate left-tail fit. The standards set by the report do not necessarily uniquely define the parameters for any model but can be used to estimate parameters. The objective of the standard is to ensure that the left tail and the center of the distribution match. The sacrifice may be a poor fit in the right tail.

The calibration exercise does not determine the precise parameters to be used in risk modeling. It is used to derive adjustments to the fitted parameters found using a relevant data set.

QUANTILES FOR ACCUMULATION FACTORS: THE EMPIRICAL EVIDENCE

Table 4.1 surprises some people. Accumulation factors such as these appear barely credible, given the recent history of stock markets in North America. Is it really possible that over a 10-year period an investment in the TSE 300 index could fall by 15 percent? In fact, the data on 10-year accumulation factors is very limited. Since the introduction of the TSE index in 1956, we have seen only four nonoverlapping 10-year periods. We therefore have little empirical evidence on the lower percentiles of the 10-year accumulation factor distribution. For the five-year accumulation factors, we have eight nonoverlapping observations, and for the one-year accumulation factors we have 43 nonoverlapping observations. Since it is possible to choose different starting points for the accumulation factors, there are several different series to choose from; for example, for the annual factors there are 12 sets corresponding to the different monthly starting points. But we cannot treat the 12 sets as giving a sample of 12×43 independent observations, when for each successive value 11 out of 12 months are repeated. This is an often repeated error.

TABLE 4.2 Observed and fitted quantiles for accumulation factors (SFTF 2000).

Accumulation Period	Quantile	Empirical Range	RSLN
1-year	$1/44 = 2.27\%$	(0.61, 0.82)	0.74
	$2/44 = 4.55\%$	(0.76, 0.85)	0.82
	$4/44 = 9.09\%$	(0.85, 0.92)	0.89
5-year	$1/9 = 11.11\%$	(0.98, 1.41) ·	1.05
10-year	$1/5 = 20.00\%$	(1.60, 2.59)	1.88

The calibration points used by the CIA Task Force were found by extrapolating from the available data. This was done by looking at a number of different models that appeared to fit well where there is more data, and using these models to generate percentiles for the longer accumulation factors where the data is sparse. (Further details are given in Appendix C of SFTF (2000).)

In Table 4.2, the range of values for the available left-tail percentiles are given. The 2.27 percentile for the one-year return is based on the worst result of 43 nonoverlapping periods of annual returns; $2.27\% = 1/44$. The 4.55 percent result is the second smallest. The final column shows the quantiles generated using a model. RSLN is the regime-switching lognormal model with two regimes, with parameters fitted to the monthly TSE 300 1956 to 1999 data by maximum likelihood. This was one of the models used to set the percentile requirements.

The instinct of some that we should be able to extract more information about the 10-year accumulation factor from 45 years of monthly data than just the 20th percentile does have some basis. We cannot, as we have mentioned, treat each overlapping 10-year period of the data as an independent observation. We may, however, use the bootstrap method of statistics to derive some information about the tails of the distribution. The bootstrap method, broadly speaking, expands the inference available from a sample of data by creating new pseudosamples. In our case, we can do this by sampling from the monthly data with replacement. So, if we have 528 monthly observations of the log-return y_t (representing the 1956 to 1999 monthly data), we can sample, with replacement, 120 values to get a new "observation" of the 10-year accumulation factor. We repeat this a number of times to construct a new "sample" of hypothetical observations of the 10-year accumulation factor. We can then use this pseudosample to estimate quantiles of the original distribution. The bootstrap method works best when successive monthly values of y_t are independent. In fact, successive values of the monthly log-return on stocks are positively correlated. One way of managing this is to take blocks of successive monthly values.

TABLE 4.3 Bootstrap estimates of accumulation factor quantiles.

Accumulation Period	Bootstrap Estimate			Approx. Standard Error
	2.5%	5%	10%	
1-year	0.75	0.83	0.90	0.011
5-year	0.76	0.86	1.00	0.014
10-year	0.92	1.08	1.32	0.025

Rather than sample 120 individual months for each hypothetical 10-year accumulation factor, we have used 20 six-month blocks of successive values with random starting points to generate bootstrap estimates of quantiles for the 10-year accumulation factors from the TSE 300 monthly data. We have also generated bootstrap estimates of quantiles for the one-year and five-year accumulation factors, again using six-month blocks. The bootstrap estimates are given in Table 4.3. They are remarkably consistent with the factors used in the SFTF (2000) report, which were derived using stochastic volatility models fitted to the data, with only the 2.5 percent factor for the 10-year accumulation factor appearing a little low in the CIA table.

Having given the case for the quantiles of the left tail of the accumulation factors, we now discuss how to adjust the model parameters to comply with the calibration requirements.

THE LOGNORMAL MODEL

For the lognormal model, with $Y_j \sim N(\mu, \sigma^2)$, the one-year accumulation factor is

$$S_{12} = \exp(Y_1 + Y_2 + \cdots + Y_{12}) \implies \log S_{12} = \sum_{i=1}^{12} Y_i$$

$$\implies \log S_{12} \sim N(12\mu, 12\sigma^2)$$

So, the one-year accumulation factor has a lognormal distribution with parameters $\mu^* = 12\mu$ and $\sigma^* = \sqrt{12}\sigma$.

It is possible to use any two of the table values to solve for the two unknown parameters μ^* and σ^*, but this tends to give values that lie outside the acceptable range for the mean. So the recommended method from Appendix A of SFTF (2000) is to keep the mean constant and equal to the empirical mean of 1.116122 (the data set is TSE 300, from 1956 to 1999). This gives the first equation to solve for μ^* and σ^*, that

$$\exp\{\mu^* + \sigma^{*2}/2\} = 1.1161 \tag{4.7}$$

Then we can use each of the nine entries in Table 4.1 as the other equation. Since each entry represents a separate test of the model, we will use the parameters that satisfy the most stringent of the tests. For the lognormal model the most stringent test is actually the 2.5 percentile of the one-year accumulation factor. This gives the second equation for the parameters:

$$\Phi\left(\frac{\log 0.76 - \mu^*}{\sigma}\right) = 0.025 \tag{4.8}$$

Together the two equations imply:

$$\log 1.1161 - \mu^* - \sigma^{*2}/2 = 0 \tag{4.9}$$

and

$$\log 0.76 - \mu^* + 1.960\sigma^* = 0 \tag{4.10}$$
$$\Longrightarrow (\log 1.1161 - \log 0.76) - 1.960\sigma^* - 0.5\sigma^{*2} = 0 \tag{4.11}$$
$$\Longrightarrow \sigma^* = 0.18714 \tag{4.12}$$

and

$$\mu^* = 0.09233 \tag{4.13}$$

So

$$\sigma = 0.05402 \quad \text{and} \quad \mu = 0.007694 \tag{4.14}$$

To check the other eight table entries, use these values to calculate the quantiles. For example, the 2.5 percentile of S_{60} must be less than 0.75, which is the same as saying that the probability that S_{60} is less than 0.75 must be greater than 2.5 percent.

$$\Pr[S_{60} < 0.75 | \mu = .007694, \sigma = .05402] = \Phi\left(\frac{\log 0.75 - 60\mu}{\sqrt{60}\sigma}\right) \tag{4.15}$$

$$= 3.67\% \tag{4.16}$$

This means that, given the parameters calculated using the 2.5 percentile for S_{12}, the probability of the five-year accumulation factor falling below 0.75 is a little over 3.6 percent, which is greater than the required 2.5 percent, indicating that the test is passed. Similarly, these parameters pass all the other table criteria. It remains to check that the standard deviation of the one-year accumulation factor is sufficiently large:

$$V[S_{12}] = (\exp(12\mu + 12\sigma^2/2))^2(\exp(12\sigma^2) - 1.0) = (21.1\%)^2 \tag{4.17}$$

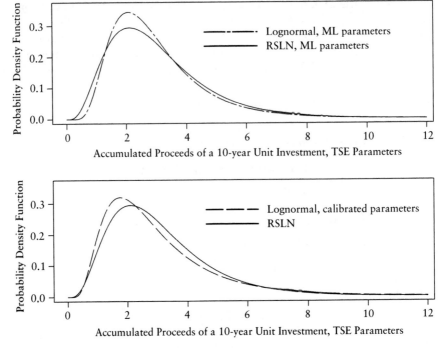

FIGURE 4.1 Comparison of lognormal and RSLN distributions, before and after calibration.

Figure 4.1 shows the effect of the calibration on the distribution for the 10-year accumulation factors. Plotted in the top diagram are the lognormal and RSLN distributions using maximum likelihood parameters. In the lower diagram, the calibrated lognormal distribution is shown against the RSLN model. The critical area is the part of the distribution below $S_{120} = 1$. The figure shows that the lognormal model with maximum likelihood parameters is much thinner than the (better-fitting) RSLN model in the left tail. After calibration, the area left of $S_{120} = 1$ is very similar for the two distributions; the distributions are also similarly centered because of the requirement that the calibration does not substantially change the mean outcome. The cost of improving the left-tail fit, as we predicted, is a very poor fit in the rest of the distribution.

ANALYTIC CALIBRATION OF OTHER MODELS

Calibration of AR(1) and the RSLN models can be done analytically, similarly to the lognormal model, though a little more complex.

AR(1)

When the individual monthly log-returns are distributed AR(1) with normal errors, the log-accumulation factors are also normally distributed. Using the AR(1) model with parameters μ, a, σ

$$\log S_n \sim N(n\mu, (\sigma \, h(a, n))^2) \qquad (4.18)$$

where

$$h(a, n) = \frac{1}{(1 - a)} \sqrt{\sum_{i=1}^{n}(1 - a^i)^2}$$

This assumes a neutral starting position for the process; that is, $Y_0 = \mu$, so that the first value of the series is $Y_1 = \mu + \sigma \varepsilon_1$.

To prove equation 4.18, it is simpler to work with the detrended process $Z_t = Y_t - \mu$, so that $Z_t = aZ_{t-1} + \sigma \varepsilon_t$.

$$\log S_n - n\mu = Z_1 + Z_2 + \cdots + Z_n \qquad (4.19)$$

$$= \sigma \varepsilon_1 + (a(\sigma \varepsilon_1) + \sigma \varepsilon_2) + (a(a(\sigma \varepsilon_1) + \sigma \varepsilon_2) + \sigma \varepsilon_3) + \cdots \qquad (4.20)$$

$$+ (a^{n-1}\sigma \varepsilon_1 + a^{n-2}\sigma \varepsilon_2 + \cdots + a\sigma \varepsilon_{n-1} + \sigma \varepsilon_n) \qquad (4.21)$$

$$= \frac{\sigma}{1 - a} \left\{ \sum_{i=1}^{n} \varepsilon_i \left(1 - a^{n+1-i}\right) \right\} \qquad (4.22)$$

The ε_t are independent, identically distributed $N(0, 1)$, giving the result in equation 4.18, so it is possible to calculate probabilities analytically for the accumulation factors.

Once again, we use as one of the defining equations the mean one-year accumulation,

$$E[S_{12}] = \exp(\mu^* + \sigma^{*2}/2) = 1.1161$$

where $\mu^* = 12\mu$ and $\sigma^* = \sigma h(a, 12)$. Use as a second the 2.5 percentile for the one-year accumulation factor for $\mu^* = .09233$ and $\sigma^* = 0.18714$ as before. Hence we might use $\mu = 0.007694$, as before. This also gives $\sigma h(a, 12) = 0.18714$. It is possible to use one of the other quantiles in the table to solve for a and, therefore, for σ. However, no combination of table values gives a value of a close to the MLE. A reasonable solution is to keep the MLE estimate of a, which was 0.082, and solve for $\sigma = 0.05224$. Checking the other quantiles shows that these parameters satisfy all nine calibration points as well as the mean and variance criteria.

TABLE 4.4 Distribution for R_{12}.

r	$\Pr[R_{12} = r]$	r	$\Pr[R_{12} = r]$
0	0.011172	7	0.041055
1	0.007386	8	0.051291
2	0.010378	9	0.063082
3	0.014218	10	0.076379
4	0.019057	11	0.091925
5	0.025047	12	0.557573
6	0.032338		

The RSLN Model

The distribution function of the accumulation factor for the RSLN-2 model was derived in equation 2.30 in the section on RSLN in Chapter 2. In that section, we showed how to derive a probability distribution for the total number of months spent in regime 1 for the n month process. Here we denote the total sojourn random variable R_n, and its probability function $p_n(r)$. Then $S_n|R_n \sim$ lognormal with parameters

$$\mu^*(R_n) = (R_n \mu_1 + (n - R_n) \mu_2) \text{ and } \sigma^*(R_n) = \sqrt{(R_n \sigma_1^2 + (n - R_n) \sigma_2^2)}$$

So

$$F_{S_n}(x) = \Pr[S_n \leq x] = \sum_{r=0}^{n} \Pr[S_n \leq x | R_n = r] p_n(r) \qquad (4.23)$$

$$= \sum_{r=0}^{n} \Phi\left(\frac{\log x - \mu^*(r)}{\sigma^*(r)}\right) p_n(r) \qquad (4.24)$$

Using this equation, it is straightforward to calculate the probabilities for the various maximum quantile points in Table 4.1. For example, the maximum likelihood parameters for the RSLN distribution for the TSE 300 distribution and the data from 1956 to 1999 are:

Regime 1 $\mu_1 = 0.012$ $\sigma_1 = 0.035$ $p_{12} = 0.037$
Regime 2 $\mu_2 = -0.016$ $\sigma_2 = 0.078$ $p_{21} = 0.210$

Using these values for p_{12} and p_{21}, and using the recursion from equations 2.20 and 2.26, gives the distribution for R_{12} shown in Table 4.4.

Applying this distribution, together with the estimators for μ_1, μ_2, σ_1, σ_2, gives

$\Pr[S_{12} < 0.76] = 0.032$ $\Pr[S_{12} < 0.82] = 0.055$ $\Pr[S_{12} < 0.90] = 0.11$

and similarly for the five-year accumulation factors:

$$\Pr[S_{60} < 0.75] = 0.036 \quad \Pr[S_{60} < 0.85] = 0.060 \quad \Pr[S_{60} < 1.05] = 0.13$$

and for the 10-year accumulation factors:

$$\Pr[S_{120} < 0.85] = 0.030 \quad \Pr[S_{120} < 1.05] = 0.057 \quad \Pr[S_{120} < 1.35] = 0.12$$

In each case, the probability that the accumulation factor is less than the table value is greater than the percentile specified in the table. For example, for the top left table entry, we need at least 2.5 percent probability that S_{12} is less than 0.76. We have probability of 3.2 percent, so the RSLN distribution with these parameters satisfies the requirement for the first entry. Similarly, all the probabilities calculated are greater than the minimum values. So the maximum likelihood estimators satisfy all the quantile-matching criteria. The mean one-year accumulation factor is 1.1181, and the standard deviation is 18.23 percent.

CALIBRATION BY SIMULATION

The Simulation Method

The CIA calibration criteria allow calibration using simulation, but stipulate that the fitted values must be adequate with a high (95 percent) probability. The reason for this stipulation is that simulation adds sampling variability to the estimation process, which needs to be allowed for. Simulation is useful where analytic calculation of the distribution function for the accumulation factors is not practical. This would be true, for example, for the conditionally heteroscedastic models.

The simulation calibration process runs as follows:

1. Simulate for example, m values for each of the three accumulation factors in Table 4.1.
2. For each cell in Table 4.1, count how many simulated values for the accumulation factor fall below the maximum quantile in the table. Let this number be M. That is, for the first calibration point, M is the number of simulated values of the one-year accumulation factor that are less than 0.76.
3. $\tilde{p} = \frac{M}{m}$ is an estimate of p, the true underlying probability that the accumulation factor is less than the calibration value. This means that the table quantile value lies at the $\tilde{p}$-quantile of the accumulation-factor distribution, approximately.

4. Using the normal approximation to the binomial distribution, it is approximately 95 percent certain that the true probability $p = \Pr[S_{12} < 0.76]$ satisfies

$$p > \tilde{p} - 1.645 \sqrt{\frac{\tilde{p}(1 - \tilde{p})}{m}} \qquad (4.25)$$

So, if $\tilde{p} - \sqrt{\frac{\tilde{p}(1-\tilde{p})}{m}}$ is greater than the required probability (0.025, 0.05, or 0.1), then we can be 95 percent certain that the parameters satisfy the calibration criterion.

5. If the calibration criteria are not all satisfied, it will be necessary to adjust the parameters and return to step 1.

The GARCH Model

The maximum likelihood estimates of the generalized autoregressive conditionally heteroscedastic (GARCH) model were given in Table 3.4 in Chapter 3. Using these parameter estimates to generate 20,000 values of S_{12}, S_{60}, and S_{120}, we find that the quantiles are too small at all durations. Also, the mean one-year accumulation factor is rather large, at around 1.128. Reducing the μ term to, for example 0.0077 per month, is consistent with the lognormal model and will bring the mean down. Increasing any of the other parameters will increase the standard deviation for the process and, therefore, increase the portion of the distribution in the left tail. The a_1 and β parameters determine the dependence of the variance process on earlier values. After some experimentation, it appears most appropriate to increase a_0 and leave a_1 and β. Here, appropriateness is being measured in terms of the overall fit at each duration for the accumulation factors.

Increasing the a_0 parameter to 0.00053 satisfies the quantile criteria. Using 100,000 simulations of S_{12}, we find 2,629 are smaller than 0.76, giving an estimated 2.629 percent of the distribution falling below 0.76. Allowing for sampling variability, we are 95 percent certain that the probability for this distribution of falling below 0.76 is at least

$$0.02629 - 1.645 \left(0.02629 \left(1 - .02629\right)/100000\right)^{\frac{1}{2}} = 0.02546$$

All the other quantile criteria are met comfortably; the 2.5 percent quantile for the one-year accumulation factor is the most stringent test for the GARCH distribution, as it was for the lognormal distribution. Using the simulated one-year accumulation factors, the mean lies in the range (1.114, 1.117), and the standard deviation is estimated at 21.2 percent.

CHAPTER 5

Markov Chain Monte Carlo (MCMC) Estimation

BAYESIAN STATISTICS

In this chapter, we describe modern Bayesian parameter estimation and show how the method is applied to the RSLN model for stock returns. The major advantage of this method is that it gives us a scientific but straightforward method for quantifying the effects of parameter uncertainty on our projections. Unlike the maximum likelihood method, the information on parameter uncertainty does not require asymptotic arguments. Although we give a brief example of how to include allowance for parameter uncertainty in projections at the end of this chapter, we return to the subject in much more depth in Chapter 11, where we will show that parameter uncertainty may significantly affect estimated capital requirements for equity-linked contracts.

The term "Bayesian" comes from Bayes' theorem, which states that for random variables A and B, the joint, conditional, and marginal probability functions are related as:

$$f(A, B) = f(A|B) f(B) = f(B|A) f(A)$$

This relation is used in Bayesian parameter estimation with the unknown parameter vector θ as one of the random variables and the random sample used to fit the distribution, X, as the other. Then we may determine the probability (density) functions for $X|\theta, \theta|X, X, \theta$ as well as the marginal probability (density) functions for X and θ.

Originally, Bayesian methods were constrained by difficulty in combining distributions for the data and the parameters. Only a small number of

---

[1]This chapter contains some material first published in Hardy (2002), reproduced here by the kind permission of the publishers.

combinations gave tractable results. However, the modern techniques described in this chapter have very substantially removed this restriction, and Bayesian methods are now widely used in every area of statistical inference.

The maximum likelihood estimation (MLE) procedure discussed in Chapter 3 is a classical frequentist technique. The parameter θ is assumed to be fixed but unknown. A random sample $X_1, X_2, \ldots, X_n$ is drawn from a population with distribution dependent on θ and used to draw inference about the likely value for θ. The resulting estimator, $\hat{\theta}$, is assumed to be a random variable through its dependence on the random sample. The Bayesian approach, as we have mentioned, is to treat θ as a random variable. We are really using the language of random variables to model the uncertainty about θ.

Before any data is collected, we may have some information about θ; this is expressed in terms of a probability distribution for θ, $\pi(\theta)$ known as the *prior distribution*. If we have little or no information prior to observing the data, we can choose a prior distribution with a very large variance or with a flat density function. If we have good information, we may choose a prior distribution with a small variance, indicating little uncertainty about the parameter. The mean of the prior distribution represents the best estimate of the parameter before observing the data. After having observed the data $x = x_1, x_2, \ldots, x_n$, it is possible to construct the probability density function for the parameter conditional on the data. This is the *posterior distribution*, $f(\theta|x)$, and it combines the information in the prior distribution with the information provided by the sample.

We can connect all this in terms of the probability density functions involved, considering the sample and the parameter as random variables. For simplicity we assume all distribution and density functions are continuous, and the argument of the density function f indicates the random variables involved (i.e., $f(x|\theta)$ could be written $f_{X|\theta}(x|\theta)$, but that tends to become cumbersome). Where the variable is θ we use $\pi()$ to denote the probability density function.

Let $f(X|\theta)$ denote the density of X given the parameter θ. The joint density for the random sample, conditional on the parameter θ is

$$L(\theta; (X_1, X_2, \ldots, X_n)) = f(X_1, X_2, \ldots, X_n|\theta)$$

This is the likelihood function that was used extensively in Chapter 3. The likelihood function plays a crucial role in Bayesian inference as well as in frequentist methods.

Let $\pi(\theta)$ denote the prior distribution of θ, then, from Bayes' theorem, the joint probability of $X_1, X_2, \ldots, X_n, \theta$ is

$$f(X_1, X_2, \ldots, X_n, \theta) = L(\theta; (X_1, X_2, \ldots, X_n)) \, \pi(\theta) \qquad (5.1)$$

Given the joint probability, the posterior distribution, again using Bayes' theorem, is

$$\pi(\boldsymbol{\theta}|X_1, X_2, \ldots, X_n) = \frac{L(\boldsymbol{\theta}; (X_1, X_2, \ldots, X_n))\, \pi(\boldsymbol{\theta})}{f(X_1, X_2, \ldots, X_n)} \qquad (5.2)$$

The denominator is the marginal joint distribution for the sample. Since it does not involve $\boldsymbol{\theta}$, it can be thought of as the constant required so that $\pi(\boldsymbol{\theta}|X_1, \ldots, X_n)$ integrates to 1.

The posterior distribution for $\boldsymbol{\theta}$ can then be used with the sample to derive the *predictive distribution*. This is the marginal distribution of future observations of x, taking into consideration the information about the variability of the parameter $\boldsymbol{\theta}$, as adjusted by the previous data. In terms of the density functions, the predictive distribution is:

$$f(x|x_1, \ldots, x_n) = \int_{\boldsymbol{\theta}} f(x|\boldsymbol{\theta})\pi(\boldsymbol{\theta}|x_1, \ldots, x_n)\, d\boldsymbol{\theta} \qquad (5.3)$$

In Chapter 11, some examples are given of how to apply the predictive distribution using the Markov chain Monte Carlo method, described in this chapter, as part of a stochastic simulation analysis of equity-linked contracts.

We can use the moments of the posterior distribution to derive estimators of the parameters and standard errors. An estimator for the parameter $\boldsymbol{\theta}$ is the expected value $E[\boldsymbol{\theta}|X_1, X_2, \ldots, X_n]$. For parameter vectors, the posterior distribution is multivariate, giving information about how the parameters are interrelated.

Both the classical and the Bayesian methods can be used for statistical inference—estimating parameters, constructing confidence intervals, and so on. Both are highly dependent on the likelihood function. With maximum likelihood we know only the asymptotic relationships between parameter estimates; whereas, with the Bayesian approach, we derive full joint distributions between the parameters. The price paid for this is additional structure imposed with the prior distribution.

MARKOV CHAIN MONTE CARLO—AN INTRODUCTION

For all but very simple models, direct calculation of the posterior distribution is not possible. In particular, for a parameter vector $\boldsymbol{\Theta}$, an analytical derivation of the joint posterior distribution is, in general, not feasible. For some time, this limited the applicability of the Bayes approach. In the 1980s the Markov chain Monte Carlo (MCMC) technique was developed. This technique can be used to simulate a sample from the posterior distribution of $\boldsymbol{\theta}$. So, although we may not know the analytic form for the posterior distribution, we can generate a sample from it, to give us any information required, including parameter estimates, confidence intervals, and parameter correlations.

Technically, the MCMC algorithm is used to construct a Markov chain $\{\Theta^{(0)}, \Theta^{(1)}, \Theta^{(2)}, \ldots\}$, which has as its stationary distribution the required posterior, π_θ. So, if we generate a large number of simulated values of the parameter set using the algorithm, after a while the process will reach a stationary distribution. From that point, the algorithm generates random values from the posterior distribution for the parameter vector. We can use the simulated values to estimate the marginal density and distribution functions for the individual parameters or the joint density or distribution functions for the parameter vector.

The early values for the chain, before the chain achieves the limiting distribution, are called the "burn in." These values are discarded. The remaining values, $\{\theta^{(k+1)}, \theta^{(k+2)}, \theta^{(k+3)}, \ldots, \theta^{(N)}\}$ are a random, nonindependent sample from the posterior distribution π_θ, enabling estimation of the joint moments of the posterior distribution.

One of the reasons that the MCMC method is so effective is that we can update the parameter vector one parameter at a time. This makes the simulation much easier to construct. For example, assume we are estimating a three-parameter distribution $\Theta = (\mu, \alpha, \beta)$. We can update $\Theta^{(r)}$ to $\Theta^{(r+1)}$ by changing only one parameter at a time, conditioning on the current values of the other parameters. In other words, given the data y and

$$\Theta^{(r)} = (\mu^{(r)}, \alpha^{(r)}, \beta^{(r)})$$

we find

$$\pi(\mu \,|\, y, \alpha^{(r)}, \beta^{(r)})$$

and simulate a value $\mu^{(r+1)}$ from this distribution; we can then use this value in the next distribution and so proceed, simulating:

$$\alpha^{(r+1)} \sim \pi(\alpha | y, \mu^{(r+1)}, \beta^{(r)}) \tag{5.4}$$

$$\beta^{(r+1)} \sim \pi(\beta | y, \mu^{(r+1)}, \alpha^{(r)}) \tag{5.5}$$

This gives us $\theta^{(r+1)} = (\mu^{(r+1)}, \alpha^{(r+1)}, \beta^{(r+1)})$, and the iteration proceeds.

The problem then reduces to simulating from the posterior distributions for each of the parameters, assuming known values for all the remaining parameters.

For a general parameter vector $\Theta = (\theta_1, \theta_2, \ldots, \theta_n)$, the posterior distribution of interest with respect to parameter θ_i is

$$\pi(\theta_i | y, \boldsymbol{\theta}_{\sim i}) \propto f(y|\boldsymbol{\theta}) \, p(\boldsymbol{\theta}) \tag{5.6}$$

where $\boldsymbol{\theta}_{\sim i}$ represents the set of parameters excluding θ_i, and $p(\theta_i)$ is the prior distribution for θ_i (we assume the prior distributions for the individual parameters are independent). The joint density $f(y|\boldsymbol{\theta})$ is the likelihood function described in Chapter 3. If we can find a closed form for the conditional probability function, we can simulate directly from that distribution (This is the Gibbs sampler method). In many cases, however, there is no closed form available for any of the posterior distributions; in these cases, we may be able to use the Metropolis-Hastings algorithm. Both of these methods are described in much more detail, along with full derivations for the algorithms, in Gilks, Richardson, and Spiegelhalter (1996). Their book also gives other examples of MCMC in practice and discusses implementation issues around, for example, convergence, which are not discussed in detail here.

THE METROPOLIS-HASTINGS ALGORITHM (MHA)

The Metropolis-Hastings algorithm (MHA) is relatively straightforward to apply, provided the likelihood function can be calculated. The algorithm steps are described in the following sections. Prior distributions are assigned before the simulation; the other steps are followed through in turn for each parameter for each simulation. In the descriptions below, we assume that the rth simulation is complete, and we are now generating the $(r + 1)$th values for the parameters.

Prior Distributions $\pi(\theta_i)$

For each parameter in the parameter vector we need to assign a prior distribution. These can be independent, or if there is a reason to use joint distributions for subsets of parameters that is also possible. In the examples that we use, the prior distributions for all the parameters are independent.

The center of the prior distribution indicates the best initial estimate of where the parameter lies. If the maximum likelihood estimate is available, that will be a good starting point. The variance of the prior distribution indicates the uncertainty associated with the initial estimate. If the variance is very large, then the prior distribution will have little effect on the posterior distribution, which will depend strongly on the data alone. If the variance is small, the prior will have a large effect on the shape and location of the posterior distribution. The exact form of the prior distribution depends on the parameter under consideration. For example, a normal distribution may be appropriate for a mean parameter, but not for a variance parameter, which we know must be greater than zero. In practice, prior distributions and candidate distributions for parameters will often be the same family. The choice of candidate distributions is discussed in the next section.

The Candidate Distribution $q(\xi|\theta_i)$

The algorithm uses an *acceptance-rejection* method. This requires a random value, ξ say, from a *candidate distribution* with probability density function $q(\xi|\theta_i)$. This value will be accepted or rejected as the new value $\theta_i^{(r+1)}$ using the acceptance probability α defined below.

For the candidate distribution we can use any distribution that spans the parameter space for θ_i, but some candidate distributions will be more efficient than others. "Efficiency" here refers to the speed with which the chain reaches the stationary distribution. Choosing a candidate distribution usually requires some experimentation. For unrestricted parameters (such as the mean parameter for an autoregressive [AR], autoregressive conditionally heteroscedastic [ARCH], or generalized autoregressive conditionally heteroscedastic [GARCH] model), the normal distribution centered on the previous value of the parameter has advantages and is a common choice. That is, the candidate value ξ for the $(r + 1)$th value of parameter θ_i is a random number generated from the $N(\theta_i^{(r)}, \sigma_i^2)$ distribution for some σ_i^2, chosen to ensure that the acceptance probability is in an efficient region.

The normal distribution can sometimes be used even if the parameter space is restricted, provided the probability of generating a value outside the parameter space is kept to a near impossibility. For example, with the AR(1) model, the normal distribution works as a candidate distribution for the autoregressive parameter a, even though we require $|a| < 1$. This is because we can use a normal distribution with variance of around 0.1 with generated values for the parameter in the range $(-0.1, 0.2)$.

For variance parameters that are constrained to be strictly positive, popular distributions in the literature are the gamma and inverted gamma distributions. Again, there are advantages in centering the candidate distribution on the previous value of the series.

The Acceptance-Rejection Procedure

The candidate value, ξ, may be accepted as the next value, $\theta_i^{(r+1)}$, or it may be rejected, in which case the next value in the chain is the previous value, $\theta_i^{(r+1)} = \theta_i^{(r)}$. Acceptance or rejection is a random process; the algorithm provides the probability of acceptance.

For the $(r + 1)$th iteration for the parameter θ_i, we have the most recent value denoted by $\theta_i^{(r)}$; we also have the most current value for parameter set excluding θ_i:

$$\boldsymbol{\theta}_{\sim i}^{(r+1,r)} = (\theta_1^{(r+1)}, \ldots, \theta_{i-1}^{(r+1)}, \theta_{i+1}^{(r)}, \ldots, \theta_n^{(r)}) \qquad (5.7)$$

The value from the candidate distribution is accepted as the new value for θ_i with probability

$$\alpha = \min\left(1, \frac{\pi(\xi|y, \boldsymbol{\theta}_{\sim i}^{(r+1,r)})\, q(\theta_i^{(r)}|\xi)}{\pi(\theta_i^{(r)}|y, \boldsymbol{\theta}_{\sim i}^{(r+1,r)})\, q(\xi|\theta_i^{(r)})}\right) \tag{5.8}$$

where $\pi(\theta_i|y, \boldsymbol{\theta}_{\sim i}^{(r+1,r)})$ is the posterior distribution for θ_i, keeping all other parameters at their current values, and conditioning on the data, y. From equation 5.2:

$$\frac{\pi(\xi|y, \boldsymbol{\theta}_{\sim i}^{(r+1,r)})}{\pi(\theta_i^{(r)}|y, \boldsymbol{\theta}_{\sim i}^{(r+1,r)})} = \frac{L_i(\xi, \boldsymbol{\theta}_{\sim i}^{(r,r+1)})\, \pi(\xi)}{f(y)}\, \frac{f(y)}{L_i(\theta_i^{(r)}\boldsymbol{\theta}_{\sim i}^{(r,r+1)})\, \pi(\theta_i^{(r)})} \tag{5.9}$$

where $L_i(z, \boldsymbol{\theta}_{\sim i})$ is the likelihood calculated using z for parameter θ_i; all other parameters are taken from the vector $\boldsymbol{\theta}_{\sim i}$; and the $\pi()$ terms give the values of the prior distribution for θ_i, evaluated at the current and the candidate values. The acceptance probability then becomes:

$$\alpha = \min\left(1, \frac{L_i(\xi, \boldsymbol{\theta}_{\sim i}^{(r,r+1)})\, \pi(\xi)\, q(\theta_i^{(r)}|\xi)}{L_i(\theta_i^{(r)}\boldsymbol{\theta}_{\sim i}^{(r,r+1)})\, \pi(\theta_i^{(r)})\, q(\xi|\theta_i^{(r)})}\right) \tag{5.10}$$

If $\alpha = 1$, then the candidate ξ is assigned to be the next value of the parameter $\theta_i^{(r+1)}$. If $\alpha < 1$, then we sample a random value U from a uniform $(0,1)$ distribution. If $U < \alpha$, set $\theta_i^{(r+1)} = \xi$; otherwise set $\theta_i^{(r+1)} = \theta_i^{(r)}$.

It is worth considering equation 5.10. If the prior distribution is disperse, it will not have a large effect on the calculations because it will be numerically much smaller than the likelihood. So a major part of the acceptance probability is the ratio of the likelihood with the candidate value to the likelihood with the previous value. If the likelihood improves, then $\alpha \approx 1$, depending on the q ratio, and we probably accept the candidate value. If the likelihood decreases very strongly, α will be small and we probably keep the previous value. If the likelihood decreases a little, then the value may or may not change. So the process is very similar to a Monte Carlo search for the joint maximum likelihood, and the posterior density for $\boldsymbol{\theta}$ will be roughly proportional to the likelihood function. The results from the MHA with disperse priors will therefore have similarities with the results of the maximum likelihood approach; in addition, we have the joint probabilities of the parameter estimates.

Did It Work?

It is important to look at the sample paths and the acceptance frequencies to assess the appropriateness of the distributions. A poor choice for the candidate distribution will result in acceptance probabilities being too low or too high. If the acceptance probability is too low, then the series takes a long time to converge to the limiting distribution because the chain will frequently stay at one value for long periods. If it is too large, the values tend not to reach the tails of the limiting distribution quickly, again resulting in slow convergence. Roberts (1996) suggests acceptance rates should lie in the range [0.15,0.5].

In Figure 5.1 are some examples of sample paths for the mean parameter generated for an AR(1) model, using the MHA sample of parameters and using the TSE 300 data for the years 1956 to 1999. In the top figure, the candidate distribution is $N(\mu^{(r)}, 0.05^2)$. The acceptance probability is very low; the relatively high variance of the candidate distribution means that candidates tend to generate low values for the likelihood, and are therefore

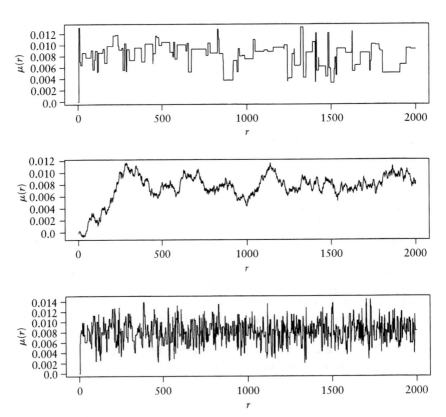

FIGURE 5.1   Sample paths for μ parameter for AR(1) model.

usually rejected. The process gets stuck for long periods, and convergence to the stationary distribution will take some time. In the middle figure, the candidate distribution has a very low standard deviation of 0.00025. The process moves very slowly around the parameter space, and it takes a long time to move from the initial value ($\mu^{(0)} = 0$) to the area of the long-term mean value (around 0.009). Values are very highly serially correlated. The bottom figure uses a candidate standard distribution of 0.005. This looks about right; the process appears to have reached a stationary state and the sample space appears to be fully explored. Serial correlations are very much lower than the other two diagrams. The correlation between the rth and $(r + 5)$th values is 0.73 for the top diagram, 0.96 for the second, and 0.10 for the third. These correlations ignore the first 200 values.

MCMC FOR THE RSLN MODEL

In this section, the application of the MCMC method to the RSLN model is described in detail. Many other choices of prior and candidate distribution would work equally well and give very similar results. The choices listed were derived after some experimentation with different distributions and parameters. Without strong prior information, it is appropriate to set the variances for the prior distributions to be large enough that the effect of the prior on the acceptance probability is very small in virtually all cases.

μ_1, μ_2

For the means of the two regimes, we use identical normal prior distributions; that is $\mu_1, \mu_2 \sim N(0, 0.02^2)$. The candidate distribution for the first regime is $N(\mu_1^{(r)}, 0.005^2)$ and for the second regime is $N(\mu_2^{(r)}, 0.02^2)$. The candidate density for μ_1 is therefore:

$$q(\lambda|\mu_1) = \frac{1}{0.005} \sqrt{(2\pi)} \exp\left(-\frac{1}{2}\left(\frac{\lambda - \mu_1}{0.005}\right)^2\right) \qquad (5.11)$$

This is an example of a random-walk Metropolis algorithm, where the ratio

$$\frac{q(\mu_1|\lambda)}{q(\lambda|\mu_1)} = 1$$

and the acceptance probability for μ_1 reduces to

$$\alpha = \min\left(1, \frac{L_1(\lambda, \Theta_{\sim 1})}{L_1(\mu_1^{(r)}, \Theta_{\sim 1}^{(r)})} \frac{\phi(\lambda/.02)}{\phi(\mu_1^{(r)}/.02)}\right) \qquad (5.12)$$

and similarly for μ_2.

The candidate variance is chosen to give an appropriate probability of acceptance. The acceptance probabilities for μ_1 and μ_2 depend on the distributions used for the other parameters; using those described below, we have acceptance probabilities of around 40 percent for both variables.

σ_1, σ_2

It is conventional to work with the inverse variance, $\tau = \sigma^{-2}$, known as the precision. The prior distribution for τ_1 is the gamma distribution with prior mean 865 and variance 849^2; the prior distribution for τ_2 is gamma with mean 190 and variance $1{,}000^2$. The prior distributions are centered around the likelihood estimates, but are both very disperse, providing little influence on the final distribution.

The candidate distributions are also gamma; for $\tau_1^{(r+1)}$, we use a distribution with mean $\tau_1^{(r)}$ and standard deviation $\tau_1^{(r)}/2.75$. For $\tau_2^{(r+1)}$, we use a distribution with mean $\tau_2^{(r)}$ and standard deviation, $\tau_2^{(r)}/1.5$. The different coefficients of variation (CV = variance/mean^2) are determined heuristically to give acceptance probabilities within the desired range. The acceptance probabilities for τ_1 and τ_2 candidates are approximately 20 percent to 35 percent.

$p_{1,2}, p_{2,1}$

Obviously, the $p_{i,j}$ parameters are constrained to lie in $(0, 1)$, which indicates the beta distribution for prior and candidate distributions. The prior distributions used for the transition probabilities are $p_{1,2} \sim \text{Beta}(2, 48)$ and $p_{2,1} \sim \text{Beta}(2, 6)$, giving prior means of 0.04 and 0.25 and standard deviations of 0.027, 0.145 respectively for $p_{1,2}$ and $p_{2,1}$.

The candidate distributions are also beta, with $\lambda \sim \text{Beta}(1.2, 28.8)$ for $p_{1,2}$, and for $p_{2,1}$, candidate $\lambda \sim \text{Beta}(1, 3)$. These have the same means as the prior distributions but are more widely distributed, to ensure that candidates from the tails of the distribution are adequately sampled.

The acceptance rates for $p_{1,2}$ and $p_{2,1}$ are approximately 35 percent.

MCMC Results for RSLN Model

The results given here are from 10,000 simulations of the parameters, separately for the TSE and S&P data. The first 500 simulations are ignored in both cases to allow for burn-in.

Table 5.1 gives the means and standard deviations of the posterior parameter distributions. The means of the posterior distributions are Bayesian point estimates for the individual parameters. These are very similar to the maximum likelihood estimates in Table 3.5. This is not surprising,

TABLE 5.1 MCMC mean parameters, with standard deviations.

	TSE 300	
$\tilde{\mu}_1 = 0.0122\ (0.002)$	$\tilde{\sigma}_1 = 0.0351\ (0.002)$	$\tilde{p}_{1,2} = 0.0334\ (0.012)$
$\tilde{\mu}_2 = -0.0164\ (0.010)$	$\tilde{\sigma}_2 = 0.0804\ (0.009)$	$\tilde{p}_{2,1} = 0.2058\ (0.065)$
	S&P 500	
$\tilde{\mu}_1 = 0.0121\ (0.002)$	$\tilde{\sigma}_1 = 0.0355\ (0.002)$	$\tilde{p}_{1,2} = 0.0286\ (0.014)$
$\tilde{\mu}_2 = -0.0167\ (0.014)$	$\tilde{\sigma}_2 = 0.0802\ (0.016)$	$\tilde{p}_{2,1} = 0.2835\ (0.098)$

because the method is very close to maximum likelihood, especially with such disperse prior distributions. Although the standard deviations also correspond closely to the estimated standard errors of the maximum likelihood estimates, these slightly understate the standard errors for the parameters because the estimates are serially correlated. The effect of this is reduced by using every 20th value in the standard deviation calculations. With this spacing, the serial correlations are very small.

Figure 5.2 shows the estimated marginal density functions for the parameters. The solid lines show the TSE results, and the broken lines show the results for the S&P 500 data. The results for regime 1 (the low-volatility regime) are very similar. For the high volatility, the two sets of data appear different. An analysis of the timing of regime switches shows that whenever the S&P 500 is in regime 2, so is the TSE 300, but the TSE also makes the occasional foray into the high-volatility regime when the S&P is comfortably in the low-volatility regime. The explanation appears to be that jitters in the U.S. market affect the Canadian market at the same time, but there are also influences specific to the Canadian market that can cause a switch into the high-volatility regime, but that do not affect the U.S. market.

Figure 5.2 demonstrates one of the advantages of the MCMC methodology in this case; typically, using maximum likelihood methods, we assume estimates are normally distributed (which is approximately true for very large sample sizes). Here, our sample size is small and it is clear from the graphs that the parameter estimates are not all normally distributed.

Table 5.2 gives the correlations for the parameters, but Figure 5.3 demonstrates the relationships between the parameters more clearly than the correlations. This figure shows, for example, that higher values of the transition probability from regime 1 to regime 2 are associated with higher values for the opposite transition from regime 2 to regime 1. It also shows that higher values for the regime 1 to regime 2 transition probability seem to

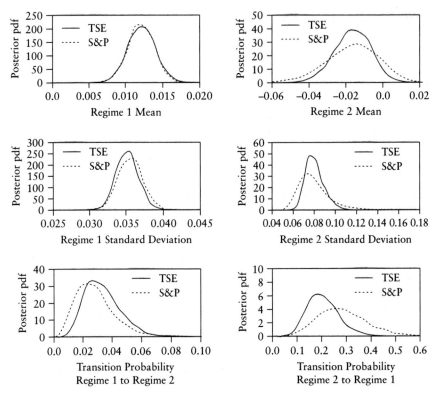

FIGURE 5.2   Simulated marginal posterior parameter distributions.

be compatible only with lower values for the regime 2 standard deviation, and with relatively high values for the regime 2 mean.

In Figure 5.4, we show the sample paths for the MCMC estimation for the six parameters of the TSE data. These are useful for an indication of the serial correlations, and to assess whether the candidate densities are

TABLE 5.2   Parameter correlations using MCMC estimation.

				TSE 300		
	μ_1	σ_1	$p_{1,2}$	μ_2	σ_2	$p_{2,1}$
μ_1	1.0000	−0.1630	0.1681	−0.1043	−0.1678	0.0552
σ_1		1.0000	−0.3438	−0.1094	0.2235	−0.0374
$p_{1,2}$			1.0000	0.0796	−0.2517	0.3385
μ_2				1.0000	−0.1476	−0.1433
σ_2					1.0000	0.1238
$p_{2,1}$						1.0000

appropriate (is the process reasonably stable). It is always important to check the sample paths when using the MHA. The paths for the parameters appear satisfactory; they resemble the third diagram of Figure 5.1, and not either of the first two. Determining when the process has converged to the ultimate stationary distribution is complex and technical. In practice, a way of checking is to rerun the simulations from a few different seed values, to ensure that the results are stable.

The log-likelihood using the MCMC mean parameter estimates for the TSE 300 data is 922.6 compared with the maximum of 922.7. In Figure 5.5, some contour plots of the likelihood function for the S&P data are given, with the point (posterior mean) MCMC estimate also marked. This shows

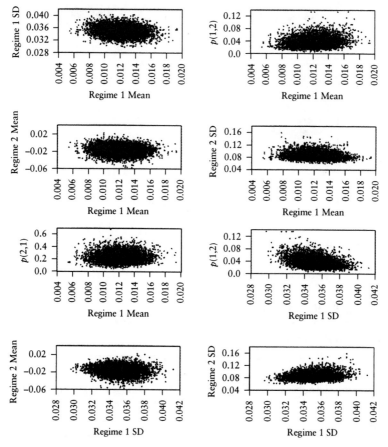

FIGURE 5.3 Two-way joint distributions for TSE data.

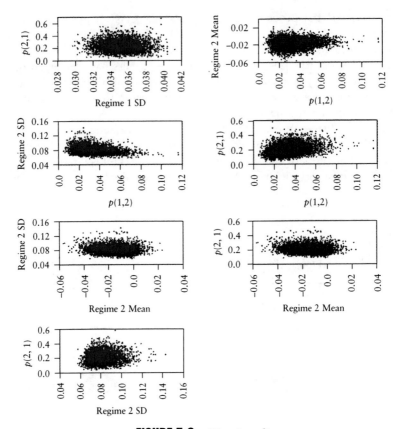

FIGURE 5.3 *(Continued)*

the relationship between the MCMC point estimates and the maximum likelihood estimates.

SIMULATING THE PREDICTIVE DISTRIBUTION

The Predictive Distribution

Once we have generated a sample from the posterior distribution for the parameter vector, we can also generate a sample from the predictive distribution, which was defined in equation 5.3. This is the distribution of future values of the process X_t, given the posterior distribution $\pi(\boldsymbol{\theta})$ and given the data x. Let $Z = (Y_1, Y_2, \ldots, Y_m)$ be a random variable representing m consecutive monthly log-returns on the S&P/TSX composite

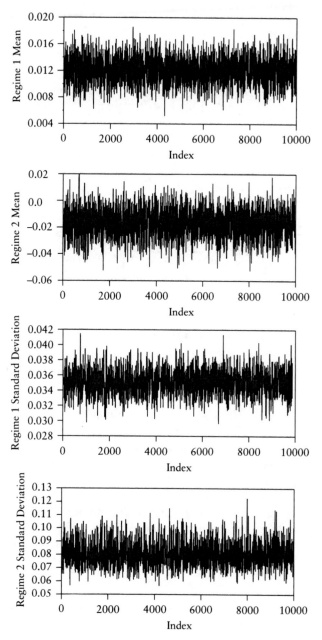

FIGURE 5.4 Sample paths, TSE data.

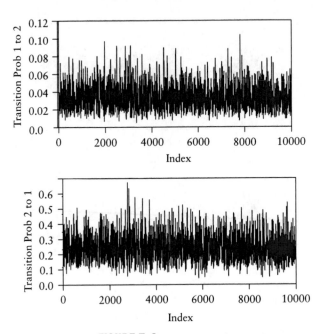

FIGURE 5.4 *(Continued)*

index. Let y represent the historic data used to simulate the posterior sample under the MHA. The predictive distribution is

$$f(z|y) = \int_{\theta} f(z|\theta, y)\pi(\theta|y)d\theta \qquad (5.13)$$

This means that simulations of the m future log-returns under the regime-switching lognormal process, generated using a different value for θ for each simulation, (generated by the MCMC algorithm) form a random sample from the predictive distribution.

The advantage of using the predictive distribution is that it implicitly allows for parameter uncertainty. It will be different from the distribution for z using a central estimate, $E[\theta|y]$, from the posterior distribution—the difference is that the predictive distribution can be written as

$$E_{\theta|y}\big[f(z|\theta, y)\big] \qquad (5.14)$$

while using the mean of the posterior distribution as a point estimate for θ is equivalent to using the distribution:

$$f(z|E[\theta|y]) \qquad (5.15)$$

Around the medians, these two distributions will be similar. However, since the first allows for the process variability and the parameter variability,

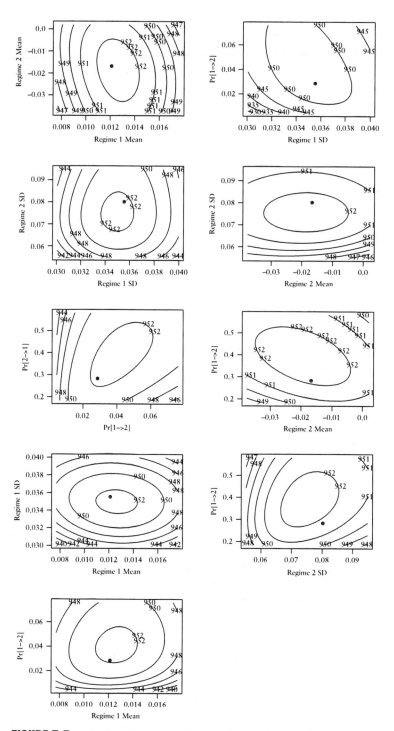

FIGURE 5.5 Likelihood contour plots, with MCMC point estimates; S&P data.

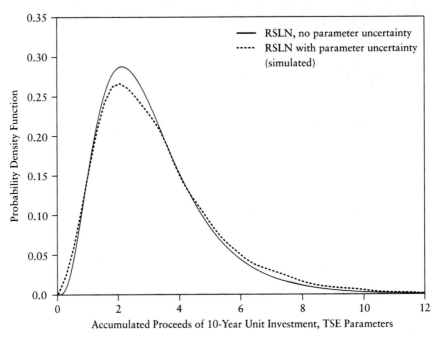

FIGURE 5.6   Ten-year accumulation factor density function; with and without parameter uncertainty (TSE parameters).

whereas the second only allows process variability, we would expect the variance of the predictive distribution to be higher than the second distribution.

Simulating the Predictive Distribution for the 10-Year Accumulation Factor

We will illustrate the ideas of the last section using simulated values for the 10-year accumulation factor, using TSE parameters. First, using the approach of equation 5.15, the point estimates of the parameters given in Table 5.1 were used to calculate the density plotted as the unbroken curve in Figure 5.6. We then simulated 15,000 values for the accumulation factor. For each simulation of the accumulation factor, we sampled a new vector from the set of parameters generated using MCMC. The parameter sample generated by the MCMC algorithm is a dependent sample. To lessen the effect of serial correlation, only every fifth parameter set was used in the simulation of the accumulation factor. The first 300 parameter vectors generated by the MCMC algorithm were ignored as burn-in. The resulting simulated density function is plotted as the broken line in Figure 5.6.

The result is that incorporating parameter uncertainty gives a distribution with fatter left and right tails. This will have financial implications for equity-linked liabilities, which we explore more fully in Chapter 11.

CHAPTER 6

Modeling the Guarantee Liability

INTRODUCTION

Risk management of equity-linked insurance requires a full understanding of the nature of the liabilities. In this chapter, we will discuss how to use stochastic simulation to determine the liability distribution under the guarantee.

In the section on provision for equity-linked liabilities in Chapter 1, four approaches to making provision for the guarantee liability were discussed. Two of these, the actuarial approach and dynamic hedging (or the financial engineering approach), form the subject of the next four chapters.

Under the actuarial approach to risk management, sufficient assets are placed in risk-free instruments to meet the liabilities, when they fall due, with high probability. We need to determine the distribution of the liabilities and, as the assets are assumed to be "lock-boxed," we can do this without reference to the assets held. This is the subject of this chapter.

Under the financial engineering approach, the capital requirement is used to construct a replicating portfolio that will, at least approximately, meet the guarantee when it becomes due. However, stochastic simulation of the liabilities is also important to the financial engineering approach to risk management for the following reasons: there will be transactions costs; the rebalancing of the hedge will be at discrete time intervals rather than continuously; and the stock returns will not precisely follow the model assumed or the parameters assumed. In this case, the assets and liabilities are very closely linked, and we need to model both simultaneously. Nevertheless, many of the issues raised in this chapter will also be important in Chapter 8, where the financial engineering approach to risk management is discussed in more detail.

THE STOCHASTIC PROCESSES

The liability under an individual equity-linked contract depends largely on two stochastic processes. The first is the equity process on which the guarantee is based. We assume a suitable equity model is available, selected perhaps from the models of Chapter 2. We also assume parameters have been estimated for the equity model. Given the model and parameters, it is possible to simulate an equity process modeling the returns earned by the separate fund account before the deduction of charges. In other words, we may simulate individual realizations of the accumulation factors for each time unit $t - 1$ to t, $\{R_t\}$, so that an equity investment of \$1 at $t - 1$ accumulates to R_t at t.

The second stochastic process models policyholder transitions—that is, whether the contract is still fully in force or whether the policyholder has died, surrendered a proportion of the fund, or withdrawn altogether. We could construct a stochastic process to model the policyholder behavior and simulate the policyholder transition process. In general we do not do this. For mortality it is usually sufficient to take a deterministic approach, provided the portfolio is sufficiently large. The underlying reason for this is that mortality is diversifiable, which means that for a large portfolio of policyholders the experienced mortality will be very close to the expected mortality.

Withdrawals are more problematic. Withdrawals are, to some extent, related to the investment experience, and the withdrawal risk is, therefore, not fully diversifiable. However, there is insufficient data to be confident of the nature of the relationship. We also know a reasonable amount about the withdrawal experience of pure investment contracts, such as mutual funds, but, crucially, we do not know how this translates to the separate account contract with maturity guarantees. It is certainly to be expected that the guarantee would materially affect the withdrawal behavior. The relatively recent surge in the sale of contracts carrying maturity guarantees, both in Canada and in the United States, means that the data available to companies is all based on recent investment experience. For example, despite having many thousands of contracts, we still only have around 10 years of data on segregated fund policyholder behavior in Canada.

The usual approach to all this uncertainty about withdrawals is to use a very simple approach, but bear in mind the possible inaccuracy in analyzing the results. The simplest approach is to treat withdrawals deterministically. Some work on stochastic modeling of withdrawals has been done, for example, Kolkiewicz and Tan (1999), but until some substantial relevant data is available, all models (including the deterministic constant withdrawal rate model) are highly speculative.

SIMULATING THE STOCK RETURN PROCESS

For most of the univariate equity models described in Chapter 2, it is fairly easy to simulate scenarios. The first requirement is a reliable random number generator; most models will need values generated from the standard normal distribution, but some may need Uniform(0,1) values. Many commercial software packages offer random number generators, some of which are more reliable than others. It is very important to check any generator you use for accuracy (does it actually produce the distribution it is supposed to, with serial independence?) and periodicity.

All random number generators use deterministic principles to generate numbers that behave as if they were truly random. All generators will eventually repeat themselves; the number of different values generated before the sequence starts again is called the period of the generator. Some generators have very high periodicity. However, software that is not designed for serious statistical purposes may use built-in generators with rather low periodicity. This can have a significant effect on the accuracy of inference from a simulation exercise. For more information on the generation of uniform and other random numbers, a good text is Ross (1996); the *Numerical Recipes* books (e.g., Press et al. 1992) also provide reliable algorithms for programming random number generators.

Given the appropriate random number generator, generating the stock price or return process is straightforward for many models. For example, for the lognormal (LN) model with parameters μ and σ per time unit, the process is as follows:

1. Generate a standard random normal deviate z_1.
2. $Y_1 = \mu + \sigma z_1$ gives the log-return in the first time unit, and $S_1 = S_0 \exp(Y_1)$ is the stock price at $t = 1$.
3. Repeat (1) and (2) for $t = 2, 3, \ldots, n$ where n is the projection period for the simulation.
4. Repeat (1) to (3) for N scenarios, where N is chosen to give the desired accuracy for the inference required.

For the generalized autoregressive conditionally heteroscedastic, or GARCH(1,1), model, the distribution of Y_t depends on the value of Y_{t-1} and σ_{t-1}, which causes problems at the start of the simulation. If the simulation is designed to apply at a specific date, then the current values of Y and σ at that time may be used for Y_0 and σ_0, though σ_0 must be estimated because it is unobservable directly. If the simulation is not for inference relating to a specific starting date, then "neutral" starting values may be used; in this case, reasonable starting values would be the long-term mean values of the variables, that is set

$$Y_0 = \mu \qquad \sigma_0^2 = \frac{\alpha_0}{1 - \alpha_1 - \beta}$$

Given the starting values and generated independent standard normal random deviates, apply the GARCH equation to generate the log-returns:

$$Y_t = \mu + \sigma_t \varepsilon_t \qquad\qquad (6.1)$$

$$\sigma_t^2 = \alpha_0 + \alpha_1 (Y_{t-1} - \mu)^2 + \beta \sigma_{t-1}^2 \qquad\qquad (6.2)$$

For the regime-switching LN (RSLN-2) model with two regimes, the distribution of Y_t depends on the starting regime. This is unobservable, but the probability that the process is in a specific regime can be estimated based on the information from current and previous returns. The probability is

$$p(\rho_0 \mid y_0, y_{-1}, \ldots, \boldsymbol{\theta}) \qquad\qquad (6.3)$$

and it was used in the calculation of the likelihood function for the RSLN-2 model in the section on maximum likelihood estimation (MLE) for the RSLN-2 model in Chapter 3, where the description of the calculation of this function is described.

A neutral starting value that does not assume a specific starting date would use the stationary distribution of the regime-switching process for the probability for the starting regime. That is,

$$\Pr[\rho_0 = 1] = \pi_1 = \frac{p_{12}}{p_{12} + p_{21}}$$

So the simulation for the RSLN-2 model could go as follows:

1. Generate a uniform random number $u \sim U(0, 1)$.
2. If $u < \Pr[\rho_0 = 1]$, assume $\rho_0 = 1$; otherwise assume $\rho_0 = 2$.
3. Then generate $z \sim N(0, 1)$.
4. $Y_1 = \mu_{\rho_0} + \sigma_{\rho_0} z$ gives the log-return in the first time unit and $S_1 = S_0 \exp(Y_1)$ is the stock price at $t = 1$.
5. Generate a new $u \sim U(0, 1)$.
6. If $u < p_{\rho_0,1}$, then assume $\rho_1 = 1$; otherwise assume $\rho_1 = 2$.
7. Repeat from (3) on for $t = 2, \ldots, n$.
8. Repeat (1) to (7) for the required number of scenarios.

NOTATION

In this section, we set out some of the notation used in this chapter. A full list of the actuarial notation is given in Appendix C. Let $_t p_x^\tau$, $_t q_x^w$, and

$_tq^d_x$, $_{u|t}q^d_x$ denote the double decrement survival and exit probabilities for a life aged x, where w denotes withdrawal and d denotes death. The term variables u and t are measured in the time step used in the simulation—this is months for all the examples of this and subsequent chapters, which is playing loose with standard actuarial notation.

The fund and cash-flow variables are as follows:

- G denotes the guarantee level per unit investment, subscripted G_t if it can change over time.
- F_t denotes the market value of the separate account at t assuming the policy is still fully in force. We assume that the management charge or management expense ratio (MER) is deducted from the fund at the beginning of each month; also for the guaranteed accumulation benefit, the fund may be increased at some month ends. It is convenient sometimes to distinguish between the fund immediately before these month-end transactions and the fund immediately after. Let F_{t^-} denote the month-end fund at t before these transactions, and let F_{t^+} denote the month-end fund after the transactions. Where the sign $-$ or $+$ is missing, assume $+$.
- S_t denotes the value of the underlying equity investment at t, where S_0 is assumed for convenience to be equal to 1.0; that is, S_t is the accumulation factor from 0 to t. S_t is randomly generated from an appropriate distribution. Y_t is the associated log-return process, so that $S_t \exp\{Y_t + Y_{t+1} + \cdots + Y_{t+r-1}\} = S_{t+r}$.
- m denotes the management charge rate deducted from the separate account, per month. The portion available for funding the guarantee cost is m_c, called the *margin offset*. This may be split by benefit so that, for example, for a joint guaranteed minimum maturity benefit (GMMB) and guaranteed minimum death benefit (GMDB) contract the total risk charge per month would be $m_c = m_m + m_d$, where m_m is allocated to the GMMB and m_d is allocated to the GMDB.
- M_t represents the income at t from the guarantee risk charge.
- C_t represents the liability cash flow at t from the contract, net of the income from M_t, allowing for deaths and withdrawals.
- L_0 is the present value of future liabilities, discounted at a constant risk-free force of interest of r per year.

The relationships between these variables, assuming that the margin offset is collected monthly in advance, are

$$F_t = \frac{S_t}{S_{t-1}} F_{t-1^+} \tag{6.4}$$

$$F_{t^+} = F_{t^-}(1 - m) = F_{(t-1)}(1 - m)\frac{S_t}{S_{t-1}} \tag{6.5}$$

so, for integer t and u, and assuming no cash injections into the fund between t and $t + u$,

$$F_{(t+u)^+} = F_t \frac{S_{t+u}(1-m)^u}{S_t} \tag{6.6}$$

Now, let F_{0^-} be the fund at the valuation date (or at policy issue date, in which case it is the policy single premium), then

$$F_t = F_{0^-} \frac{S_t (1-m)^t}{S_0} \tag{6.7}$$

The margin offset income, which is the income allocated to funding the guarantee, is

$$M_t = (F_{t^-}) \, m_c \tag{6.8}$$

$$= m_c \, F_{0^-} \frac{S_t(1-m)^t}{S_0} \tag{6.9}$$

GUARANTEED MINIMUM MATURITY BENEFIT

In this section, we show how to generate the distribution of the present value of the guarantee liability for a simple GMMB policy held by a life aged x with remaining duration n years. We assume a monthly discrete time model for equity returns and management charges. Withdrawals and deaths are assumed to occur at month ends. As discussed, exits are treated deterministically, so the only random process simulated is the equity price process.

Clearly other assumptions and approaches are possible; the aim here is to demonstrate the basic principles. Since S_t is a stock index, we assume $S_0 = 1.0$ so that S_t is the accumulation factor for the period from time 0 to time t. Recall that $(G - F_n)^+ = \max(0, G - F_n)$. Then,

$$C_t = -{}_t p_x^\tau M_t \qquad t = 0, 1, \ldots, n-1 \tag{6.10}$$

and

$$C_n = -{}_n p_x^\tau \left(G - F_n\right)^+ \tag{6.11}$$

Then,

$$L_0 = \sum_{t=0}^{n} C_t \, e^{-rt} \tag{6.12}$$

Example **101**

So C_t and L_0 can be calculated for each stock index scenario, and distributions for the cash flows in different years and for the present value random variable can all be simulated.

GUARANTEED MINIMUM DEATH BENEFIT

Assume no reset or rollover benefit; the death benefit is the greater of the initial investment and the fund value at death. Using a deterministic approach to the death benefit is equivalent to assuming that $_tq_x$ lives per policy die in the interval $(0, t)$. (See Appendix C for an explanation of the actuarial notation used here.) The liability cash flow for the benefit at t is therefore:

$$C_t = -_tp_x^\tau M_t + _{t-1|1}q_x^d (G - F_t)^+ \quad t = 0, 1, \ldots, n \tag{6.13}$$

$$C_t = -_tp_x^\tau F_0 \, S_t(1 - m)^{t-1}m_d + _{t-1|1}q_x^d (G - F_0 \, S_t (1 - m)^t)^+ \tag{6.14}$$

M_t^d is the risk charge income in respect of the death benefit.

EXAMPLE

We will work through an example of a combined GMMB and GMDB contract to show how easy this is. All the details to follow this example are given in Appendix A. For any useful information, we would need at least 1,000 simulated stock return scenarios, but for the purpose of demonstrating the calculation we will use just one.

Suppose we have a contract with a GMMB and a GMDB at a fixed guarantee level, with the following features:

- Let $x = 50$, $F_0 = 100$, $G = 100$, $m = .02/12$ per month, and $m_c = .005/12$ per month.
- Let the remaining contract term be 12 months.
- Let the dependent death and withdrawal rates be as given in Appendix A.
- Let the equity index given be a single, randomly generated scenario, generated using the RSLN model.

The result of the single scenario is given in Table 6.1. The margin offset is received in advance, so there is no income at the end of the final month. The death benefit under the guarantee is greater than zero only on death in the first or last months; for the rest of the period the fund is larger than the guarantee. At the end of the contract, the fund is worth slightly less than the guarantee, so a small GMMB is due.

TABLE 6.1   GMMB/GMDB liability cash flow projection, single random stock scenario.

Month t	Equity Index S_t (Simulated)	F_t	${}_t p_x^\tau$	${}_{t|1} q_x^d$	Margin Offset Income	DB and MB Outgo	C_t
0	1.0000	100.00	1.0000	0.0003	0.042		−0.042
1	.9935	99.19	0.9931	0.0003	0.041	0.0002	−0.041
2	1.0227	101.93	0.9862	0.0003	0.042	0	−0.042
3	1.0399	103.48	0.9793	0.0003	0.042	0	−0.042
4	1.0761	106.90	0.9725	0.0003	0.043	0	−0.043
5	1.1095	110.03	0.9658	0.0003	0.044	0	−0.044
6	1.0800	106.93	0.9591	0.0003	0.043	0	−0.043
7	1.1195	110.65	0.9524	0.0003	0.044	0	−0.044
8	1.2239	120.77	0.9458	0.0003	0.048	0	−0.048
9	1.0894	107.32	0.9392	0.0003	0.042	0	−0.042
10	1.0865	106.86	0.9327	0.0003	0.042	0	−0.042
11	1.0573	103.81	0.9262	0.0003	0.040	0	−0.040
12	1.0150	99.49	0.9198	0.0003	0.000	0.471	0.471

At a risk-free annual rate of interest of 6 percent per year, the net present value of future liability for this scenario (the sum of the cash flow present values) is −0.145. The negative sign implies a net income.

GUARANTEED MINIMUM ACCUMULATION BENEFIT

Under a guaranteed minimum accumulation benefit (GMAB) policy there may be multiple maturity dates. The design offers guaranteed renewal of the contract. On renewal the minimum term applies (typically 10 years). There may be an upper limit to the number of allowable renewals.

The effect of renewal is that if the guarantee is in-the-money, $G > F_T$, then the insurer must pay out the difference. Then, on renewal, the fund value is G. The contract then starts again at the same guarantee level. If the guarantee is out-of-the-money, that is $G < F_T$, the guarantee is automatically reset at renewal to the fund value at that time. So, the minimum of F_T and G is always increased to the maximum of F_T and G at renewal, with a cash payment due if $G > F_T$. This is sometimes referred to as a rollover option. Although expense charges are typically not guaranteed, increases are rare and it is prudent to assume no changes. Some policyholders may choose not to renew. This can be allowed for in the decrement rate q^w.

Assume that the next renewal is in n_1 months, and subsequent renewals occur at times $n_2, \ldots, n_k$, given that the contract is in force at those dates. Since the fund may increase at the renewal dates, we distinguish between the fund before and after the injection of cash, denoting by $F_{n_r}^-$ the fund immediately before renewal and by F_{n^+} the fund immediately after renewal.

The guarantee in force at the start of the projection period is $G_0 = F_{n_0^+}$ from the last reset before the projection. Subsequently,

$$G_1 = \max(G_0, F_{n_1}^-) = G_0 \max\left(1.0, \ 1.0 + \frac{F_{n_1}^-}{F_{n_0^+}}\right) \qquad (6.15)$$

$$G_2 = \max(G_1, F_{n_2}^-) = G_0 \prod_{r=1}^{2} \max\left(1.0, \ 1.0 + \frac{F_{n_r}^-}{F_{n_{r-1}^+}}\right) \qquad (6.16)$$

$$\vdots$$

$$G_k = \max(G_{k-1}, F_{n_k}^-) = G_0 \prod_{r=1}^{k} \max\left(1.0, \ 1.0 + \frac{F_{n_r}^-}{F_{n_{r-1}^+}}\right) \qquad (6.17)$$

Now the fund growth between renewal dates arises from the underlying index growth, $S_{n_r}/S_{n_{r-1}}$, with management charges deducted, so that

$$\frac{F_{n_r}^-}{F_{n_{r-1}^+}} = (1 - m)^{n_r - n_{r-1}} \frac{S_{n_r}}{S_{n_{r-1}}} \qquad (6.18)$$

So the guarantee in force can be tracked through each individual projection.

Between maturity dates, say at month t where $n_r < t < n_{r+1}$, the income is from the risk charge and the outgo is from the death benefit, which applies at guarantee level G_r. The liability cash flow then is:

$$C_t = {}_{t-1|1}q_x^d (G_r - F_t)^+ - {}_tp_x^\tau M_t \qquad n_r < t < n_{r+1} \qquad (6.19)$$

At renewal or maturity dates $n_1, \ldots, n_k$ the cash flow is

$$C_{n_r} = {}_{n_r-1|1}q_x^d(G_r - F_{n_r}^-)^+ + {}_{n_r}p_x^\tau (G_r - F_{n_r}^-)^+ - {}_{n_r}p_x^\tau M_{n_r} \qquad (6.20)$$

where the first term allows for the GMDB in the final month, the second term is the maturity benefit, and the third term is the risk-charge income at renewal.

GMAB EXAMPLE

In this section, we will again work through a single scenario to show how the process described above works in practice. The scenario is set out in a spreadsheet format because this gives a convenient layout for following an individual projection. In practice, spreadsheets are generally not the most suitable framework for a large number of simulations. The main reasons for this are, first, that a spreadsheet approach may be very slow compared with other methods. A spreadsheet approach may, therefore, limit the maximum number of simulations that can be carried out in a reasonable time much more severely than using a more direct programming approach. Secondly, the built-in random number generators of proprietary spreadsheets are often not suitable for a large number of simulations or for complex problems. The example we show is a GMAB benefit with the following contract details:

- The separate fund value at the beginning of the projection period is $100.
- The guarantee level at the start of the projection is $80.
- There are rollover dates where the fund is made up to the guarantee, or vice versa, in two years, in 12 years with final maturity, and in 22 years from the start of the projection.
- Management charges of 3 percent per year are deducted monthly in advance.
- A margin offset of 0.5 percent per year, collected monthly from the management charge, is available to fund the guarantee liability.

Stochastic simulation has been used to generate a stock index path using the RSLN-2 model with MLE parameters as shown in Table 6.2[1]. Mortality is assumed to follow the Canadian Institute of Actuaries (CIA) insured lives summarized in Appendix A. Lapses are assumed to be constant at two-thirds percent per month. The precise mortality rates used in the example are given in full in Appendix A.

TABLE 6.2 RSLN parameters for examples.

Regime 1	$\mu_1 = 0.012$	$\sigma_1 = 0.035$	$p_{12} = 0.037$
Regime 2	$\mu_2 = -0.016$	$\sigma_2 = 0.078$	$p_{21} = 0.210$

---

[1] These are maximum likelihood parameters for TSE 300 data, 1956 to 1999 period. These parameters are used for most of the examples in this and subsequent chapters.

TABLE 6.3 Fund cash flows under example scenario assuming contract is in force.

$(t-1) \to t$	F_{t-1}	M_{t-1}	I_t	F_t	G	$(G-F_t)^+$
0–1	100.00	0.0417	−0.427%	99.32	80	0
1–2	99.32	0.0414	4.70%	103.73	80	0
2–3	103.73	0.0432	−0.770%	102.67	80	0
3–4	102.67	0.0428	−1.685%	100.69	80	0
4–5	100.69	0.0420	−1.428%	99.00	80	0
5–6	99.00	0.0413	1.530%	100.27	80	0
6–7	100.27	0.0418	8.098%	108.12	80	0
7–8	108.12	0.0450	−6.316%	101.03	80	0
8–9	101.03	0.0421	−0.879%	99.89	80	0
9–10	99.89	0.0416	10.708%	110.31	80	0
10–11	110.31	0.0460	−6.302%	103.40	80	0
$\vdots$						
23–24	148.47	0.0619	7.356%	158.99	80	0
24–25	158.99	0.0662	1.917%	161.63	158.99	0
25–26	161.63	0.0673	−7.004%	149.94	158.99	9.05
26–27	149.94	0.0625	4.738%	156.65	158.99	2.34
27–28	156.65	0.0653	0.546%	157.11	158.99	1.88
$\vdots$						
141–142	107.01	0.0446	12.339%	119.91	158.99	39.08
142–143	119.91	0.0500	1.251%	121.11	158.99	37.88
143–144	121.11	0.0505	1.206%	122.26	158.99	36.73
144–145	158.99	0.0662	−1.649%	155.98	158.99	3.01
145–146	155.98	0.0650	4.362%	162.38	158.99	0
$\vdots$						
263–264	471.99	0.1967	6.755%	512.61	158.99	0

In Table 6.3, we show the fund at the start of the month, before management charges are deducted, F_{t-1}; the income from the risk premium, M_{t-1}; the interest rate earned on the fund in the tth month, I_t; and the end-year fund, F_t, after deducting management charges and adding the year's interest. All these figures are calculated assuming that the contract is still in force. In this table F_0 starts at \$100 at time $t = 0$. The total management charge deducted at the start of the year is 0.25, of which 0.0417 ($= M_0$) is received as risk-premium income to offset the guarantee cost. The net fund after expenses is \$99.75, which earns a return of $I_1 = -0.427$ percent, leading to an end-year fund of $F_1 = \$99.32$. This is still greater than the current guarantee of \$80, so there is no guarantee liability for death benefits in the first month.

All through the first two years, the fund exceeds the guarantee at the end of each month. At the end of the 24th month the first renewal date applies. In this scenario $F_{24} = 158.99$, compared with the guarantee of \$80. There is, therefore, no survival benefit due, and the guarantee value is increased for the renewed 10-year contract to the month-end fund value, \$158.99.

In the 10 years following the first renewal under this single stock return scenario, the index rises very slowly. After the guarantee has been reset to the fund value, the fund value drifts below the new guarantee level, leaving a potential death benefit liability. In fact, over the entire 10-year period the accumulation is only 3.8 percent. Since expenses of 0.25 percent per month are deducted from the fund, by the end of 144 months the fund has fallen \$36.73 below the guarantee that was set at the end of 24 months.

At the second renewal, then, the insurer must pay the difference to make the fund up to the guarantee, provided the policy is still in force. Therefore, at the start of the 145th month the fund has been increased to the guarantee value of \$158.99.

Since the fund was less than the guarantee at the renewal date, the guarantee remains at \$158.99 for the final 10 years of the contract. After the 145th month the fund is never again lower than the guarantee value, and there is no further liability. However, the risk-premium portion of the management charge continues to be collected at the start of each month. In Table 6.4, we show the liability cash flows under this particular scenario.

Each month a negative cash flow comes from the income from the risk-premium management charge. The amount from the third column of Table 6.3 is multiplied by the survival probability $_{t-1}p_x^{(\tau)}$ for the expected cash flow.

A death benefit liability arises in months for which $(G - F_t)$ is greater than zero at the month end. For example, if the policyholder dies in the 26th month, the death benefit due at the month end would be $(G - F_{26}) = \$9.05$. Since we allow for mortality deterministically, we value this death benefit at the month end by multiplying by the probability of death in the 26th month, $_{25|}q_x^{(d)}$, which is an expected payment of \$0.00273. The probability of the policyholder's surviving, in force, to the second renewal date is $_{144}p_x^{(\tau)} = 0.35212$, and the payment due under the survival benefit is \$36.73, leading to an expected cash flow under the survival benefit of $_{144}p_x^{(\tau)} 36.73 = \$12.93$.

In the final column, the cash flows from the tth month are discounted to the start of the projection at the assumed risk-free force of interest of 6 percent per year. The management charge income is discounted from the start of the month, and any death or survival benefit is discounted from the end of the month.

TABLE 6.4 Expected nonfund cash flows allowing for survivorship.

$(t-1) \rightarrow t$	In-Force Probability $_{t-1}p_x^\tau$	Mortality Probability $_{t-1}\|q_x^d$	Expected Death Benefit	Expected Survival Benefit	C_t	$C_t v^t$
0–1	1.00000	0.000287	0		−0.0417	−0.0417
1–2	0.99307	0.000288	0		−0.0411	−0.0409
2–3	0.98619	0.000289	0		−0.0426	−0.0422
3–4	0.97934	0.000289	0		−0.0419	−0.0413
4–5	0.97255	0.000290	0		−0.0408	−0.0400
5–6	0.96580	0.000290	0		−0.0398	−0.0389
6–7	0.95909	0.000291	0		−0.0401	−0.0389
7–8	0.95243	0.000292	0		−0.0429	−0.0414
8–9	0.94581	0.00029	0		−0.0398	−0.0383
9–10	0.93923	0.000293	0		−0.0391	−0.0374
10–11	0.93270	0.000293	0		−0.0429	−0.0408
$\vdots$						
23–24	0.85157	0.000301	0		−0.0527	−0.0470
24–25	0.84561	0.000301	0	0	−0.0560	−0.0497
25–26	0.83970	0.000302	0.00273		−0.0538	−0.0475
26–27	0.83382	0.000303	0.00071		−0.0514	−0.0451
27–28	0.82797	0.000303	0.00057		−0.0535	−0.0467
$\vdots$						
141–142	0.36032	0.000359	0.01402		−0.0021	−0.0010
142–143	0.35757	0.000359	0.01360		−0.0043	−0.0021
143–144	0.35483	0.000359	0.01319	12.932	12.9276	6.2925
144–145	0.35212	0.000359	0.00183		−0.0222	−0.0108
145–146	0.34942	0.000360	0		−0.0228	−0.0110
$\vdots$						
263–264	0.12938	0.000351	0	0	−0.0254	−0.0068

For this example scenario, the net present value (NPV) of the guarantee liability is $2.845. The contribution of the death benefit guarantee is $1.338, and the survival benefit expected present value is $6.295. The management charge income offsets these expenses by $4.788.

In fact, this example is unusual; in most scenarios there is no survival benefit at all, and the management charge income generally exceeds the expected outgo on the death benefit, leading to a negative NPV of the guarantee liability.

STOCHASTIC SIMULATION OF LIABILITY CASH FLOWS

For a stochastic analysis of the guarantee liability, we repeat the calculations described in the previous section many times using different sequences of investment returns. If we consider a contract with monthly cash flows over, say, 22 years (such as the example above), applying 10,000 different simulations will give a lot of information and there are different ways of analyzing the output. In this section, we examine how to summarize that information and give an example of the simulated liability for the GMAB contract of the example in Tables 6.3 and 6.4.

The NPV of the Liability

One method of summarizing the output is to look at the simulated NPVs for the liability under each simulation. As an example, we have repeated the GMAB example above for 10,000 simulations, all generated using the same stock return model. The range of net liability present values generated is −$24.6 to $37.0. The number of NPVs above zero (implying a raw loss on the contract) is 1,380. The mean NPV is −$4.0.

The principle of stochastic simulation is that the simulated empirical distribution function is taken as an estimate of the true underlying distribution function. This means that, for example, since 8,620 projections out of 10,000 produced a negative NPV, the probability that the NPV is negative is estimated at 0.8620. We can, therefore, generate a distribution function for the NPVs. Let $\tilde{F}(x)$ denote the empirical distribution function for the NPV at some value x. Then

$$\tilde{F}(x) = \frac{\text{Number of simulations giving NPV} < x}{10,000}$$

This gives the distribution function in Figure 6.1.

It may be easier to visualize the distribution from the simulated density function. The density can be estimated from the distribution using the procedure:

1. Partition the range of the NPV output into, say, 100 intervals, indicated by $(x_0, x_1, \ldots, x_{100})$. The intervals do not have to be equal; for best results use wider intervals in the tails and smaller intervals in the center of the distribution.
2. The estimated density function at the partition midpoints is

$$\tilde{f}\left(\frac{x_t + x_{t+1}}{2}\right) = \frac{\tilde{F}(x_{t+1}) - \tilde{F}(x_t)}{x_{t+1} - x_t}$$

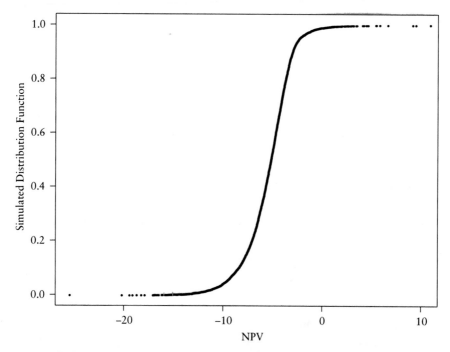

FIGURE 6.1 Simulated distribution function for GMAB NPV example.

Altering the partition will give more or less smoothness in the function. The simulated density function for the 10,000 simulations of the GMAB NPV of the liability is presented in the first diagram of Figure 6.2; in the right-hand diagram we show a smoothed version.

The density function demonstrates that although most of the distribution lies in the area with a negative liability value, there is a substantial right tail to the distribution indicating a small possibility of quite a large liability, relative to the starting fund value of $100. We can compare the distribution of liabilities under this contract with other similar contracts—for example, with a two-year contract with no renewals, otherwise identical to that projected in Figures 6.1 and 6.2.

A set of 10,000 simulations of the two-year contract produced a range of outcomes for the NPV of the liability of −$1.6 to $37.1, compared with −$24.6 to $37.0 for the contract including renewals. The mean of the NPVs under the two-year contract is −$0.30 compared with −$4.00 when renewals are taken into consideration. Thus, at first inspection it looks advantageous to incorporate the renewal option—after all, if the contract continues for 20 years, that's a lot more premium collected with only a relatively small risk of a guarantee payout. But, when we take risk into consideration, the situation does not so clearly favor the with-renewal

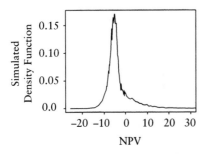 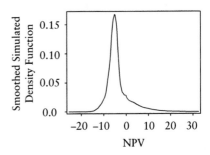

FIGURE 6.2   Simulated probability density function for GMAB NPV example; original and smoothed.

contract. The simulated probability of a positive liability NPV under the two-year contract is 7.5 percent, compared with 13.8 percent for the contract with renewals. So, if we ignore the renewal option, we ignore both upside (an extra 20 years of premiums) and downside (two further potential liabilities under the maturity guarantee).

Liability Cash-Flow Analysis

In addition to the NPV, which is a summary of the nonfund cash flows for the contract, we can use simulation to build a picture of the pattern of cash flows that might be expected under a contract. In the GMAB example, the nonfund cash flows are the management charge income, the death benefit outgo, and the maturity benefit outgo. Any picture of all three sources is dominated by the rare but relatively very large payments at the renewal dates. In Figure 6.3, we show 40 example projections of the cash flows for the GMAB contract. The income and the death benefit outgo are on the same scale, but the maturity benefit outgo is on a very different scale. For this contract, the death benefit rarely exceeds the management charge. An interesting feature of the death benefit outgo is the fact that the larger payments increase after each renewal. As the guarantee moves to the fund level, both the frequency and severity of the death benefit liability increase. In most projections there is no maturity benefit outgo, but when there is a liability, it may be very much larger than the management charge income. The cash flows plotted allow for survival and are not discounted.

This type of cash-flow analysis can help with planning of appropriate asset strategy, as well as product design and marketing. We can also examine the projections to explore the nature of the vulnerability under the contract. For a simple GMMB with no resets or renewals, the risk is clearly that returns over the entire contract duration are very low. For the GMAB, there is an additional risk that returns start high but become weaker after the fund and guarantee have been equalized at a renewal date. By isolating the

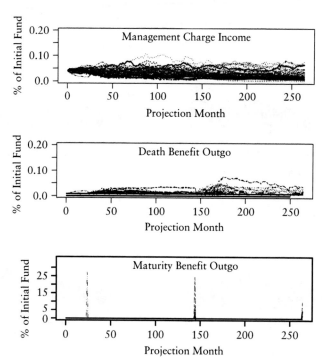

FIGURE 6.3 Simulated projections of nonfund cash flows for GMAB contract.

stock return projections for those cases where a maturity benefit was paid, we may be able to identify more accurately what the risks are in terms of the stock returns.

In Figure 6.4, we show the log stock index for the simulations leading to a maturity benefit at the first, second, and third renewal date. In the final diagram we show 100 paths where there was no maturity benefit liability.

The risk for the two-year maturity benefit is, essentially, a catastrophic stock return in the early part of the projection. This is simply a two-year put option, well out-of-the-money because at the start of the projection the guarantee is assumed to be only 80 percent of the fund value. For the second and third maturity benefits, the stock index paths are flat or declining, on average, from the previous renewal date to the payment date. For this contract the 10-year accumulation factor has a substantial influence on the overall liability. In addition, the two-year accumulation factor plays the major role in the liability at the first renewal date. The calibration procedure discussed in Chapter 4 considers accumulation factors between 1 and 10 years to try to capture this risk. However, the right-tail risk is not tested in that procedure.

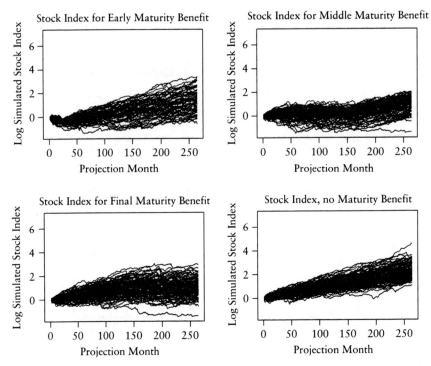

FIGURE 6.4   Simulated projections of log-stock index separated by maturity benefit liability.

THE VOLUNTARY RESET

A common feature of the more generous segregated fund contracts in Canada is a voluntary reset of the guarantee. The policyholder may opt at certain times to reset the guarantee to the current fund value, or some percentage of it; the term would normally be extended.

The simple way to explain the voluntary reset is as a lapse and reentry option. Suppose that a policyholder is six years into a GMAB contract, with, say, two rollover dates before final maturity. The next rollover date is in four years. Stocks have performed well, and the separate fund is now worth, say, 180 percent of the guarantee. If the same contract is still offered, the policyholder could lapse the contract, receive the fund value, and immediately reinvest in a new contract with the same fund value but with guarantee equal to the current fund value. The term to the next rollover under a new contract would generally be 10 years, so the policyholder replaces the rollover in 4 years with another in 10 years with a higher guarantee.

Perhaps in order to avoid the lapse and reentry issue, many insurers wrote the option into the contract. A typical reset feature would allow the policyholder to reset the guarantee to the current fund value; the next rollover date is, then, extended to 10 years from the reset date. The number of resets per year may be restricted, or the option may be available only on certain dates.

The reset feature can be incorporated in the liability modeling without too much extra effort, although we need to make some somewhat speculative assumptions about how policyholders will choose to exercise the option. The assumptions used to produce the figures in this section are described below, but it should be emphasized that modeling policyholder behavior is an enormous open problem.

So, we adapt the GMAB contract described in the previous section to incorporate resets. We assume the same true term for the contract, and that the policyholder does not reset in the final 10 years. We assume also that the policyholder will reset when the ratio of the fund to the guarantee hits a certain threshold—we explore the effect of varying this threshold later in this section. We also assume the effect of restricting the maximum number of resets each year. The figures given are for a GMAB with a 10-year nominal term (between rollover terms, if the policyholder does not reset) and a 30-year effective term. The starting fund to guarantee ratio is 1.0.

In Table 6.5, some quantiles of the NPV distributions are given for the various reset assumptions. These result from identical sets of 10,000 scenarios. Figures are per $100 starting fund.

This table shows that the effect of the reset option is not very large, although the right-tail difference is sufficiently significant that it should be taken into consideration. This will be quantified in Chapter 9. The effect of different threshold choices is relatively small, as is the choice in the policy design of restricting the number of resets permitted per year, although that will clearly affect the expenses associated with maintaining the policy. Having a restricted number of possible resets does not matter much because infrequent use of the reset appears to be the best strategy.

TABLE 6.5 Quantiles for the NPV of the guarantee liability for a GMAB contract with resets; percentage of starting-fund value.

Reset Assumption	Threshold	5%	25%	50%	75%	95%
No resets		−10.7	−7.0	−5.2	−3.3	5.1
2 resets per year	115%	−9.9	−6.2	−4.2	−1.1	7.8
No limit	105%	−9.5	−5.8	−3.9	−1.1	8.2
No limit	115%	−9.7	−6.2	−4.2	−1.3	8.0
No limit	130%	−10.1	−6.5	−4.4	−1.6	7.6

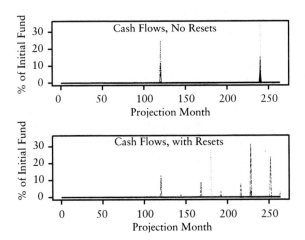

FIGURE 6.5   Simulated cash flows, with and without resets.

Resetting every time the fund exceeds 105 percent of the guarantee may lead to lost rollover opportunities, so that the contract may pay out less than the contract without resets.

From these figures it does not appear that the reset feature is all that valuable, on average, but the tail risk is significantly increased (as represented by the 95th percentile). In addition, the reset will constrain the risk management of the contract, for two major reasons. The first is a liquidity issue—without the reset option, the maturity benefit is due at dates set at issue. Allowing resets means that the maturity benefit dates could arise at any time after the first 10 years of the contract have expired. This will make planning more difficult. For example, in Figure 6.5 we show 50 simulated cash flows from a contract without resets; then, with everything else equal, the same contract cash flows are plotted if resets are permitted, and a threshold of 105 percent is used as a reset threshold.

The other problem with voluntary resets is that the option has the effect of concentrating risk across cohorts. Consider a GMAB policy written in 2000 and another written in 2003. Without resets, there is a certain amount of time diversification here, because the first rollover dates for these contracts are 2010 and 2013, respectively, and it is unlikely that very poor stock returns will affect both contracts. Now assume that both policies carry the reset option and that stocks have a particularly good year in 2004. Both policyholders reset at the end of 2004, which means that both now have identical rollover dates at the end of 2014, and the time diversification is lost. In the light of these problems, the voluntary reset feature is becoming less common in new policy design.

For a more technical discussion of the financial engineering approach to risk management for the reset option see Windcliff et al. (2001) and (2002).

CHAPTER 7

A Review of Option Pricing Theory

INTRODUCTION

In Chapter 1 we discussed how the investment guarantees of equity-linked insurance may be viewed as financial options. Since the seminal work of Black and Scholes (1973) and Merton (1973), the theory and practice of option valuation and risk management has expanded phenomenally. Actuaries in some areas have been slow to fully accept and implement the resulting theory. Although some actuaries feel that the no-longer-new theory of option pricing and hedging is too risky to use, for contracts involving investment guarantees it may actually be more risky not to use it.

In this chapter, we revise the elementary results of the financial economics of option or contingent claims valuation. Many readers will know this well, and they should feel free to skip to the next chapter. For readers who have not studied any financial economics (or who may be a little rusty), the major assumptions, results, and formulae of the theory of Black, Scholes, and Merton are all discussed. We do not prove any of the valuation formulae; there are plenty of books that do so. Boyle et al. (1998) and Hull (1989) are two excellent works that are well known to actuaries.

This chapter will demonstrate the crucial concepts of no-arbitrage pricing with a simple binomial model. Using this very simple model all of the major, often misunderstood, results of financial economics can be clearly derived and discussed, including:

- The ideas of valuation through replication.
- The difference between the true probability distribution for the risky asset outcome (the *P*-measure), and the risk-neutral distribution (the *Q*-measure), and why it is correct to use the latter when it is clearly not realistic.
- The idea of rebalancing the replicating portfolio without cost.

All of these concepts are demonstrated in the section on replication and no-arbitrage pricing. Even though it is very elementary, any reader who does not feel confident about these issues should study that section.

In the section on the Black-Scholes-Merton assumptions, later in this chapter, we write down the important assumptions underlying the theory. We then show how to determine the valuation and replicating portfolio for a general uncertain liability, based on an underlying risky asset.

In the final sections of the chapter, we give the formulae and methods for the options that arise in the context of equity-linked insurance. We find in later chapters that knowing the formulae for European call and put options is surprisingly helpful for more complicated benefits.

THE GUARANTEE LIABILITY AS A DERIVATIVE SECURITY

A European put option is a derivative security based on an underlying asset with (random) value F_t at t. If T is the maturity date of the option and K is the strike price, then the put option pays at time T, either $(K - F_T)$ if $K \geq F_T$ or nothing if $K < F_T$. This structure is identical to the standard guaranteed minimum maturity benefit (GMMB), where K is the guarantee, T is the maturity date, and F_T is the segregated fund value at T, so the payoff under the guarantee is $(K - F_T)^+$.

In fact, all of the financial guarantees that were described in Chapter 1 can be viewed as derivative securities, based on some underlying asset. In the segregated fund or variable-annuity (VA) contract, the underlying security is the separate fund value. Similarly to derivative securities in the banking world, financial guarantees in equity-linked insurance can be analyzed using the framework developed by Black, Scholes, and Merton.

REPLICATION AND NO-ARBITRAGE PRICING

First, we give a very simplified example of option pricing, using a binomial model for stock returns, to illustrate the ideas of replication and no arbitrage pricing.

Suppose we have a liability that depends on the value of a risky asset. The risky asset value at any future point is uncertain, but it can be modeled by some random process, which we do not need to specify.

The no-arbitrage assumption (or law of one price) states that two identical cash flows must have the same value. Replication is the process of finding a portfolio that exactly replicates the option payoff—that is, the market value of the replicating portfolio at maturity exactly matches the option payoff at maturity, whatever the outcome for the risky asset. So, if it is possible to construct a replicating portfolio, then the price of that portfolio at any time t must equal the price of the option at time t, because there can only be one price for the same cash flows.

For example, suppose an insurer has a liability to pay in one month an amount exactly equal to the price of one unit of the risky asset at that time. The amount of that liability at maturity is uncertain. The insurer might take the expected value of the risky asset price in one month, using some realistic probability distribution, and discount the expected value at some rate. That method of calculation would be the traditional actuarial approach. The beautiful insight of no-arbitrage pricing says that such a calculation is essentially worthless in terms of a market valuation of the liability. If the insurer buys one unit of the risky asset now, it will have enough to precisely meet the liability due in one month. If the liability is valued at any amount lower or higher than the current price of one unit of the risky asset, then an arbitrage opportunity exists that would quickly be exploited and therefore eliminated. So, the replicating portfolio is one unit of risky asset, and the valuation is the price of one unit of risky asset. Replication and valuation are inextricably linked.

To see how the theory is applied to a more complicated contingent liability, such as an option, we use a simple binomial model in which two assets are traded:

1. A risk-free asset that earns a risk-free force of interest of $r = .05$ per time unit, so an investment of $100e^{-r}$ at time $t = 0$ will pay 100 at $t = 1$.
2. A risky asset (or a stock) that pays $S_u = 110$ if the market goes up over one time unit, and $S_d = 85$ if the market goes down. No other outcomes are possible in this simple model. Assume that the time 0 price of the risky asset is $S_0 = 100$.

Suppose we sell a put option on the stock. The option gives the buyer the right to sell the stock at a fixed price of, say, 100 at time $t = 1$. This right will be exercised if the stock price goes down, because in that case the purchaser receives 100 under the contract compared with 85 in the market. If the stock price goes up, the purchaser can sell the asset in the market for 110 and, therefore, has no incentive to exercise the option and sell for only 100. The option seller then has a liability of $K - S_d = 15$ if the market goes down (since they have to buy the stock at K but end up with an asset worth only S_d) and 0 if the market goes up.

Now assume the option seller buys a mixed portfolio of the risk-free asset and the risky asset; the portfolio has a units of the risk-free asset and b units of the risky asset, so its value at $t = 0$ is $P_0 = ae^{-r} + bS_0$ and at $t = 1$ its value is

$$P_1 = \begin{cases} a + bS_u & \text{if the market goes up} \\ a + bS_d & \text{if the market goes down} \end{cases}$$

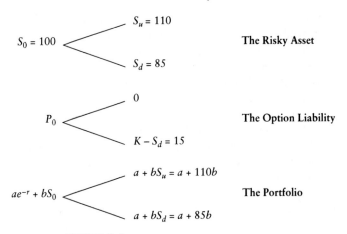

FIGURE 7.1   One-period binomial model.

The situation is illustrated in Figure 7.1.

Now, we can make the portfolio exactly match the option liability by solving the two equations for a and b:

$$a + bS_u = 0 \tag{7.1}$$

$$a + bS_d = K - S_d \tag{7.2}$$

That is,

$$a + 110b = 0 \tag{7.3}$$

$$a + 85b = 15 \tag{7.4}$$

$$\Longrightarrow \quad a = 66 \quad b = -0.6 \tag{7.5}$$

This solution means that if the option seller buys the portfolio at time 0 that consists of a short holding of –0.6 units of stock (with price –$60, since $S_0 = 100$) and a long holding of $ae^{-r} = 62.78114$ in the risk-free asset, then whether the stock goes up or down, the portfolio will exactly meet the option liability. The option is perfectly hedged by this portfolio. Since the portfolio and the option have the same payout at time $t = 1$, then they must, by the no-arbitrage principle, also have the same price at time $t = 0$. Hence the price of the option at $t = 0$ must be the same as the price of the matching portfolio at $t = 0$; the option price is 2.78114.

A very interesting feature of the result is that we never needed to know or specify the probability that the stock rises or falls. We have not used the expected value of the payoff anywhere in this argument.

In general, this binomial setup for the put option gives a price:

$$P_0 = (K - S_d)\frac{S_u e^{-r} - S_0}{S_u - S_d} \tag{7.6}$$

$$= (K - S_d)e^{-r}p^* \tag{7.7}$$

$$\text{where} \quad p^* = \frac{S_u - S_0 e^r}{S_u - S_d} \tag{7.8}$$

In fact, if we consider a more general option in this framework, where the payoff in the up-state is C_u and the payoff in the down state is C_d, then the replicating portfolio will always have value at time $t = 0$

$$P = (C_u(1 - p^*) + C_d p^*)e^{-r}$$

Based on our results, we know that $S_d < S_0 e^r < S_u$ (since any other ordering breaches the no-arbitrage assumption) so that $0 < p^* < 1$. Now p^* looks like a probability and the portfolio value P looks like an expected present value, because if we treat p^* as the probability that the market falls and $(1 - p^*)$ is the probability that the market rises, $(C_u(1 - p^*) + C_d p^*)$ is the expected payoff at $t = 1$ under the option, and the e^{-r} term discounts the expected payoff to the time zero value at the risk-free force of interest. So, even though we have not used expectation anywhere, and even though p^* is not the true probability that the market falls, we can use the language of probability to express the option as an expectation under this artificial probability distribution.

This illustrates the third concept of option valuation: the *risk-neutral probability measure*. Using the artificial probabilities p^* for the down market and $(1 - p^*)$ for the up market, the expected value of the risky asset at time $t = 1$ is

$$p^* S_d + (1 - p^*)S_u = \frac{S_u - S_0 e^r}{S_u - S_d}S_d + \frac{S_0 e^r - S_d}{S_u - S_d}S_u = S_0 e^r$$

So under this artificial probability distribution, the expected value of S_0 at $t = 1$ is the same as if the stock earned the risk-free rate of interest. This is why the probability distribution p^* and $(1 - p^*)$ is known as the *risk-neutral probability distribution*. In financial economics literature, it is also commonly known as the *Q-measure* (measure is just used to mean probability distribution). The real probability distribution for the stock price (which we have not needed here) is known as "nature's measure," the "true measure," or the "subjective measure," but is always shortened in the finance literature to the *P-measure*.

The difference between the Q and P probability distributions is very important, and is the source of much misunderstanding. In particular, the theory does *not* assume that equities earn the risk-free rate of interest on average, even though the Q-measure might give this impression. The Q-measure is a device for a simple formulation for the price of an option as an expected value, even though we are not using expectation to value it but replication. The Q-measure is therefore crucial to pricing, but also, crucially, is *only* relevant to pricing and replication. Any attempt to project the true distribution of outcomes for an equity-type fund or portfolio must be based on an appropriate P-measure. Say we wanted to predict how frequently the option in the binomial example above ends up in-the-money, which is the probability that the stock ends up in the "down" state, the Q-measure "down" probability p^* is quite irrelevant to this frequency, and can give us no useful information.

The derivation of the risk-neutral measure from the market model, in general, does require some information about the underlying P-measure:

1. The risk-neutral measure must be *equivalent* to the P-measure. Equivalence means (loosely) that the two measures have the same null space—or in simple terms, that all outcomes that are feasible under the P-measure are also feasible under the Q-measure, and vice versa.
2. The expected return on the risky asset using the Q-measure must be equal to the return on the risk-free asset.

These two requirements are sufficient in the binomial example to determine the risk-neutral probabilities. The first requires that the only possible outcomes under the Q-measure are p_u, the probability of moving to the "up" state, and p_d, the probability of moving to the "down" state. Clearly, under the first requirement,

$$p_u + p_d = 1 \qquad (7.9)$$

The second requirement states that

$$p_u S_u + p_d S_d = S_0 e^r \qquad (7.10)$$

These equations together give the probability distribution in equation 7.8.

Now we extend the binomial model above to two periods to illustrate the principle of *dynamic hedging*. The term *hedging* is used to mean replication of a liability.

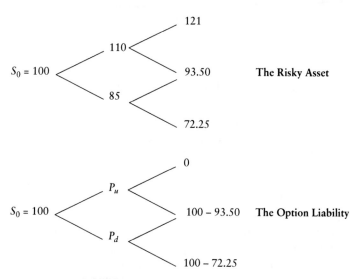

FIGURE 7.2 Two-period binomial model.

We keep the same structure so that, over each time period, the price of the risky asset rises by 10 percent or falls by 15 percent, and we make no assumptions about the relative probabilities of these events. The stock worth 100 at $t = 0$ then follows one of the paths in the top diagram of Figure 7.2.

Now consider a put option that matures after two time units. The strike price is $K = 100$, giving a liability at the end of the period of 0 if the stock has risen in both time units, 6.50 if it has risen once and fallen once, and 27.75 if the stock price fell in both time units. We can replicate the option payoff in this model by working backwards through the various paths. The idea is to break the two-period model down into two one-period models. At time 1 we know if we are in the up state or the down state. If we are in the up state, then we need a portfolio

$$P_u = a_u e^{-r} + b_u S_u \qquad (7.11)$$

which will exactly meet the liabilities after the next time step, that is:

$$a_u + 121 b_u = 0 \qquad (7.12)$$
$$a_u + 93.5 b_u = 6.5 \qquad (7.13)$$
$$\implies \quad a_u = 28.6 \quad b_u = -6.5/27.5 \qquad (7.14)$$

which gives a portfolio value at time $t = 1$ of $P_u = a_u e^{-r} + b_u S_u = 1.20516$.

Similarly, if we are in the down state at time 1, we need a portfolio

$$P_d = a_d e^{-r} + b_d S_d \qquad (7.15)$$

which will exactly meet the liabilities after the next time step, that is:

$$a_d + 93.5 b_d = 6.5 \qquad (7.16)$$

$$a_d + 72.25 b_d = 27.75 \qquad (7.17)$$

$$\implies \quad a_d = 100 \quad b_d = -1.0 \qquad (7.18)$$

which gives a portfolio value at time 1 of $P_d = a_d e^{-r} + b_d S_d = 10.12294$.

Now move back one time step; at $t = 0$ we need a portfolio P_0 that will give us exactly P_u at time 1 if the asset price rises, which will enable us to set up the portfolio $P_u = a_u e^{-r} + b_u S_u$ and will give us exactly P_d at time 1 if the asset price falls, so that we can construct the portfolio $P_d = a_d e^{-r} + b_d S_d$. Say

$$P_0 = a e^{-r} + b S_0 \qquad (7.19)$$

then

$$a + b S_u = P_u \quad \text{that is } a + 110b = 1.20516 \qquad (7.20)$$

$$a + b S_d = P_d \quad \text{that is } a + 85b = 10.12294 \qquad (7.21)$$

$$\implies \quad a = 40.44340 \quad b = -0.356711 \qquad (7.22)$$

So $P_0 = 2.7998$.

This example demonstrates that if we invest $a e^{-r} = 38.4709$ in the risk-free asset and $b S_0 = -35.6711$ in the risky asset, we will have enough to fund P_u if the market rises and P_d if the market falls. Then at time 1 we rearrange the portfolio, investing $a_u e^{-r}$ in the risk-free asset and $b_u S_u$ in the risky asset if the risky-asset value rises, or $a_d e^{-r}$ in the risk-free asset and $b_d S_d$ in the risky-asset if the risky asset price falls. Either way, no extra money is required at time 1. The rearranged portfolio will exactly meet the option liability at time 2, regardless of whether the market rises or falls. Note that, even with the two time steps, we have not used any probability in the pricing argument.

The previous example illustrates a *dynamic hedge* of the option; it is a hedge because the option liability is exactly met by the rearranged portfolio, and dynamic because the hedge portfolio needs to be adjusted according to the outcome of the risky-asset price process.[1] It is important to note that no extra funds are needed during the term of the contract. Such hedges are called *self-financing*.

Note also that we do not have to construct the replicating portfolio to find the price of the option. We can use the artificial, risk-neutral probabilities p^* and $1 - p^*$ to find the expected payoff under the Q-measure, and then discount at the risk-free rate to give

$$P_0 = e^{-2r}E_Q[(100 - S_2)^+] = \left\{ 2p^*(1 - p^*)6.5 + (p^*)^2 27.75 \right\} \quad (7.23)$$

$$= 2.7998$$

where E_Q denotes expectation under the artificial, risk-neutral probability measure, and p^* is defined in equation 7.8. Equation 7.23 gives the same cost as that derived by working through the replicating portfolio, in equations 7.12 through 7.22, but it does not give the strategy required to hedge the liability.

In these two simple examples we have demonstrated four very important concepts from financial economics:

1. Replication of the option payoff with a mixed portfolio of the risky and the risk-free assets.
2. The no-arbitrage assumption, which requires that the replicating portfolio has the same price as the option.
3. The risk-neutral probability distribution, which allows us to use the shorthand of expectation for the option value, even though we are not using (and do not need) the true probabilities.
4. Dynamic hedging, which requires rearrangement of the portfolio as the stock price process evolves.

All of these concepts carry directly into the more general framework, where stocks may take infinitely many values, and where prices are changing continuously, not just over a single time unit.

THE BLACK-SCHOLES-MERTON ASSUMPTIONS

The binomial model, of course, has its limitations. In particular, for real-world application it is reasonable to assume that the stochastic process

---

[1]A static hedge is one that does not have to be rearranged; a trivial example would be if the seller of the option bought an identical option at the contract inception.

describing the price of a risky asset is a continuous time process. The Black-Scholes-Merton framework for option valuation is a continuous time model, and is based on more sophisticated market assumptions. In this section, we list the major assumptions underlying the theory. The major assumptions are as follows:

- The asset price S_t follows a geometric Brownian motion (GBM) with constant variance σ^2. This implies that asset returns over any period have a lognormal distribution, and that asset returns over two disjoint periods of equal length are independent and identically distributed.
- Markets are assumed to be "frictionless"—that is, no transactions costs or taxes and all securities are infinitely divisible.
- Short selling is allowed without restriction, and borrowing and lending rates of interest are the same.
- Trading is continuous.
- Interest rates are constant.

All of these assumptions are clearly unrealistic to some extent. In Chapter 3, we have shown that the lognormal model is not a very accurate model for stock prices historically. Clearly, markets are not open continuously and trading costs money. Nevertheless, the Black-Scholes-Merton model has proved to be remarkably robust to such departures from the assumptions.

In Chapter 8, in the section on unhedged liability, we discuss how to quantify and manage the risks associated with departures from the assumptions.

THE BLACK-SCHOLES-MERTON RESULTS

The framework created from the assumptions listed in the previous section can be used to value any option (though some require numerical methods). The most famous equations are the Black-Scholes equations for a European call or put option.

The Price

The most general result from the Black-Scholes-Merton framework is that any derivative security can be valued using the discounted expected value under the artificial, risk-neutral probability distribution, where the force of interest for discounting is the risk-free rate, denoted r. That is, for a security with a payoff W at time T, where the payoff is contingent on a risky asset with price process S_t, the cost of the self-financing, replicating portfolio at $t < T$ is

$$P_t = e^{-r(T-t)} E_Q[W] \tag{7.24}$$

where Q represents the risk-neutral measure. I emphasize here that the Q-measure does not in any sense represent the true distribution of outcomes for the equity. It is a valuation device for the option.

The Hedge

The price P_t represents the cost of the replicating portfolio at t. The general Black-Scholes result goes further than this, telling us exactly how to construct a hedging portfolio out of the underlying risky asset S_t and the risk-free asset. Let

$$\Psi_t = \frac{\partial P_t}{\partial S_t} \tag{7.25}$$

The portfolio that comprises $\Psi_t S_t$ in the risky asset and $P_t - \Psi_t S_t$ in the risk-free asset at time t will exactly replicate the option, and will be self-financing, under the Black-Scholes assumptions. By self-financing we mean that the change in value of the stock part of the hedge in each infinitesimal time step must be precisely sufficient to finance the change in bond price in the hedge.

The Risk-Neutral Probability Distribution (*Q*-Measure)

Under the first assumption of the previous section on the Black-Scholes-Merton assumptions, the stock price process is assumed to follow a GBM, with drift parameter μ and variance parameter σ^2. This is assumed to be the true probability distribution, or P-measure.

We derive the risk-neutral distribution using the same requirements as used in the binomial model, described in the section on replication and no-arbitrage pricing. The risk-neutral distribution must be equivalent to the P-measure, and the expected annual return under the risk-neutral distribution must be at the risk-free rate r (continuously compounded).

For a given risk-free force of interest r per unit time, the risk-neutral distribution generated by the GBM is another GBM, with drift parameter $r - \sigma^2/2$ and with variance parameter σ^2. This gives a risk-neutral distribution that is lognormal over any period of length t time units. It is convenient to work with the accumulation factor $A_t = S_t/S_0$ (where $t = 0$ is any arbitrary starting point). Under the risk-neutral distribution, $A_t \sim \text{lognormal}(t(r - \sigma^2/2), t\sigma^2)$. Note that the mean of this distribution is

$$\exp(t(r - \sigma^2/2) + t\sigma^2/2) = e^{tr}$$

which is the accumulation factor at the risk-free rate of interest.

The original drift parameter μ does not affect the risk-neutral distribution. This is analogous to the redundancy of the true up and down probabilities in the binomial example. It is important to remember that the Q-measure is just as artificial a probability distribution as the p^* probabilities above; it does not represent the true underlying probability distribution for the stock returns. This is a subtle but crucially important point that is often misunderstood.

The stock price process may be assumed to follow a more complex process than GBM, for example with stochastic variance parameter (such as GARCH or regime-switching distribution). In this case, there is no unique risk-neutral distribution. In fact, there are infinitely many risk-neutral distributions. Pricing using these distributions will not, in general, have the self-financing property that we have in the GBM case.

THE EUROPEAN PUT OPTION

In this section, we derive the value of a put option at time t using the principle of discounted expected value under the Q-measure. Let t denote the current time; T the time of maturity of the contract; σ^2 the constant variance per unit time of the GBM; S_t the price process of the underlying risky asset on which the option is written; and $\Phi()$ the standard normal distribution function (often denoted by $N()$ in the financial literature). The payoff is $(K - S_T)^+$. Let $f_Q()$ denote the risk-neutral density for the accumulation factor A_{T-t}. Then the price of the replicating portfolio at time $t < T$ is denoted BSP_t (for Black-Scholes put) where:

$$BSP_t = E_Q[(K - S_T)^+]e^{-r(T-t)} \tag{7.26}$$

$$= S_t E_Q[(K/S_t - A_{T-t})^+]e^{-r(T-t)} \tag{7.27}$$

$$= e^{-r(T-t)} S_t \int_0^{K/S_t} (K/S_t - s)f_Q(s)ds \tag{7.28}$$

Evaluation of this integral is relatively straightforward, since A_{T-t} has a lognormal distribution with mean parameter $(T - t)(r - \sigma^2/2)$ and variance parameter $\sigma\sqrt{T - t}$ (see, for example, Appendix A of Klugman, Panjer, and Willmot 1998), giving

$$BSP_t = \left\{ K\Phi\left(\frac{\log(K/S_t) - (r - \sigma^2/2)(T - t)}{\sigma\sqrt{T - t}}\right) \right.$$
$$\left. - S_t e^{r(T-t)}\Phi\left(\frac{\log(K/S_t) - (r + \sigma^2/2)(T - t)}{\sigma\sqrt{T - t}}\right) \right\} e^{-r(T-t)}$$
$$= Ke^{-r(T-t)}\Phi(-d_2) - S_t\Phi(-d_1) \tag{7.29}$$

where d_1 and d_2 are functions:

$$d_1 = \frac{\log(S_t/K) + (T-t)(r + \sigma^2/2)}{\sqrt{T-t}\,\sigma} \tag{7.30}$$

$$d_2 = \frac{\log(S_t/K) + (T-t)(r - \sigma^2/2)}{\sqrt{T-t}\,\sigma} = d_1 - \sigma\sqrt{T-t} \tag{7.31}$$

The terms d_1 and d_2 are the common terms from the finance literature. It is important to remember, however, that these are functions of the variables S_t, K, time to expiry, r, and σ. This is particularly relevant for the next step: establishing the hedge portfolio.

The stock part of the hedge portfolio is $S_t \Psi_t$ where

$$\Psi_t = \frac{\partial}{\partial S_t} \text{BSP}_t$$

$$= -\Phi(-d_1) - S_t \frac{\partial(-d_1)}{\partial S_t} \phi(-d_1) + Ke^{-r(T-t)} \frac{\partial(-d_2)}{\partial S_t} \phi(-d_2)$$

where $\phi(\ )$ is the standard normal density function. Since $d_2 = d_1 - \sigma\sqrt{(T-t)}$, the partial derivatives of d_1 and d_2 with respect to S_t are the same. Also,

$$\phi(-d_1) = \frac{e^{-d_1^2/2}}{\sqrt{2\pi}} \tag{7.32}$$

and

$$\phi(-d_2) = \frac{e^{-(d_1 - \sqrt{(T-t)}\sigma)^2/2}}{\sqrt{2\pi}}$$

$$= \phi(-d_1)\exp\{d_1\sigma\sqrt{(T-t)} - \sigma^2(T-t)/2\}$$

$$= \phi(-d_1)\exp\{(\log(S_t/K) + r(T-t) + \sigma^2(T-t)/2) - \sigma^2(T-t)/2\}$$

$$= \phi(-d_1)\left(\frac{S_t}{K}e^{r(T-t)}\right)$$

so that

$$\Psi_t = -\Phi(-d_1) - \frac{\partial(-d_1)}{\partial S_t}\phi(-d_1)\left\{S_t - Ke^{-r(T-t)}\left(\frac{S_t}{Ke^{-r(T-t)}}\right)\right\} \tag{7.33}$$

$$= -\Phi(-d_1) \text{ since } \left\{S_t - Ke^{-r(T-t)}\left(\frac{S_t}{Ke^{-r(T-t)}}\right)\right\} = 0 \tag{7.34}$$

Now, this result is actually fairly obvious from the form of the Black-Scholes equation; this shows that the hedge portfolio is always $-\Phi(-d_1)$ units of the underlying risky asset together with $\Phi(-d_2)Ke^{-r(T-t)}$ invested in the risk-free asset. The purpose of the derivation of Ψ_t is to demonstrate how to find the stock part of the hedge portfolio, with emphasis on the fact that d_1 and d_2 are both functions of the risky-asset price.

THE EUROPEAN CALL OPTION

Most of the options in this book most closely resemble put-type options. However, call options are also relevant, especially for the equity-indexed annuities (EIAs), which are discussed in Chapter 13.

Under a European call option, the holder has the right to buy a share in the underlying stock at the strike price K at a fixed maturity date T. If the share price at maturity S_T is higher than the strike price K, the option holder buys the share for K, and may immediately sell for S_T, giving a payoff at maturity of $(S_T - K)$. Obviously, if $K > S_T$, then the option is not exercised and the contract expires with zero payoff.

The price of the call option at time $t < T$ is found in the same way as for the put option, shown earlier, by taking the expectation under the risk-neutral measure of the payoff, discounted at the risk-free rate. If we also use the standard Black-Scholes-Merton assumption for S_t that the process is a GBM, so that S_T has a lognormal distribution, then the standard Black-Scholes price at time t for a call option is denoted BSC (for Black-Scholes call), where

$$\text{BSC}_t = E_Q[e^{-r(T-t)}(S_T - K)^+] = S_t\Phi(d_1) - Ke^{-r(T-t)}\Phi(d_2) \qquad (7.35)$$

where d_1 and d_2 are defined exactly as in equations 7.30 and 7.31.

As with the put option, the Black-Scholes equation for a call option immediately provides the hedge portfolio at time $t > 0$ for replicating the option. It comprises a long position of $\Phi(d_1(t))$ units of stock and a short position of $\Phi(d_2(t))$ units of zero-coupon bond, face value K, and therefore price at t of $Ke^{-r(T-t)}$.

PUT-CALL PARITY

Put-call parity was mentioned in Chapter 1, but it is relevant to give a reminder here. Suppose an investor buys a put option on a unit of stock and holds a unit of the stock. The option has strike price K, and the stock has price S_t at t. The option matures at T. The total value of the stock plus the put option at maturity is

$$S_T + (K - S_T)^+ = \max(S_T, K)$$

Now suppose the investor holds a call option on the same stock with the same strike price K, maturing at T, together with a risk-free zero-coupon bond that matures at T with face value K. The bond plus call option pays at T:

$$K + (S_T - K)^+ = \max(S_T, K)$$

So, the two portfolios—stock plus put and bond plus call—have exactly the same payoff, and must therefore have the same price (remember the law of one price).

The price at t of a unit of stock is S_t; the price at t of the zero-coupon bond with face value K is $K e^{-r(T-t)}$. Put-call parity implies that:

$$Ke^{-r(T-t)} + \text{BSC}_t = S_t + \text{BSP}_t$$

This identity can be easily verified for the equations for BSP and BSC.

DIVIDENDS

In most of the contracts examined in this book, the equity linking is by reference to a stock index in which dividends are reinvested. In this case, we do not need to consider the effect of dividends on the hedging of the embedded option. However, for some insurance options, notably those associated with the EIAs of Chapter 13, the payout is linked to an index that does not allow for reinvested dividends. In this case the replicating portfolio, which comprises a holding in the underlying stocks and a holding in bonds, must make allowance for the receipt of dividends on the stock holding. For a call option, where the replicating portfolio includes a long position in the stock, the incoming dividends allow the option seller to hold less stock in the hedge portfolio, anticipating the future dividend income. The dividends are assumed to be proportional to the stock price. This is a reasonable assumption that makes allowance for dividends easier to incorporate.

As a simple example, assume we have a one-year call option on one unit of stock, with strike price 1.10 and current price 1.00, and with volatility $\sigma = 20$ percent and risk-free rate $r = .06$. The replicating portfolio for this call option with no dividend income is (from equation 7.35)

$$1.0\,\Phi(d_1) - 1.1e^{-(0.06)}\,\Phi(d_2)$$

That is, the hedge comprises a long holding of $\Phi(d_1)$ units of stock and a short holding of bonds. But, if we have incoming dividends guarantees of, say, 2 percent of the stock, delivered at $t = 1$, when the contract matures, then we can reduce the long stock position by .02 units of stock. So the net stock position for the replicating portfolio is only $1.0\,\Phi(d_1) - 0.02$, making the replication cheaper.

In practice, we will assume that dividend income is a continuous stream. This is a rough approximation for a single stock, but is more reasonable for an index comprising a large variety of stocks with a range of dividend dates. If we assume a dividend stream at a fixed rate of d per year, then a stock holding of 100 units at time 0 accumulates through reinvesting the dividend income to $100e^{dT}$ units at time T; therefore, if we need S_T in stock at T, then at time $t = 0$ we need only $S_0\,e^{-dT}$.

The call-option value allowing for dividend income can then be obtained by replacing S_t in equation 7.35 by $S_t\,e^{-d(T-t)}$, remembering to replace the stock price in the calculation of d_1 and d_2.

The option price for a Black-Scholes call option at time $t = 0$ allowing for dividend income, is then:

$$S_0\,e^{-dT}\Phi(d_1) - K\,e^{-rT}\,\Phi(d_2) \qquad (7.36)$$

where, now,

$$d_1 = \frac{\ln\left(\frac{S_0\,e^{-dT}}{K}\right) + (r + \sigma^2/2)T}{\sigma\,\sqrt{T}}$$

$$= \frac{\ln\left(\frac{S_0}{K}\right) + (r - d + \sigma^2/2)T}{\sigma\,\sqrt{T}}$$

and $d_2 = d_1 - \sigma\sqrt{T}$.

EXOTIC OPTIONS

The put and call options featured in the previous sections are sometimes called "plain vanilla" contracts, being the simplest forms of derivative contracts. However, there are many other forms of option contracts. One more complex option is the GMAB benefit valued in Appendix B. Other examples will arise in Chapter 13, where we look at more complicated guarantees associated with U.S. EIA contracts. Options that are more complicated than the plain vanilla forms are often referred to as "exotic." These might include options based on the average value of the underlying stock price process S_t over some period, rather than simply the end value (these are also called Asian options). That is, where the payoff for a call option is

$$(S^{\text{ave}} - K)^+$$

where S^{ave} is the average value of the stock process over a defined period (which may be the entire term). Another form of exotic option uses the maximum value of the stock price process over some period of the contract term, so that the payoff is

$$\left(\max_{t \in (t_0, t_1)} \{S_t\} - K\right)^+$$

This is a form of "lookback" option.

Valuation and risk management of exotic options follows exactly the same principles as used for the plain vanilla contracts. For the value, we take the expectation of the option payoff discounted at the risk-free rate of interest. For the delta-neutral hedge, we differentiate the value of the option with respect to the price of the risky asset, that is the underlying stock or equity index. In some cases differentiation can be done analytically. This is true for the GMAB option, for Asian options if the geometric average is used rather than the arithmetic, and for the lookback option provided the lookback feature is continuous; that is, it is true if we consider the maximum of all values of S_t to be viewed as a process in continuous time. If we consider the maximum only at discrete points, then no analytic solution is available.

Where no analytic solution is available, it is still possible to determine a value and a hedge for exotic options. Boyle (1977) introduced the Monte Carlo method for option valuation. For many options the expectation that cannot be derived analytically can be accurately estimated by simulation. Using the risk-neutral distribution, we can simulate a large number of outcomes for the option, and discount at the risk-free rate. The simulated expectation is simply the mean of the individual simulated-payout present values. As with all simulation, the estimate is subject to random-sampling uncertainty (which is discussed in detail in Chapter 11), but the sampling error and price uncertainty can be calculated and minimized by using a sufficiently large number of simulations or other techniques to reduce sampling error (*variance reduction*).

Using simulation it is also possible to find the hedge portfolio by determining the Monte Carlo estimate of the derivative of the simulated price with respect to the underlying stocks. This simply requires a sensitivity test of the mean value, changing the starting value of the stock price process, but using the same random numbers.

The work by Boyle, Broadie, and Glasserman (1997) provides a full review of the use of simulation for option valuation.

CHAPTER 8

Dynamic Hedging for Separate Account Guarantees

INTRODUCTION

In this chapter, we apply the theory of Chapter 7 to separate account products such as variable annuities and unit-linked and segregated fund contracts.

In the section on Black-Scholes formulae for segregated fund guarantees, we derive valuation formulae using option pricing for the guaranteed minimum maturity benefit (GMMB), the guaranteed minimum death benefit (GMDB), and guaranteed minimum accumulation benefit (GMAB) contracts described in Chapter 1. These formulae will include allowances for mortality and exits.

In the section on pricing by deduction from the separate account, we show how the price of the option can be translated into a regular amount of charge deducted from the policyholder's fund. This "margin offset" is the usual method of charging for the guarantee in separate account products in North America.

The section on the unhedged liability is where we utilize both actuarial and financial engineering techniques to quantify the additional costs associated with the dynamic-hedging approach to risk management that are not allowed for in the option valuation. This includes allowance for deviation from the Black, Scholes, and Merton assumptions of Chapter 7. This is an important part of the book, and the ideas from this section are used again in all the subsequent chapters.

Finally, we follow all these ideas through for some examples of GMMB, GMDB, and GMAB contracts in the final section of the chapter.

BLACK-SCHOLES FORMULAE FOR SEGREGATED FUND GUARANTEES

Adapting the Black-Scholes results for guarantees embedded in insurance contracts requires a little work. In this section, we continue to assume the Black-Scholes framework, including all the assumptions listed in Chapter 7.

We need to adapt the formula for the put option to reflect the fact that the underlying asset is not the stock price itself, but the segregated fund value, and that this differs from the stock price through the deduction of the management charge. In addition, for the GMDB, the option matures at death, giving a random term to maturity rather than the fixed term of a European option. For the GMAB, payable on death or maturity, the payoff of the option is more complicated than the standard put option.

Black-Scholes Formula for the GMMB

The GMMB is a straightforward put option on the segregated fund. Assume a fund value at the valuation date $t = 0$ of F_0. Let G denote the guarantee, and assume first that the guarantee is fixed. The insurer's liability under the GMMB at maturity in, say, T years is $(G - F_T)^+$. This is identical to the put option, with strike price G and underlying asset F_t. Under standard Canadian contract terms for policies of this type, G is typically 75 percent or 100 percent of the initial single premium for the contract. Let m denote the monthly management charge deducted. Then

$$F_T = F_0 \frac{S_T}{S_0}(1 - m)^T$$

where S_t is the stock index used for equity linking. The payoff under the GMMB is $W = (G - F_T)^+$. Let $F_0 = S_0$, then the option price is

$$P_0 = e^{-rT} E_Q[(G - F_T)^+]$$

$$= e^{-rT} E_Q[(G - S_T(1 - m)^T)^+] \tag{8.1}$$

$$= (1 - m)^T \{ e^{-rT} E_Q[(G(1 - m)^{-T} - S_T)^+] \} \tag{8.2}$$

Either of equations 8.1 and 8.2 can be used to determine the Black-Scholes price allowing for the management charge. Using equation 8.1 we just use $S_0(1 - m)^T$ in place of S_0 in the Black-Scholes formula. Using equation 8.2 we increase the guarantee G to $G(1 - m)^{-T}$ and multiply the whole formula by $(1 - m)^T$; this seems the more complicated approach.

Using the first approach, that is, replacing S_0 by $S_0(1 - m)^T$ in the standard Black-Scholes formula, the put option price at time $t = 0$ is:[1]

$$P_0 = Ge^{-rT}\Phi(-d_2) - S_0(1 - m)^T\Phi(-d_1) \qquad (8.3)$$

where

$$d_1 = \frac{\log(S_0(1 - m)^T/G) + (r + \sigma^2/2)T}{(\sigma\sqrt{T})}$$

$$= \frac{\log(S_0/G) + (r + \log(1 - m) + \sigma^2/2)T}{(\sigma\sqrt{T})}$$

and $d_2 = d_1 - \sigma\sqrt{T}$. This price does not allow for mortality or lapses; not all policyholders will survive in force to maturity. The mortality risk (that is, the risk that more than the expected number of policyholders survive to maturity) can be hedged by diversification. In other words, by selling a sufficiently large number of contracts, the mortality experience will be known accurately, with decreasing relative error. This provides a justification for a deterministic approach. This was used in the context of guaranteed death benefits by Boyle and Schwartz (1977) and Brennan and Schwartz (1976).

The lapse risk is also treated as diversifiable in most applications. However, this is only true to the extent that lapses are independent of the guarantee liability. It is known that lapses are, to some extent, related to the segregated fund performance, but no credible model has yet been proposed. In the absense of a satisfactory stochastic model of lapsation, we adopt a deterministic model, treating lapses similarly to mortality. We therefore assume that lapses are also diversifiable and that exits may be treated as independent of the guarantee liability under the Q-measure. This assumption just means that if BSP_0 is the option price with no allowance for lapses, and $_Tp_x^\tau$ is the probability that the contract is in force at maturity, then the option price allowing for lapses is simply $_Tp_x^\tau \mathrm{BSP}_0$.

In general, the GMMB replicating portfolio allowing for exits may be found by multiplying the option price by the survival probability. That is, if the probability that the policyholder lapses or dies before the maturity date is $_Tq_x^\tau = 0.25$, and we know that BSP_0 is the amount required for a guaranteed maturity benefit with no allowance for exits, then the amount required allowing for exits is simply $0.75\mathrm{BSP}_0$.

---

[1] This is identical to the standard adaptation of the Black-Scholes formula to allow for dividends on the risky asset.

TABLE 8.1   Example hedge costs, percentage of fund at the valuation date, for a GMMB, with allowance for policyholder exits following Appendix A.

Guarantee	Term to Maturity T		
% of Fund	5	10	20
60	0.552	0.607	0.218
80	2.341	1.704	0.477
100	5.883	3.438	0.833
120	11.125	5.747	1.270
$_Tp^\tau_{50}$	0.65520	0.42247	0.15972

This relationship may be demonstrated with an example. Consider a 50-year-old life holding a separate account product with GMMB. Assume that mortality and lapses follow those of the double decrement table in Appendix A.

The GMMB matures in 5, 10, or 20 years. We assume that the annual volatility of the underlying segregated fund is $\sigma = 20$ percent, the risk-free force of interest is $r = 6$ percent and the management charge is 3 percent nominal per year, deducted monthly. The replicating portfolio cost for various guarantee levels are given in Table 8.1, for a fund of $100 at the valuation date.

The table shows that, even for a fund that is significantly less than the guarantee (i.e., the option is in-the-money) at the valuation date, if the term is long enough, the hedge cost is small. This happens because the cost of a put option decreases over the long term (though it increases in the short term) and because of the survival effect. On the other hand, the shorter-dated options have substantial cost, even when the guarantee is only 80 percent of the fund value at the valuation date.

Black-Scholes Formula for the GMDB

Under the GMDB the liability is identical to the GMMB, except that the maturity date is contingent on the policyholder's death rather than his or her survival. The term of the option is, therefore, itself a random variable.

Let $BSP_0(T)$ denote the cost at time 0 of a put option that matures in T years. Under the GMDB, T is a random variable representing the future lifetime of the policyholder, corresponding to T_x in actuarial literature. Let $E_T[\ ]$ denote expectation over the distribution of T, then the cost of the hedge portfolio is simply the expected value of $BSP_0(T)$ over the distribution of T. Let $_Tp^\tau_x$ denote the double decrement survival probability, as before, and let $\mu^{(d)}_{x,t}$ represent the force of mortality at time t for a life aged x at time

$t = 0$. Then the cost of the hedge portfolio at time $t = 0$ for a contract with a maximum term n time units is

$$E_T[BSP_0(T)] = \int_0^n BSP_0(t) \, _tp_x^\tau \, \mu_{x,t}^{(d)} \, dt \tag{8.4}$$

and this can be easily evaluated numerically. An approximation would be to use

$$H(0) = \sum_{t=1}^n BSP_0(t) \, _{t-1}p_x^\tau \, _1q_{x,t-1}^d \tag{8.5}$$

where t is measured in a suitably small time step (perhaps months), $_{t-1}p_x^\tau$ is the survival probability for $t - 1$ time units, and $_1q_{x,t-1}^{(d)}$ is the probability that the policyholder dies in the time interval $t - 1$ to t, given that she or he has survived for $t - 1$ time units.

Sample values are given in Table 8.2, using the same parameters as for Table 8.1. These values were calculated using equation 8.5 with monthly time steps. Decrement rates are from Appendix A.

The hedge portfolio can be found by splitting $BSP_0(t)$ in equation 8.5 into the risky asset part and the risk-free asset part. That is, the total hedge cost allowing for mortality at time 0 is

$$H(0) = \int_0^n BSP_0(t) \, _tp_x^\tau \mu_{x,t}^{(d)} dt \tag{8.6}$$

$$= \int_0^n (Ge^{-rT}\Phi(-d_2) - S_0(1-m)^t\Phi(-d_1)) \, _tp_x^\tau \, \mu_{x,t}^{(d)} dt \tag{8.7}$$

$$= \int_0^n (Ge^{-rT}\Phi(-d_2)) \, _tp_x^\tau \, \mu_{x,t}^{(d)} dt$$

$$+ \int_0^n (-S_0(1-m)^t\Phi(-d_1)) \, _tp_x^\tau \, \mu_{x,t}^{(d)} dt \tag{8.8}$$

TABLE 8.2 Example hedge costs, percentage of fund, for GMDB.

Guarantee % of Fund	Term to Maturity T		
	5	10	20
60	0.0062	0.0307	0.0957
80	0.0393	0.1194	0.2758
100	0.1395	0.3154	0.6058
120	0.3329	0.6426	1.1045

so the first part is the risk-free asset portion of the hedge portfolio, whereas the second part is the risky asset portion.

The GMDB costs are rather less than the GMMB for this sample contract, even for an in-the-money option, because the mortality rates are fairly low for a 50-year-old life. The cost of hedging a combination of options is simply the sum of the individual options. This is easily seen because the option cost is an expected value, and the expected value of the sum of contingent payoffs is simply the sum of the expected values of the contingent payoffs. For example, for a contract offering both a GMMB and GMDB, the cost of the hedge portfolio is the sum of the individual hedge portfolio costs.

Equation 8.5 can be easily adapted for more complex death benefits simply by adapting the definition of $BSP_0(T)$. We have assumed in equation 8.8 that $BSP_0(T)$ is the price of a straightforward European put option with fixed strike price G. A common feature of variable-annuity contracts is a death benefit guarantee that increases at a compound rate. Suppose, for example, that the death benefit increases at 5 percent per year. In this case the put option, contingent on death in the Tth month, has a strike price

$$G_T = G_0(1.05)^{T/12}$$

If the guarantee is increased at the end of each year, then use the integer part of the exponent: $G_T = G_0(1.05)^{[T/12]}$.

In Table 8.3 we show the hedge costs for a GMDB identical to that of Table 8.2 except that the guarantee is increasing at 5 percent per year; in

TABLE 8.3 Example hedge costs expressed as a percentage of fund for variable-annuity GMDB with guarantee increasing at 5 percent per year.

Initial Guarantee % of Starting Fund	Term to Maturity T		
	5	10	20
80	0.088	0.360	1.299
100	0.249	0.754	2.227
120	0.509	1.296	3.363
Monthly guarantee increases			

Initial Guarantee % of Starting Fund	Term to Maturity T		
	5	10	20
80	0.078	0.333	1.229
100	0.233	0.694	2.016
120	0.472	1.218	3.205
Annual guarantee increases			

the top part of the table, the increase is applied at each month end, and in the bottom part the increases apply annually.

Black-Scholes Formula for the GMAB

The GMAB is a more complicated option with curious put- and call-type features. Ignoring exits for the moment, we will derive the hedge portfolio at time $t = 0$ for a GMAB with renewals at $t_1 > 0$ and at $t_2 > t_1$, maturing at $t_3 > t_2$. The starting guarantee is G, and the starting separate fund is F_0. At t_1, if the fund value is more than G, then the guarantee is reset to the fund level. On the other hand, if the guarantee is greater than the fund at t_1, then the insurer pays the difference into the fund so that the next period starts with the fund and guarantee equal. The process is repeated at time t_2, similarly. At t_3 the policy matures, and the insurer must pay the difference between the final guarantee and final fund value if the guarantee exceeds the fund amount at that time.

Let S_0 be the stock price at $t = 0$ for the underlying stock, and let

$$P(t) = \mathrm{BSP}((1 - m)^t, 1, t) \quad \text{and} \quad P_S(t_1) = \mathrm{BSP}(S_0(1 - m)^{t_1}, G, t_1)$$

where $\mathrm{BSP}(S, K, T)$ represents the price of a European put option using the standard Black Scholes formula, equation 7.29, with time zero stock price S, strike price K, and term T. So $P(t)$ is the price of a European put option with strike price of 1, starting stock price of $(1 - m)^t$, and term t; $P_S(t)$ is the price of a European put option with strike price G, the starting guarantee value, with starting stock price $S_0 (1 - m)^t$ and term t. Note that $P_S(t)$ depends on the stock price S_t, but $P(t)$ does not.

With these two straightforward European put-option price formulae, we can construct the option price formula for the much more complicated GMAB benefit. The derivation is given in Appendix B; the principle is the same as used for all the options of Chapters 7 and 8, that is, to take the expected value of the payout under the risk-neutral measure and discount at the risk-free rate of interest.

The total hedge cost at $t = 0$ for the GMAB survival benefit, assuming final maturity at t_3 is, then,

$$
\begin{aligned}
H(0, t_3) = &(P_S(t_1) + S_0(1 - m)^{t_1}) \\
&\times \{1 + P(t_2 - t_1)(1 + P(t_3 - t_2)) + (1 - m)^{t_2 - t_1} P(t_3 - t_2)\} \\
&- S_0(1 - m)^{t_1}
\end{aligned} \tag{8.9}
$$

Generally the dates between renewals are fixed at 10-year intervals, in which case $t_3 - t_2 = t_2 - t_1 = 10$, giving:

$$H(0) = (P_S(t_1) + S_0(1 - m)^{t_1})\{1 + P(10)(1 + P(10) + (1 - m)^{10})\} - S_0(1 - m)^{t_1}$$

If, in addition, the management charge is set to zero, $H(0, t_3)$ reduces to the form:

$$(S_0 + P_S(t_1))(1 + P(10))^2 - S_0$$

We can split equation 8.9 into the benefit due at each maturity (or renewal or rollover) date, which allows us to apply survival probabilities. Furthermore, we can generalize to include the death benefit under the GMAB contract. On death between t_1 and t_2, say, the insurer is liable for the first rollover benefit at t_1 as part of the survival benefit; the insurer is also liable for the guarantee liability at the date of death, when the amount due is the guarantee (which has been reset at t_1) less the fund value at t. We define $P_k(t)$ for $t = t_k$ to be the option price at time $t = 0$ for the survival benefit due at t_k, given that the policy is still in force at that time, and $P_k(t)$ for $t_k < t \leq t_{k+1}$ to be the option price at $t = 0$ for the death benefit due if the life dies at time t, after k rollovers. Then $H(0, t_3) = P_1(t_1) + P_2(t_2) + P_3(t_3)$, and:

$$P_1(t) = P_S(t) \tag{8.10}$$

$$P_2(t) = (S_0(1 - m)^{t_1} + P_S(t_1)) P(t - t_1) \qquad t > t_1 \tag{8.11}$$

$$P_3(t) = \{S_0(1 - m)^{t_2} + P_S(t_1)(1 - m)^{t_2 - t_1} + (S_0(1 - m)^{t_1} + P_S(t_1))P(t_2 - t_1)\} P(t - t_2) \qquad t > t_2 \tag{8.12}$$

The only terms in $H(0, t)$ that involve the stock price S_0 are $P_S()$, and the terms in $S_0(1 - m)^t$. The first is a straightforward put option, and the derivative with respect to S_0 was derived in Chapter 7, so deriving the split between stocks and bonds for the hedge portfolio for the GMAB is not difficult, giving the stock part of the hedge at time $t = 0$ as:

$$S_0 \frac{\partial H(0, t_3)}{\partial S_0} = (-S_0 \Phi(-d_1(t_1)) + S_0(1 - m)^{t_1})$$
$$\times \{1 + P(t_2 - t_1)(1 + P(t_3 - t_2)) + (1 - m)^{t_2 - t_1} P(t_3 - t_2)\}$$
$$- S_0(1 - m)^{t_1}$$

Allowing for exits, the cost of the GMAB survival benefit hedge for a policyholder age x, assuming final maturity at age t_3, is

$$P_1(t_1) \, {}_{t_1}p_x^\tau + P_2(t_2) \, {}_{t_2}p_x^\tau + P_3(t_3) \, {}_{t_3}p_x^\tau$$

For the additional death benefit, the hedge price at time $t = 0$ is

$$\int_0^{t_1} P_1(w) \, {}_wp_x^\tau \, \mu_{x,w}^{(d)} dw + \int_{t_1}^{t_2} P_2(w) \, {}_wp_x^\tau \, \mu_{x,w}^{(d)} dw + \int_{t_2}^{t_3} P_3(w) \, {}_wp_x^\tau \, \mu_{x,w}^{(d)} dw$$

TABLE 8.4 Example hedge price, percentage of fund, for GMAB death and survival benefit.

Guarantee	$t_1/t_2/t_3$		
% of Fund	2/12/22	5/15/25	10/20/30
60	4.232	3.789	2.702
80	5.797	5.713	3.959
100	11.053	9.556	6.001
120	20.638	15.289	8.787

All this formula does is sum over all relevant dates of death the probability that the policyholder dies at w, multiplied by the option cost for the contingent benefit due at w, given that the life dies at that time. The benefit depends on the previous rollovers, so the term of the contract is split into periods between rollover dates.

Some values for the GMAB, including both death and survival benefits, are given in Table 8.4, per $100 of fund value at valuation. The withdrawal and mortality rates are from Appendix A, as used for the tables of the previous sections. The option costs for the GMAB are much higher than the longer-term GMMB and GMDB benefits, even where the option begins well out-of-the-money. The nature of the contract is that at each renewal date the next option becomes at-the-money, so only the first payout is reduced substantially by starting out-of-the-money.

The costs without the renewal option (that is, assuming the policy matures at t_1) are given in Table 8.5, for comparison. These figures are simply the sum of the GMMB and GMDB for each term and guarantee level. The difference between the figures in Table 8.4 and Table 8.5 indicate how costly the guaranteed renewal option may be. Note however that the costs may be greatly reduced if a substantial proportion of policyholders choose not to exercise the option.

TABLE 8.5 Example hedge price, percentage of fund, for death and survival benefit with no renewals or rollover.

Guarantee	Term t_1		
% of Fund	2	5	10
60	0.137	0.558	0.638
80	1.626	2.380	1.823
100	6.625	6.022	3.753
120	15.747	11.458	6.390

PRICING BY DEDUCTION FROM THE SEPARATE ACCOUNT

The Black-Scholes-Merton framework that has been used in the previous sections to calculate the lump-sum valuation of embedded options in insurance contracts can also be employed to calculate the price under the more common pricing arrangement for these contracts, where the income comes from a charge on the separate account. The charge for the option forms part of the MER (management expense ratio), which is a proportion of the policyholder's fund deducted at regular intervals to cover expenses and other outgo; the part allocated to fund the guarantee liability is called the *margin offset*. The resulting price is found by equating the arbitrage-free valuation of the fund deductions with the arbitrage-free valuation of the embedded option.

Assume that a monthly margin offset of 100α percent is deducted from the fund at the end of each month that the policy is in force. Suppose that the value of the option at time $t = 0$ is calculated using the techniques of the previous section, and is denoted by B. Then the arbitrage-free value for α is found by equating the expected present value of the total margin offset to B, using the risk-neutral measure. That is, measuring t in months and using r for the monthly risk-free force of interest,

$$B = E_Q\left[\sum_{t=0}^{n-1} \alpha\, F_t\, e^{-rt}\, {}_tp_x^{\tau}\right] \tag{8.13}$$

Now, $F_t = S_t(1 - m)^t$ where S_t is the stock process for the separate fund account, and m is the monthly management charge deduction (assumed constant). But under any risk-neutral measure, the expected rate of increase of the stock index is the risk-free rate, so that

$$E_Q[S_t e^{-rt}] = S_0$$

which gives us:

$$B = S_0\, \alpha \sum_{t=0}^{n-1} (1 - m)^t\, {}_tp_x^{\tau} = S_0\, \alpha\, \ddot{a}_{x:\overline{n}|i'}^{\tau} \tag{8.14}$$

where $\ddot{a}_{x:\overline{n}|i'}^{\tau}$ is an n-month annuity factor, using standard actuarial notation, evaluated at rate of interest $i' = (1 - m)^{-1} - 1$. The superscript τ indicates that the annuity takes both death and withdrawals into consideration. So the appropriate margin offset rate for the contract is

$$\alpha = \frac{B}{S_0\, \ddot{a}_{x:\overline{n}|i'}^{\tau}} \tag{8.15}$$

TABLE 8.6 Example annual rate of hedge costs using monthly deduction from the fund, for a GMDB with monthly increases of 5 percent per year.

	Term to Maturity T (years)		
	5	10	20
Value of option B	0.249	0.754	2.227
Value of annuity of $1 per month $\ddot{a}^\tau_{x:\overline{m}|i'}$	45.9	71.7	93.3
Annual margin offset rate (basis points) $100(12\alpha)$	6	13	29

For example, consider a variable-annuity GMDB with annual increases of 5 percent applied monthly to the guaranteed minimum payment. Under the mortality assumptions of Appendix A and using a volatility of 20 percent per year, as before, the values of the option on the 5-, 10-, and 20-year contract, with both initial guarantee and fund values set at $100, are given in Table 8.3. In Table 8.6 the annuity rates and annual rates of margin offset are given; the annual rate is simply 12 times the monthly rate. The initial guarantee level is assumed to be equal to the initial fund value of $100. One basis point is 0.01 percent.

Note that we have assumed that increasing the margin offset does not increase the total management charge m from which α is drawn. If increasing α also increases m, then B will also be affected and the solution (if it exists) will generally require numerical methods.

THE UNHEDGED LIABILITY

The reaction of many actuaries to the idea of applying dynamic hedging to investment guarantees in insurance is that it couldn't possibly work in practice—the assumptions are so simplified, and the uncertainty surrounding models and parameters is so great. Although there is some truth in this, both experience and experiment indicate that dynamic hedging actually works remarkably well, even allowing for all the difficulty and uncertainties of practical implementation. By this we mean that it is very likely that the hedge portfolio indicated by the Black-Scholes analysis will, in fact, be sufficient to meet the liability at maturity (or liabilities for the GMAB contract), and it will be close to self-funding; that is, there should not be substantial additional calls for capital to support the hedge during the course of the contract. Of course, we do need to estimate transactions costs; these are not considered at all in the Black-Scholes price.

In this section, an actuarial approach is applied to the quantification and management of the unhedged liability. The unhedged liability comprises the additional costs on top of the hedge portfolio for a practical dynamic-hedge strategy. For a more detailed analysis of discrete hedging error and transactions costs from a financial engineering viewpoint, see Boyle and Emmanuel (1980), Boyle and Vorst (1992), and Leland (1995).

Discrete Hedging Error with Certain Maturity Date

The Black-Scholes-Merton (B-S-M) approach assumes continuous trading; every instant, the hedge portfolio is adjusted to allow for the change in stock price. Under the B-S-M framework each instant the adjustment required to the stock part of the hedge portfolio is exactly balanced by the adjustment required to the bond part of the hedge. In practice we cannot trade continuously, and would not if we could, since that would generate unmanageable transactions costs.

Discrete hedging error is introduced when we relax the assumption of continuous trading. With discrete time gaps, between which the hedge is not adjusted, the hedge may not be self-financing; the change in the stock part of the hedge over a discrete time interval will not, in general, be the same as the change in the bond part of the hedge. The difference is the *hedging error*. It is also known as the tracking error.

In Chapter 6 we used stochastic simulation to estimate the distribution of the cost of the guarantee liability, assuming that the insurer does not use a dynamic-hedging strategy, and invests the required funds in risk-free bonds. In this section we use the same approach, but we apply it only to the part of the liability that is not covered by the hedge itself. Then, the total capital requirement for a guarantee will be the sum of the hedge cost and the additional requirement for the unhedged liability.

The frequency with which a hedge portfolio is rebalanced is a trade-off between accuracy and transactions costs. Hedging error may be modeled assuming a *time-based strategy* or a *move-based strategy*. The time-based approach assumes the hedge portfolio is rebalanced at regular intervals. The move-based approach assumes the hedge portfolio is rebalanced when the stock price moves by some specified triggering percentage. The move-based approach has been shown to be more efficient, that is, generating less hedging error for a given level of expected transactions costs. However, it is more straightforward to demonstrate the method using regular time steps, and that is the approach adopted here. One reason that it is more straightforward is that it makes it simpler to incorporate mortality costs. We will use monthly time steps, as we did in Chapter 6.

For a general option liability, let Y_t be the value at t (in months) of the bond part of the hedge, and let $S_t \Psi_t$ be the stock part. Bonds are assumed to earn a risk-free rate of interest of $r/12$ per month. In the month t to $t+1$, the stock price changes from S_t to $S_t + 1$. The option price at t is:

$$H(t) = Y_t + \Psi_t S_t$$

Immediately before rebalancing at t, the hedge portfolio from $t-1$ has accumulated to

$$H(t^-) = Y_{t-1}e^{r/12} + \Psi_{t-1}S_t$$

and the hedge required is $H(t)$. The difference $H(t) - H(t^-)$ is the hedging error. If this difference is negative, then the hedging error is a source of profit. This means that the replicating portfolio brought forward is worth more than we need to set up the rebalanced portfolio.

As an example, in Table 8.7 we show the results from a single simulation of the hedging error for a two-year GMMB or European put option with monthly hedging. The strike price or guarantee at $t = 0$ is $K = \$100$, which is equal to the fund at the start of the two-year projection. Management charges of 3 percent per year are deducted from the fund. The risk-free force of interest is assumed to be 6 percent; the volatility for the hedge is 20 percent per year.

The stock prices in the second column are calculated by simulating an accumulation factor each month from a regime-switching lognormal (RSLN) distribution. This is the real-world measure, not the Q-measure, because we are interested in the real-world outcome. The Q-measure is only used for pricing and constructing the hedge portfolio.

In column 3, the stock part of the hedge is calculated; this is

$$-S_t (0.97)^2 \Phi\left(-\left(\frac{\ln(S_t (0.97)^2/K) + (r + \sigma^2/2)(2 - t/12)}{\sigma\sqrt{2 - t/12}}\right)\right)$$

In column 4, the bond part of the hedge is given:

$$Ke^{-r(2-t/12)}\Phi\left(-\left(\frac{\ln(S_t (0.97)^2/K) + (r - \sigma^2/2)(2 - t/12)}{\sigma\sqrt{2 - t/12}}\right)\right)$$

Column 5 is the sum of columns 3 and 4; this is the Black-Scholes price at t months, using the projected stock price at that time $(H(t))$. This represents the cost of the hedge required to be carried forward to the next month.

TABLE 8.7 Single simulation of the hedging error for a two-year GMMB.

Time (Months) t	S_t	Stock Part of Hedge	Bond Part of Hedge	BSP $H(t)$	Hedge b/f $H(t^-)$	HE
0	100.000	−34.160	41.961	7.801	0.000	
1	99.573	−35.145	43.096	7.951	8.157	−0.206
2	104.250	−31.296	37.708	6.412	6.516	−0.105
3	103.447	−32.577	39.209	6.632	6.842	−0.210
4	101.703	−34.901	42.081	7.180	7.377	−0.197
5	100.251	−37.081	44.759	7.679	7.889	−0.211
6	101.784	−36.104	43.203	7.099	7.336	−0.237
7	107.445	−30.419	35.665	5.246	5.308	−0.062
8	106.365	−32.111	37.603	5.492	5.730	−0.238
9	107.996	−30.682	35.618	4.936	5.188	−0.252
10	119.560	−18.480	20.823	2.343	1.829	0.513
11	118.520	−19.363	21.755	2.393	2.608	−0.215
12	120.944	−16.811	18.714	1.903	2.106	−0.202
13	119.696	−17.767	19.718	1.951	2.171	−0.219
14	128.840	−9.442	10.280	0.838	0.693	0.145
15	131.346	−7.209	7.782	0.573	0.706	−0.133
16	133.677	−5.248	5.618	0.370	0.484	−0.114
17	136.096	−3.478	3.692	0.214	0.303	−0.089
18	141.205	−1.456	1.529	0.074	0.102	−0.028
19	150.057	−0.239	0.249	0.009	−0.010	0.019
20	154.164	−0.040	0.042	0.001	0.004	−0.003
21	165.900	0.000	0.000	0.000	−0.002	0.002
22	159.486	0.000	0.000	0.000	0.000	0.000
23	179.358	0.000	0.000	0.000	0.000	0.000
24	192.550	0.000	0.000	0.000	0.000	0.000

Column 6 is the value of the hedge brought forward from the previous month. This is found by allowing the stock part to move in proportion to the stock price from $t - 1$ to t, and the hedge part accumulates for one month at the risk-free rate. This means, for example, that the hedge brought forward from $t = 0$ to $t = 1$ is

$$H(1^-) = -34.160\frac{S_1}{S_0} + 41.961\, e^{r/12} = 8.157$$

The hedging error in column 7 is, then, $H(t) - H(t^-)$. So, for example, at $t = 1$ we need a hedge costing \$7.951, and we have \$8.157 available from the previous rebalancing. Then, the error is −\$0.206.

We can calculate the total discounted hedging error; in this case, discounting at the risk-free force gives a present value of $-\$2.0$. Over a large number of simulations the hedging error will be approximately zero on average, if the volatility used for projections is the same as the Q-measure volatility used for hedging. In this example, the P-measure volatility is actually less than the Q-measure (for this simulation); we are using the RSLN model, and for the two years of the projection the process is mainly in the low-volatility regime. The volatility experienced in this scenario is the standard deviation of the log-returns, and is approximately 14 percent per annum. Because this is much lower than the 20 percent used in the hedge, the hedging error tends to be negative. If we had used a scenario that experienced more months of the high-volatility regime, then the 20 percent volatility used to calculate the hedge would be less than the experienced volatility, and the hedging error would be positive.

This example demonstrates the point that the vulnerability of the loss using dynamic hedging is different in nature to the vulnerability using the actuarial approach. In dynamic hedging the risk is large market movements in either direction (i.e., high volatility). Using the actuarial approach of Chapter 6, the source of loss is poor asset performance, and the volatility does not, in itself, cause problems.

If the real-world and risk-neutral measures used are consistent, then the mean hedging error is zero. By consistent we mean that Q is the unique equivalent risk-neutral measure for P. This is not the case for this example.

Discrete Hedging Error: Life-Contingent Maturity

The hedging error for an option contingent on death or maturity must take survival into consideration. The specific example worked in this section is a guarantee payable on death or maturity, that is a combined GMMB/GMDB contract, but the final formulae translate directly to other similar embedded options.

For the combined GMMB/GMDB contract, the death benefit $(G - F_t)^+$ is paid at the end of the month of death, if death occurs in the month $t - 1 \rightarrow t$, and the maturity benefit $(G - F_n)^+$ is paid on survival to the end of the contract. Let $P(t, w)$ be the Black-Scholes price at t for a put option maturing at $w \geq t$, and let $_{w-t}|q^d_{x,t}$ denote the probability that a life age x years and t months survives as a policyholder for a further $w - t$ months, and dies in the following month. Let $_{n-t}p^\tau_{x,t}$ denote the probability that a policyholder age x years and t months survives, and does not lapse, for a further $n - t$ months. Then the total hedge price at t for a GMMB/GMDB contract, *conditional on the contract being in force at t*, is

$$H^c(t) = \sum_{w=t}^{n-1} {}_{w-t}|q^d_{x,t}P(t, w) + {}_{n-t}p^\tau_{x,t}P(t, n) \qquad (8.16)$$

The hedge price at t unconditionally (that is, per policy in force at time $t = 0$) is determined by multiplying (8.16) by ${}_t p_x^\tau$ to give

$$H(t) = \sum_{w=t}^{n-1} {}_w|q_x^d P(t, w) + {}_n p_x^\tau P(t, n) \tag{8.17}$$

The hedging error is calculated as the difference between the hedge required at t, including any payout at that time, and the hedge brought forward from $t - 1$. Using the conditional payments, we split the hedge $H(t)$ into the stock and bond components: S_t, Ψ_t^c is the stock component of the hedge required at t conditional on the contract being in force at t, and Y_t^c is the bond part of the hedge required at t conditional on the policy being in force at that time:

$$H^c(t) = Y_t^c + \Psi_t^c S_t$$

where

$$\Psi_t^c = \frac{\partial}{\partial S_t} H^c(t) \quad \text{and} \quad Y_t^c = H^c(t) - S_t \Psi_t^c \tag{8.18}$$

Similarly,

$$H(t) = Y_t + \Psi_t S_t$$

where $\Psi_t = {}_t p_x^\tau \Psi_t^c$ and, similarly, $Y_t = {}_{n-t} p_{x,t}^\tau Y_t^c$ for the split of the unconditional hedge price between stocks and bonds. The unconditional values are the expected amounts required per policy in force at $t = 0$. Similarly to the certain maturity date case, before rebalancing at t, the hedge portfolio from $t - 1$ accumulates to

$$H(t^-) = Y_{t-1} e^{r/12} + \Psi_{t-1} S_t$$

exactly as before, whether or not the contract remains in force.

Now consider the hedging error at t given that the contract is in force at $t - 1$. If the life survives, the hedging error is the difference between the hedge portfolio required at t and the hedge portfolio brought forward from $t - 1$. If the life dies or lapses, the hedging error is the difference between the benefit at t (if any) and the hedge brought forward. Taking each of these cases and multiplying by the appropriate probability, which is conditional on survival in force to $t - 1$, gives the hedging error at t conditional on surviving to $t - 1$. The term $q^l_{x,t-1}$ is the probability that the life withdraws in the month $t - 1$ to t, given that the policy is in force at time $t - 1$. The hedging error conditional on surviving to $t - 1$ then is

$$p^\tau_{x,t-1}(H^c(t) - H^c(t^-))$$
$$+ q^d_{x,t-1}((G - F_t)^+ - H^c(t^-))$$
$$+ q^l_{x,t-1}(-H^c(t^-))$$
$$= p^\tau_{x,t-1}H^c(t) + q^d_{x,t-1}((G - F_t)^+) - H^c(t^-)$$

The unconditional hedging error at t, denoted HE_t, is found by multiplying by the probability that the contract is in force at $t - 1$, that is the survival probability from age x to age x plus $t - 1$ months, giving:

$$\mathrm{HE}_t = {}_{t-1}p^\tau_x \{ p^\tau_{x,t-1}H^c(t) + q^d_{x,t-1}((G - F_t)^+) - H^c(t^-) \}$$
$$= H(t) + {}_{t-1}|q^d_x((G - F_t)^+) - H(t^-) \tag{8.19}$$

This equation shows that it is not necessary to apply lapse and survival probabilities individually each month. For the GMMB described in the previous section, the hedging error, allowing for life contingency, is found simply by multiplying the hedging errors calculated for the certain maturity date by the probability of survival for the entire term of the contract.

Transactions Costs

Transactions costs on bonds are negligibly small for institutional investors. It is common in finance to assume transactions costs are proportional to the absolute change in the value of the stock part of the hedge. That is, for an option with certain maturity date, assume transaction costs of τ times the change in the stock part of the replicating portfolio at each hedge. Then, the transactions costs arising at the end of the tth month are

$$\tau S_t \left| \Psi_t - \Psi_{t-1} \right| \tag{8.20}$$

To allow for life-contingent maturity, let Ψ^c_t now be defined as in equation 8.18, that is, calculated assuming the contract is in force at t and allowing for life contingencies from t to final maturity n. Let Ψ_t be the unconditional equivalent, then $\Psi_t = {}_tp^\tau_x \Psi^c_t$ is the stock portion of the projected hedge required at t. The expected stock amount required at t if the contract is in force at $t - 1$ is

$$p^\tau_{x,t-1} \Psi^c_t S_t$$

The transactions costs at t conditional on survival to $t-$ are

$$\tau S_t \left| p^\tau_{x,t-1} \Psi^c_t - \Psi^c_{t-1} \right| \tag{8.21}$$

Multiply by the $t - 1$ month survival probability for the unconditional transactions costs at t:

$$\begin{aligned}
\text{TC}_t &= {}_{t-1}p^\tau_x \left\{ \tau S_t \left| p^\tau_{x+t-1} \Psi^c_t - \Psi^c_{t-1} \right| \right\} \\
&= \tau S_t \left| \Psi_t - \Psi_{t-1} \right|
\end{aligned} \tag{8.22}$$

In the examples that follow, transactions costs are assumed to be $\tau = 0.2$ percent of the change in the stock component of the hedge.

Model Error

In the example given in Table 8.7, we simulated the stock price assuming an RSLN process. Under any stochastic volatility process, such as the RSLN model, the Black-Scholes hedge loses the self-financing property, and we use simulation to derive the distribution of additional hedging costs where the hedge is not self-financing. In fact, this emerges naturally from the simulation process as part of the hedging error, and examples are given in the following section. This is the approach we will follow through the rest of the book when we look at the implications of following a dynamic-hedging strategy. That is, we calculate the hedge using a constant volatility assumption, then project the hedge using the stochastic volatility RSLN model. The resulting hedging errors then capture both the error arising from discrete hedging and the error arising from the fact that the real-world measure assumes stochastic volatility.

Another approach is to calculate a hedge using a Q-measure consistent with the stock model. For example, with the RSLN-2 model a consistent Q-measure would be another RSLN-2 model with the same parameters for the variance and the transition probabilities, but with the mean parameters for the two regimes adjusted to give the risk-neutral property (it is necessary that $E[S_t|S_{t-1}] = e^r S_{t-1}$). Option prices calculated using this Q-measure are derived in Hardy (2001), and do reflect the structure of market prices more accurately than the lognormal distribution. However, the process of calculating the hedge portfolio is much more complex, and the benefits in terms of accuracy are limited. Also, for any stochastic volatility model there are infinitely many risk-neutral measures that we may use to price the option. Only in the constant volatility model is the price unique and self-financing. So whatever price we use for the stochastic volatility projection, it will be necessary to assess the distribution of the possible hedge shortfall.

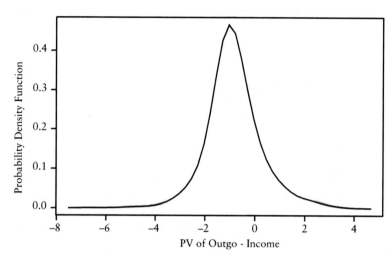

FIGURE 8.1   Simulated probability density function for net present value of outgo of the joint GMMB/GMDB contract, using hedging, expressed as percentage of premium.

EXAMPLES

Joint GMMB and GMDB Contract

In Figure 8.1 we show the probability density function for the net present value of outgo random variable for a straightforward contract offering a guarantee of 100 percent of premium on death or survival. The contract details are as follows:

Mortality:	See Appendix A
Premium:	$100
Guarantee:	100 percent of premium on death or maturity
MER:	0.25 percent per month
Margin offset:	0.06 percent per month
Term:	10 years

The simulation details are as follows:

Number of simulations:	5,000
Volatility used to calculate the hedge:	20 percent per year
Stock price process:	RSLN-2, with parameters from Table 6.2
Transactions costs:	0.2 percent of the change in market value of stocks
Rebalancing frequency:	Monthly

At each month end, the outgo is calculated as the sum of any mortality payout, plus transactions costs from rebalancing the hedge, plus the hedge required in respect of future guarantees minus the hedge brought forward from the previous month. In the first month of the contract there is no hedge brought forward, so that the initial rebalancing hedging error comprises the entire cost of establishing the hedge portfolio (around 3.8 percent of the premium in this case). Income is calculated as the margin offset multiplied by the segregated-fund value at each month end, except the last. The present value is calculated at the risk-free rate of interest, that is 6 percent per year compounded continuously. Since we are simulating a loss random variable, negative values indicate that at the risk-free rate income exceeded outgo. We can see that most of the distribution falls in the negative part of the graph. This means that, in most cases, the margin offset is adequate to meet all the hedging costs and leave some profit. However, there is a substantial part of the distribution in the positive quadrant, indicating a significant probability of a loss.

If the hedge portfolio is calculated using a volatility that is equal to the volatility of the stock price process, then the hedging error will be zero, on average. In this example, the stock price process volatility is around 15.5 percent, whereas the hedge is calculated using a 20 percent volatility assumption. This leads in most cases to *overhedging,* so that the average hedging error is negative.

On the other hand, the stock price process here is assumed to be following a regime-switching (RS) model. The process occasionally moves to the high-volatility regime, under which the volatility is approximately 26 percent per year. During these periods, the hedging error may be positive and relatively large. The consequence is that the path of monthly hedging errors under these simulations generally lies below zero, with spikes arising from the short periods of high volatility. Some sample paths are given in Figure 8.2.

It is worth nothing that, in practice, hedging error will also be generated by deviations from the lapse and mortality assumptions in the model.

GMAB

In Chapter 6, in the section on stochastic simulation of liability cash flows, the cash flows for a GMAB contract were simulated assuming no hedging strategy is followed. In this section, the same GMAB contract cash flows are projected assuming a Black-Scholes hedge is used, with monthly rebalancing. As with the GMMB/GMDB example in the previous section, deviations from the strict Black-Scholes assumptions are explicitly modeled in the form of transactions costs (at 0.2 percent of the change in market value of stocks), plus hedging error (allows for discrete hedging and model error). The hedge

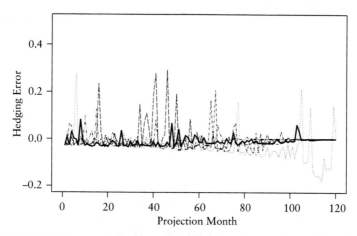

FIGURE 8.2 Simulated hedging errors for GMMB/GMDB contract, given in five simulations; percentage of premium.

portfolio assumes lognormal stock price process with volatility 20 percent, whereas the stock price is simulated as an RSLN process with parameters from Table 6.2. This is assumed to be an ongoing product, and we project the future cash flows under stochastic simulation. It is assumed that an amount equal to the initial hedge portfolio is available at the start of the simulation. All values are percentages of the fund value at the start of the projection. The guarantee value at that time is assumed to be 80 percent of the market value.

Contract Details

Guarantee   GMAB with:
- 10-year terms between rollover dates
- two years to next rollover
- maximum of two further rollovers
- guarantee paid on death or maturity

Mortality: Canadian Institute of Actuaries (CIA),
                   see Appendix A

Initial guarantee: 80 percent of starting market value

Hedging

Black-Scholes hedge using formula in Appendix B, with:

Volatility: 20 percent
Risk-free rate: 6 percent continuously compounded

Rebalancing frequency: Monthly
Transactions costs: 0.2 percent of change in market value
                           of stocks
Hedge brought forward: 5.797 percent of fund (see Table 8.4)

Asset-Liability Simulation

Asset model: RSLN
Parameters: From Table 6.2
No. of simulations: 2,000

The resulting simulated probability density function for the future net costs is given in Figure 8.3. Most of the distribution is in the negative cost sector; that is, there is little probability of a future loss. This is because the hedge already purchased has substantially reduced future liability risk; all that remains is from hedging error and transactions costs. The hedge portfolio acts to immunize the insurer against the guarantee liability.

An interesting feature of the GMAB contract emerges from the individual cash-flow analysis. The GMAB hedge portfolio is more complex than the "plain vanilla" GMMB and GMDB contracts. For the simple European option, the hedge always comprises a long position in bonds and a short position in equities. The GMAB may be long or short in equities at different times, and it is liable to swing dramatically from long to short at the rollover dates.

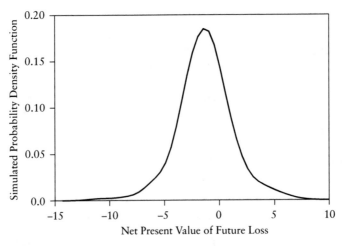

FIGURE 8.3   Simulated probability density function for net present value of outgo for the GMAB contract, using hedging; percentage of starting fund value.

We can illustrate this with a GMAB contract with one renewal in T years and maturity in $T + 10$ years. Mortality and lapses are ignored for now. Suppose the previous renewal was at $T - 10$ when the guarantee was set to K_0. The option price at t, using the notation of the section on the Black-Scholes formula for GMAB in this chapter, is

$$H = P_S((1 - m)^{10}, T) + (S_t (1 - m)^{10} + P_S((1 - m)^{10}, T)) P(10)$$

As $T \rightarrow 0$, if the fund value is greater than K_0, then $P_S((1 - m)^{10}, T) \rightarrow 0$ and the option price

$$H \rightarrow S_t (1 - m)^{10} P(10)$$

The stock part of the hedge is found from $S_t \, dP/dS_t$, which just before the rollover is just $S_t (1 - m)^{10} P(10)$, which is greater than zero. This shows that the entire option price is invested in stocks just before rebalancing at renewal, provided the fund is greater than the guarantee in force. However, immediately after rebalancing, the option becomes a straight European put with strike $S_{t+T} e^{-10m}$, for which the hedge requires a short stock position. Therefore, at renewal, the hedge moves from a long 100 percent stock position to a short stock position—that is, more than the entire option price is transacted. So transactions costs are high. Moreover, this swing from long to short makes the hedge very sensitive to stock price movements, which increases the potential hedging error compared with a standard European option. In terms of the "greeks" of financial economics, the hedge involves dramatic gamma $(d^2 P / dS^2)$ spikes at each renewal date.

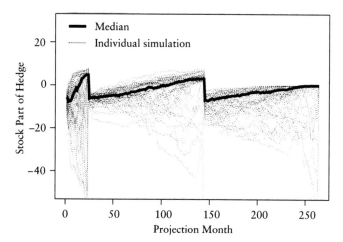

FIGURE 8.4 Simulated stock part for 100 simulations of the GMAB hedge, with median value in bold.

In Figure 8.4 the heavy line shows the median stock part of the hedge portfolio as it evolves through the simulations. The broken lines show individual simulation paths, to give a picture of the variation in this feature. The rollovers happen at 24 months and at 144 months, and these dates correspond to the plunge in the stock part seen in most of the simulations. Although these gamma spikes are a highly undesirable feature of the GMAB contract, the effect is mitgated substantially in practice where a portfolio has a spread of maturity or rollover dates over time.

CHAPTER 9

Risk Measures

INTRODUCTION

In Chapters 6 and 8, we developed the distribution of liabilities for equity-linked insurance using the actuarial and dynamic-hedging approaches, respectively. In this chapter, we discuss how to apply risk measures to the liability distribution to compare products, particularly focusing on risk and return.

A risk measure is a method of encapsulating the riskiness of a distribution in a single number or in a real-valued function. The most familiar risk measures to actuaries are premium principles, which determine how a risk distribution is to be used to set a policy premium. Most finance professionals are familiar with the *value-at-risk* (VaR) risk measure, by which the distribution of future losses on a portfolio is used to determine a capital requirement for solvency management in relation to that portfolio. Regulators use risk measures as a succinct way of quantifying risk.

More formally, a risk measure is functional, mapping a distribution to the real numbers; if we represent the distribution by the appropriate random variable X and let $\mathcal{H}$ represent the risk-measure functional, then

$$\mathcal{H} : X \rightarrow \mathbb{R}$$

In Chapter 6, the net present value (NPV) random variable for the outgo was simulated for the different contracts assuming that no risk-mitigation strategy (such as hedging) is adopted. This is known as the *actuarial* approach (though many actuaries do not use it). Because the liability is discounted at the risk-free rate, the NPV represents the amount required that, if invested at the risk-free rate, will be exactly sufficient to meet the guarantee at maturity. In Chapter 8, we also discounted the NPV of the guarantee, but this time assuming that some of the funds are used to establish and support a hedge portfolio to mitigate the liability risk. In this chapter, risk measures are applied to both of the NPV distributions derived using actuarial and dynamic-hedging risk management.

In this chapter we first introduce the *quantile* risk measure. Value-at-risk, or VaR, is a well-known financial application of the quantile risk measure. We also describe the *conditional tail expectation* (CTE) risk measure, which is related to the quantile risk measure. This risk measure is gaining ground in many financial applications. It is also known as *tail-VaR* (by Artzner et al. (1999) and as *expected shortfall*. Although exact calculation of the risk measures is discussed in these sections, the most practical method of determining the risk measure in most applications explored in this book is by stochastic simulation. The CTE measure has many advantages over the quantile measure, which we discuss. To illustrate the application of risk measures, we have used two examples in this chapter. First, we consider the liability from a guaranteed minimum accumulation benefit (GMAB) contract. Next we consider the guaranteed minimum death benefits (GMDBs) commonly embedded in variable-annuity contracts. In both cases the risk measures will be applied to the NPV of future loss random variable, denoted by L_0. If the actuarial strategy is adopted, we have an NPV random variable

$$L_0 = \text{NPV of guarantee cost} - \text{NPV of margin offset}$$

and if the insurer uses a dynamic-hedge strategy to manage the risk, then the NPV random variable is

$$L_0 = \text{Initial hedge cost} + \text{NPV of hedging errors}$$
$$+ \text{NPV of transactions costs} - \text{NPV of margin offset}$$

In either case, the question is how to use the distribution to determine a suitable reserve, to determine appropriate solvency capital[1], or to determine whether the margin offset is a suitable charge for the guarantee. All of the risk measures discussed can be equally applied to the NPV random variable with or without allowance for dynamic hedging.

Actuarial science has long experience of risk measures through premium principles, discussed for example in Gerber (1979). A premium principle describes a method of using a distribution for an insurable loss X to calculate a premium. Simple examples are the following:

The expected value principle: $\mathcal{H}[X] = (1 + \alpha)E[X]$

The variance principle: $\mathcal{H}[X] = E[X] + \alpha\, V[X]$

---

[1]The solvency capital may be the same as the reserve, but generally the reserve is determined on accounting principles and solvency capital is added to satisfy risk management and regulatory requirements.

Although we call these risk measures "premium principles," we also use them for other risk management issues, such as calculating reserves and solvency requirements.

The expected value and variance premium principles are more appropriate for diversifiable risks than for the systematic risks of equity-linked contracts. For a sufficiently large number of independent risks, the law of large numbers states that the sum of losses will be close to the mean, and the distance from the mean is a function of the distribution variance, making the expected value and variance principles both reasonable choices. For equity-linked insurance where the losses within each cohort are not diversifiable, we cannot rely on the law of large numbers. Two risk measures are in common use for this type of loss, the *quantile risk measure* (which includes VaR) and the CTE.

THE QUANTILE RISK MEASURE

Introduction

Let the random variable L_0 be the present value of losses, discounted at the risk-free rate of interest. The quantile risk measure for L is defined for parameter α, $0 \leq \alpha \leq 1$, as

$$\mathcal{H}[L_0] = V_\alpha = \inf\{V : \Pr[L_0 \leq V] \geq \alpha\} \tag{9.1}$$

So, V_α is the 100α percentile of the loss distribution, hence the quantile risk measure. This expression is easily interpreted: V_α is the smallest sum to hold in risk-free assets in order that at maturity, when combined with the fund F_n and all the margin offset received over the term $t = 0$ to $t = n$, accumulated at the risk-free rate of interest, the probability of having a sufficient amount to pay the guarantee G is at least α. For a guaranteed death benefit, this is averaged over the different possible claim dates according to the mortality rates. The probability distribution used is the real-world measure, or P-measure, because we are interested in the real-world outcome. The Q-measure is only used for pricing or determining the hedge portfolio. The quantile risk measure is the basis of the VaR calculation used in banking risk management. Generally a 99 percent quantile (or ninety-ninth percentile) for 10-day losses must be held as solvency capital.

Simulation

The quantile risk measure is very easy to estimate when the liability distribution is constructed by stochastic simulation. By ordering the simulations, the estimated α-quantile risk measure is the $(N\alpha)$th value of the ordered liability values, where N is the number of simulations. That is, if the jth smallest simulated loss present value is $L_{0(j)}$, then the estimate of the α-quantile is $L_{0(N\alpha)}$.

This α-quantile estimate will vary as a result of sampling variability. It is useful to quantify the variability in the estimate—in other words, to calculate the standard error[2] of the estimate. The quantile risk measure is an order-statistic of the loss distribution, and from the theory of order statistics we can calculate the standard error of the simulation estimate[3].

A nonparametric 100β percent confidence interval for the α-quantile from the ordered simulated loss costs $L_{0(j)}$ is given by an interval

$$(L_{0(N\alpha-A)}, L_{0(N_\alpha+A)})$$

where

$$A = \Phi^{-1}\left(\frac{1+\beta}{2}\right) \sqrt{N\alpha(1-\alpha)} \tag{9.2}$$

It is usual to round A to an integer, but it is also reasonable to interpolate for noninteger values. This formula is derived using the binomial distribution for the count of simulations below the true α-quantile. The number of simulations below the α-quantile is a random variable, M, say. It has a binomial distribution with parameters N and α, with mean $N\alpha$ and variance $N\alpha(1-\alpha)$. We use $N\alpha$ as an estimate for M, which is unknown as the true α-quantile is unknown. Then $(N\alpha - A, N\alpha + A)$ is a β-confidence interval for M where, if $F_B()$ is the distribution function of the binomial(N, α) distribution,

$$F_B(N\alpha + A) - F_B(N\alpha - A) = \beta$$

Using the normal approximation to the binomial distribution gives the equation 9.2. This is a reasonable approximation, provided $N\alpha$ is sufficiently large, that is greater than about 30.

The implementation of all this is very simple. Suppose we have a set of 10,000 simulations of the present value of loss for an equity-linked contract, and we are interested in the ninetieth percentile. Then $N = 10,000$, $\alpha = 0.9$, and the estimate of the α-quantile is the 9,000th ordered value of the simulated losses.

Now suppose we are interested in a 95 percent confidence interval for the quantile, so that $\beta = 0.95$. Calculate

$$A = \Phi^{-1}(.975) \sqrt{10,000(0.1)(0.9)} = (1.96)(30) = 58.8$$

---

[2] The standard error is the standard deviation of a random estimator.
[3] See David (1981) for a comprehensive text on order statistics theory.

Round A to 59, to give a 95 percent confidence interval of

$$(L_{0(8941)}, L_{0(9059)})$$

That is, we have 95 percent confidence that the *distribution* 0.9-quantile lies between the 0.8941 quantile and the 0.9059 quantile of the *simulation*.

Exact Calculation

In some circumstances, it is possible to calculate the quantile risk measure exactly. If the insurer does not use dynamic hedging, and stock returns follow a lognormal distribution, then the cost of the guaranteed minimum maturity benefit (GMMB) guarantee has a distribution with a probability mass at zero and a lognormal-type density above zero (because it has a censored, transformed lognormal distribution). However, once the margin offset income is added in, exact calculation becomes impractical. The present value of the GMMB net of the margin offset income is a sum of dependent lognormal random variables that is not very tractable.

For some purposes, the cost of the guarantee before allowing for margin offset income is interesting—for example, as a numerical check, for a rough calculation, or for use as a control variate in variance reduction (see Chapter 11).

The first step required is to determine whether the probability of the guarantee ending up out-of-the-money[4] is greater or less than the quantile level of interest. Using obvious notation, the present value of the guarantee, ignoring margin offset income and mortality, is

$$L_0 = \begin{cases} (G - F_n)\, e^{-rn} & G \geq F_n \\ 0 & G < F_n \end{cases} \tag{9.3}$$

and we are interested in the α-quantile of L_0. Let the stock process be denoted S_t, as usual, with $S_0 = F_0$ so that the fund at n is simply the stock reduced by the management charge, $F_k = S_k(1 - m)^k$ for integer k.

Now, define $\xi = \Pr[L_0 = 0]$. This is the probability that the final fund value is greater than the guarantee, meaning that there is no payment under the guarantee.

$$\xi = \Pr[G < F_n] = \Pr[G < S_n(1 - m)^n] = \Pr\left[\frac{G}{S_0} < \frac{S_n(1 - m)^n}{S_0}\right]$$

---

[4]Recall that *in-the-money* means that the guarantee is greater than the fund level, *out-of-the-money* means that the fund is greater than the guarantee.

If it is further assumed that stock returns follow a lognormal process, then

$$\frac{S_n (1 - m)^n}{S_0} \sim \log N(n(\mu + \log(1 - m)), n\sigma^2)$$

and we can easily calculate the probability that the guarantee cost is equal to zero, ξ, as

$$\xi = 1 - \Phi\left(\frac{\log G/S_0 - n(\mu + \log(1 - m))}{\sqrt{n}\,\sigma}\right) \tag{9.4}$$

As an example, let the term $n = 120$ months, let S_t/S_{t-1} have a lognormal distribution with parameters $\mu = .0081$ and $\sigma = 0.0451$ per month, and let $m = 0.25$ percent per month. Assume a starting fund value of $F_0 = S_0 = \$100$ and a guarantee of 100 percent of the starting fund. Then

$$\xi = 1 - \Phi\left(\frac{\log G/S_0 - n(\mu + \log(1 - m))}{\sqrt{n}\,\sigma}\right) = 1 - \Phi(-1.3594) = 0.9130$$

So, if assets follow the lognormal distribution in this example there is a probability of 0.913 that there will be no payment under the guarantee. The quantile risk measure for any α-parameter less than 91.3 percent must, therefore, be zero. We do not need to hold any extra funds to ensure a probability of 90 percent, say, of meeting the guarantee liability; that probability is adequately covered by the fund alone.

For the quantile risk measure with $\alpha > \xi$ we know that the quantile falls in the part of the distribution where $L_0 > 0$, so, from equation 9.3, $L = (G - F_n) e^{-rn}$. In this case, the quantile risk measure is V_α, defined as the smallest amount satisfying

$$\Pr[F_n + V_\alpha e^{rn} > G] \geq \alpha \tag{9.5}$$

and (assuming F_n is a continuous random variable) this gives

$$V_\alpha = (G - F_{F_n}^{-1}(1 - \alpha)) e^{-rn} \tag{9.6}$$

where $F_{F_n}()$ is the distribution function for the fund value at maturity, F_n. If we again assume that returns on the assets underlying the fund have a lognormal distribution with parameters μ and σ per year, and let $z_p = \Phi^{-1}(p)$, then

$$V_\alpha = (G - F_0 \exp(-z_\alpha \sqrt{n}\sigma + n(\mu + \log(1 - m)))) e^{-rn} \tag{9.7}$$

TABLE 9.1 Ten-year GMMB quantile risk measures with no mortality or lapses; guarantee 100 percent of starting market value.

Model/Parameters	ξ	$V_{90\%}$	$V_{95\%}$	$V_{99\%}$
Lognormal/MLE $\mu = 0.0081$ $\sigma = 0.0451$ $m = 0.0025$	0.9130	0	7.22	20.84
Lognormal/Calibrated $\mu = 0.0077$ $\sigma = 0.0542$ $m = 0.0025$	0.8541	6.90	16.18	29.02
RSLN/MLE Table 6.2 parameters $m = 0.0025$	0.8705	5.12	15.78	30.76

It is also possible to calculate the quantile risk measures for other distributions analytically. In Table 9.1 some quantile risk measure figures are given for the lognormal distribution and for the regime-switching lognormal (RSLN) distribution, in both cases using maximum likelihood parameters from the TSE 300 1956 to 1999 data. Figures are also given for the lognormal model using the calibrated parameters from Chapter 4. These parameters are found by calibrating the left tail of the lognormal distribution to the left tail of the data, rather than using maximum likelihood.

The table shows the effect of the heavier tail of the RSLN model, with higher quantiles at all three levels. The effect of calibration brings the results closer together, as intended. In the uncalibrated lognormal case, the probability of a zero liability under the guarantee is $\xi = 0.913$, so the 90 percent quantile falls in the probability mass at zero. In other words, the 90 percent quantile must be sufficient to meet the guarantee with probability 0.90; but holding zero will meet the guarantee with probability 0.9130, so the 90 percent quantile risk measure is also zero.

THE CONDITIONAL TAIL EXPECTATION RISK MEASURE

Introduction

There are some practical and theoretical problems associated with the quantile risk measure, which in some circumstances outweigh the ease of application (particularly with simulation output) and the simple interpretation. See Wirch and Hardy (1999) and Boyle, Siu, and Yang (2002) for examples.

In modern applications, a popular alternative to the quantile risk measure is the CTE risk measure. The CTE risk measure is closely connected with the quantile risk measure, and like the quantile risk measure is determined with respect to a parameter α, where α lies between 0 and 1 as in the quantile risk measure in the previous section. Given α, the CTE is defined as the expected value of the loss given that the loss falls in the upper $(1-\alpha)$ tail of the distribution.

We start with the quantile risk measure V_α. For a continuous loss distribution (or, more strictly, if $V_{\alpha+\varepsilon} > V_\alpha$ for any $\varepsilon > 0$), the CTE with parameter α, is

$$\text{CTE}_\alpha(L) = E[L_0 | L_0 > V_\alpha] \qquad (9.8)$$

where V_α is defined as in equation 9.6.

Note that this definition, though intuitively appealing, does not give suitable results where V_α falls in a probability mass. This will happen for example where $\alpha < \xi$, in which case $V_\alpha = 0$. Suppose, for example, that the loss random variable has the following distribution:

$$L = \begin{cases} 0 & \text{with probability} & 0.98 \\ 100 & \text{with probability} & 0.02 \end{cases}$$

Then the 95 percent quantile is clearly $V_{0.95} = 0$; the value of $E[L|L > 0]$ is clearly 100. But the 95 percent CTE is the mean of the losses given such that the losses fall in the worst 5 percent of the distribution, which is

$$\text{CTE}_{0.95} = \frac{(0.03)(0.0) + (0.02)(100)}{0.05} = 40$$

In the more general case, the CTE with parameter α is calculated as follows. Find

$$\beta' = \max\{\beta : V_\alpha = V_\beta\}$$

then

$$\text{CTE}_\alpha(L) = \frac{(1 - \beta') E[X|X > V_\alpha] + (\beta' - \alpha) V_\alpha}{1 - \alpha} \qquad (9.9)$$

This complication is automatically managed when the CTE is estimated by simulation.

Simulation

Using simulation output to calculate the CTE risk measure estimate is very straightforward. Start by ordering the simulated losses so that $L_{0(j)}$ is the jth smallest. To estimate CTE_α with N simulations, calculate the mean of the largest $N(1 - \alpha)$ simulations. That is, provided $(N\alpha)$ is an integer, the CTE estimate is

$$\widehat{\text{CTE}}_\alpha(L_0) = \sum_{j=N\alpha+1}^{N} L_{0(j)}\big/N(1 - \alpha) \qquad (9.10)$$

So, whereas the estimate of the α-quantile is $L_{0(N\alpha)}$, the estimate of the CTE is the average of all outcomes greater than $L_{0(N\alpha)}$.

As with the quantile estimate, with simulation output the estimate will have uncertainty attached from sampling variability. This may be quantified by the standard error or by a confidence interval, but these are much more difficult to determine for the CTE than for the quantile.

Suppose the quantile of the underlying distribution were known with certainty, V_α, say. Then apply standard statistical inference to the sample of observations of $L_0 | L_0 > V_\alpha$, and the standard error of the mean is the standard deviation of the sample divided by the square root of the sample size.

Where we use simulation to estimate V_α there is an added source of uncertainty, and that causes the problems. Ignoring the second source of uncertainty gives a biased low estimate of the standard error for the sample, of

$$\frac{\text{SD}(L_{(j)} : j > N\alpha)}{\sqrt{N(1 - \alpha)}} \qquad (9.11)$$

where $\text{SD}()$ denotes the sample standard deviation of the L's. For a more accurate estimate of the uncertainty surrounding the CTE estimate, the simplest method is to use the Monte Carlo version of the sledgehammer; repeat the simulation many times using different (independent) starting seed values for the random number generators, determine separate CTE estimates for each set of simulations and calculate the standard deviation of the estimates. Another approach, described in Manistre and Hancock (2002), is to approximate the tail of the loss distribution using a generalized Pareto distribution. This leads to quite straightforward formulae that are both practical and accurate.

Exact Calculation

As with the quantile risk measure, it is possible to calculate the CTE risk measure for a plain vanilla GMMB, with no allowance for margin offset and no dynamic hedging. The term ξ is again used as $\Pr[F_n > G]$, which is the probability that there is no payment under the guarantee. The two cases, $\alpha \geq \xi$ and $\alpha < \xi$ are dealt with separately. Assume first that $\alpha \geq \xi$, and let the fund value $F_n = S_n(1 - m)^n$ have density function and distribution function $f_{F_n}()$ and $F_{F_n}()$ respectively, then

$$\text{CTE}_\alpha(L) = E[L \mid L > V_\alpha] \tag{9.12}$$

$$= E[(G - F_n)e^{-rn} \mid F_n < (G - V_\alpha e^{rn})] \tag{9.13}$$

The probability $\Pr[F_n < (G - V_\alpha e^{rn})] = (1 - \alpha)$ from the definition of V_α, so

$$\text{CTE}_\alpha(L) = \frac{e^{-rn}}{1 - \alpha} \left\{ \int_0^{G - V_\alpha e^{rn}} (G - y)f_{F_n}(y)dy \right\} \tag{9.14}$$

$$= \frac{e^{-rn}}{1 - \alpha} \left\{ G\, F_{F_n}(G - V_\alpha e^{rn}) - \int_0^{G - V_\alpha e^{rn}} y\, f_{F_n}(y)dy \right\} \tag{9.15}$$

$$= e^{-rn} \left\{ G - \frac{1}{1 - \alpha} \int_0^{G - V_\alpha e^{rn}} y\, f_{F_n}(y)dy \right\} \tag{9.16}$$

If $S_n \sim \text{LN}(n\mu, \sqrt{n}\sigma)$, then for $\alpha \geq \xi$:

$$\text{CTE}_\alpha(L) = e^{-rn} \left\{ G - \frac{e^{n(\mu + \log(1-m) + \sigma^2/2)}}{1 - \alpha} \right.$$

$$\left. \times \Phi\left(\frac{\log(G - V_\alpha e^{rn}) - n(\mu + \log(1 - m) + \sigma^2)}{\sqrt{n}\sigma} \right) \right\}$$

$$= e^{-rn} \left\{ G - \frac{e^{n(\mu + \log(1-m) + \sigma^2/2)}}{1 - \alpha} \Phi(-z_\alpha - \sqrt{n}\sigma) \right\} \tag{9.17}$$

which is a nice simple formula.

If $S_n \sim \text{RSLN}$, then things are not much more complicated. Remember that if R denotes the number of time units spent in regime 1, then $S_n|R \sim \text{LN}(\mu^*(R), \sigma^*(R))$ where $\mu^*()$ and $\sigma^*()$ are weighted averages defined in equations 2.27 and 2.28. It is straightforward to sum over all possible values of R and multiply by the probability function for R, $p_n(k)$ from equation 2.20 to obtain the CTE for the RSLN distribution, for $\alpha \geq \xi$:

$$\text{CTE}_\alpha(L) = e^{-rn} \left\{ G - \frac{(1 - m)^n}{1 - \alpha} \sum_{k=0}^n p_n(k)(e^{\mu^*(k) + \sigma^*(k)^2/2} \Phi(Y_k)) \right\}$$

TABLE 9.2 Ten-year GMMB CTE risk measures with no mortality or lapses, no margin offset, and guarantee 100 percent of starting market value.

Model/Parameters	ξ	$CTE_{90\%}$	$CTE_{95\%}$	$CTE_{99\%}$
Lognormal/MLE	0.9130	8.89	15.50	25.77
Lognormal/Calibrated	0.8541	17.65	24.00	33.39
RSLN/MLE	0.8705	17.51	24.86	35.76

where

$$Y_k = \frac{\log(G - V_\alpha e^{rn}) - \mu^*(k) - n\log(1 - m) - \sigma^*(k)^2}{\sigma^*(k)} \tag{9.18}$$

If $\alpha < \xi$, then the quantile falls in the probability mass at zero of the loss distribution. Use equation 9.9, with $\beta' = \xi$ and $V_\alpha = V_\xi = 0$ so that $CTE_\xi(X) = E[X|X > 0]$ and

$$CTE_\alpha(X) = \frac{(1 - \xi)}{(1 - \alpha)} CTE_\xi(X) \tag{9.19}$$

For illustration, in Table 9.2 some examples of CTE measures are given using the same model/parameter combinations as in Table 9.1. Again, mortality and lapses are ignored. As with the quantiles in Table 9.1, the effect of calibration in bringing the tail measures closer together is clear.

QUANTILE AND CTE MEASURES COMPARED

Both the quantile and CTE risk measures are very simple to work with, particularly in the usual context of estimating the measure from standard stochastic simulation output. Obviously, because the CTE is related to the quantile risk measure as

$$CTE_\alpha(L_0) = E[L_0|L_0 > V_\alpha]$$

then the CTE must be greater than the quantile until the maximum value of L_0 is reached, when they will be equal.

If the distribution of $L_0|L_0 > V_\alpha$ is uniform, then $CTE_\alpha(L_0) = V_{(1+\alpha)/2}$, and this relationship is approximately true for other distributions of the tail of L_0. For most GMMB, GMDB, and GMAB contracts the right tail of the loss distribution is heavier than the uniform, so that $CTE_\alpha(L_0) > V_{(1+\alpha)/2}$.

There is an extensive literature on risk measures, including Wang (1995), Artzner et al. (1997 and 1999), and Wirch and Hardy (1999). The latter three papers are concerned with the *coherence* of risk measures. A risk measure $\mathcal{H}[X]$ is said to be coherent if it has the following, obviously desirable, properties:

Bounded above by the maximum loss: $\mathcal{H}[X] \leq \max(X)$ (9.20)

Bounded below by the mean loss: $\mathcal{H}[X] \geq E[X]$ (9.21)

Scalar additive and multiplicative: $\mathcal{H}[aX + b] = a\mathcal{H}[X] + b$ (9.22)

for $a, b > 0$

Subadditive: $\mathcal{H}[X + Y] \leq \mathcal{H}[X] + \mathcal{H}[Y]$ (9.23)

Quantile risk measures fail both property 9.21 and property 9.23. The first is easy to see—from Table 9.1 the 90 percent quantile for the GMMB loss is zero, because the probability of a nonzero loss is less than 10 percent. But the mean outgo is

$$E[L] = e^{-rn} \int_0^G (G - y) f_{F_n}(y) dy \qquad (9.24)$$

$$= e^{-rn} \left\{ G F_{F_n}(G) - \int_0^G y f_{F_n}(y) dy \right\} \qquad (9.25)$$

$$= e^{-rn} \left\{ G(1 - \xi) - F_0 \exp(n(\mu + \log(1 - m) + \sigma^2/2)) \Phi(A) \right\} \qquad (9.26)$$

where

$$A = \frac{(\log G_{F_0} - n(\mu + \log(1 - m)) - n\sigma^2)}{(\sqrt{n} \sigma)} \qquad (9.27)$$

which gives an expected discounted cost using the lognormal model of $0.90. At all quantiles up to $\alpha = 0.92$ the quantile measure will be less than the mean. This means, for example, that if the 90 percent risk measure is used as the basis for the reserve or solvency capital, on average it will be inadequate, although it will usually be sufficient.

The CTE does not suffer from this disadvantage. Clearly, $CTE_{\alpha=0}(L_0) = E[L_0]$ and for any $\alpha > 0$, $CTE_\alpha > E[L_0]$ provided L_0 is not degenerate at $E[L_0]$. In fact, the CTE satisfies all the criteria for coherence and, therefore, does not create the anomalies that are associated with the quantile measure. The quantile measure is determined by one point on the loss distribution; no consideration is taken in the quantile of the shape of the distribution either side of that point. The CTE uses all of the loss distribution to the right of the quantile; two distributions may have the same 90 percent quantile, but one may be much heavier tailed than the other beyond the ninetieth percentile of the distribution. The CTE takes this into consideration, whereas the quantile risk measure does not.

Another consideration is robustness under simulation; the quantile approach takes a single (ordered) outcome from, perhaps, 5,000 simulations to determine the risk measure. The CTE approach takes an average of a set of the largest outcomes. The average should be less sensitive to sampling variability. This is investigated further in Chapter 11.

The Canadian Institute of Actuaries (CIA) Taskforce (SFTF 2000) recommended that the CTE should form the risk measure for both the reserve and the solvency capital calculations for segregated fund contracts in Canada. This recommendation was accepted by the Office of the Superintendent of Financial Institutions (OSFI), which regulates insurers. In principle, the reserves for segregated fund contracts will be determined using the CTE with α of around 80 percent (varying according to the contract details), and total solvency capital (including the reserve) set at the CTE with $\alpha = 95$ percent. Because the liabilities are to be determined by stochastic simulation, the CTE approach has proved quite practical for insurers to implement.

RISK MEASURES FOR GMAB LIABILITY

Introduction

All the examples in this section are estimates from simulation of the liabilities of a GMAB contract. Two sets of projections are run: one using the actuarial approach, without any hedging, and the other using the dynamic-hedging approach. The basic contract details are as follows:

- A 10-year renewable contract, maximum one renewal.
- A 3 percent per year management charge, applied monthly.
- A 0.5 percent per year margin offset applied monthly.
- Guarantee 100 percent of fund immediately following previous renewal.

The following are simulation details for all projections in this section:

▨ RSLN stock returns with TSE 300 parameters from Table 6.2.
▨ Mortality follows tables in Appendix A.
▨ The same 5,000 simulations of the stock return process are used for both sets of projections (actuarial and dynamic hedge).
▨ All cash flows are discounted at the risk-free rate of interest of 6 percent per year.

The projection output is the NPV of the total outgo for the contract discounted at the risk-free rate on interest. In the case of the dynamic-hedging approach this includes the cost of the hedge.

CTE and Quantile Risk Measure for Actuarially Managed GMAB

In Figure 9.1 the quantile and CTE risk measures are compared for a 10-year GMAB contract with two renewals; both the starting fund and the starting guarantee are $100, so that the numbers can be interpreted as percentages of the fund for an at-the-money guarantee. This contract is managed according to the principles of Chapter 6—the actuarial method, which assumes solvency capital is invested in bonds. Note that $CTE_{0\%}$ is the mean loss, so that the figure shows that the quantile falls below the mean at all values of α less than around 60 percent. Clearly, the CTE curve lies above the quantile curve until the maximum value is reached.

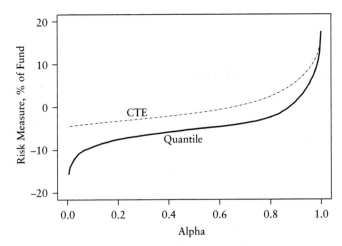

FIGURE 9.1 CTE and quantile risk measures for 10-year once-renewable, at-the-money GMAB contract.

The CTE curve is somewhat smoother than the quantile curve, though they are both plotted with the same partition of the α-values. This illustrates the robustness point mentioned in the previous section: The CTE, being mean based, will generally be more robust to sampling variability than the quantile, which is based on a single ordered value.

In Table 9.3 we show some of the tail risk measures for this GMAB contract. We also show the same risk measures for a similar contract, with the additional benefit of the voluntary reset feature described in Chapter 6. The voluntary reset allows the policyholder to reset the guarantee to the fund value at the reset date, at the expense of an extension of the term to 10 years from the reset date. We show the CTE risk measures for the contract with no resets, for the contract with monthly optional resets, and for the contract with up to two resets per year. The reset option is assumed to be exercised when the separate account fund value exceeds the guarantee by the reset threshold given in the table. The table shows a significant tail risk arising from offering the reset option, with around 3 percent of the fund value required for the reset above the requirement for the regular GMAB without the reset option at each of these CTE standards. We also see that restricting the option to two "shouts," or resets, per year does not significantly help control the tail risk; the difference between two shouts and 12 shouts is small.

Comparison of Actuarial and Hedging Approaches to Risk Management of GMAB

In the top graph of Figure 9.2, the quantile risk measures are plotted for all values of α for the GMAB contract using the actuarial and the dynamic-hedging approach. In the lower figure, the CTE risk measures are given for the same contract, with and without hedging. The risk measure using dynamic hedging includes the cost of the hedge.

Now suppose the risk is to be managed by solvency capital determined using the quantile risk measure with $\alpha = 90$ percent. This is simply the

TABLE 9.3 CTE risk measure for GMAB contract with resets with actuarial risk management; $100 starting fund value and $100 starting guarantee.

Contract	Reset Threshold	CTE		
		90%	95%	99%
No reset GMAB	—	5.92	8.60	13.61
2 resets per year	1.15	8.24	11.35	16.36
12 resets per year	1.05	8.54	11.70	16.65

4,500th value of the sorted NPVs. For the actuarial approach, this is

$$V_{90\%}^{act} = 1.29 \text{ percent of fund}$$

For the dynamic-hedging approach, it is

$$V_{90\%}^{dh} = 1.06 \text{ percent of fund}$$

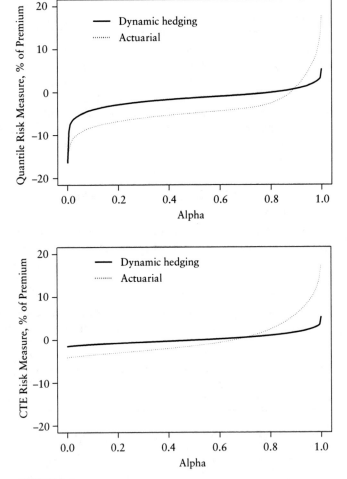

FIGURE 9.2 Risk measures for 10-year once-renewable, at-the-money GMAB contract; actuarial and hedging risk management.

These results indicate a very similar risk under the two approaches. This is deceptive, though, because it ignores the shape of the loss above the quantile.

If, instead, the CTE method is used with the same α value, the heavy right tail of the actuarial approach is taken into consideration in the mean calculation, so that the CTE values are

$$\mathrm{CTE}_{90\%}^{act} = 5.92 \text{ percent of fund}$$

$$\mathrm{CTE}_{90\%}^{db} = 1.74 \text{ percent of fund}$$

which indicates more of a difference. As the lower graph of Figure 9.2 indicates, the difference increases as the α parameter increases. At $\alpha = 95$ percent, the CTEs are

$$\mathrm{CTE}_{95\%}^{act} = 8.60 \text{ percent of fund}$$

$$\mathrm{CTE}_{95\%}^{db} = 2.32 \text{ percent of fund}$$

RISK MEASURES FOR VA DEATH BENEFITS

Many VA contracts do not carry guaranteed living benefits, and the only guarantee to be considered is a death benefit. We consider a VA-type contract with 30-year term sold to a life age 50; mortality and withdrawal rates are assumed to be the same as for the GMAB contract discussed earlier, with the actual rates given in Appendix A. Implicit in these is an assumption of 8 percent withdrawals per year; this is 8 percent of funds, so it could comprise both whole and partial withdrawals of funds. As with mortality, withdrawals are treated deterministically. It is not proposed that these are necessarily realistic, and the analysis of VA-GMDB liabilities is hampered by the lack of information on policyholder behavior, just as with GMMB.

In Figure 6.3 in the section on stochastic simulation of liability cash flows, the contributions to the net liability present value from margin offset, death benefit, and maturity benefits are shown separately for some sample cash flows. This shows that for the GMAB contract the death benefit outgo is generally small, considerably smaller than the margin offset income, except for the very rare simulation. We might infer that where the only guarantee is a death benefit, the costs are fairly low, and simulation evidence supports this.

In the figures shown later in this section, we consider net liability present value for a GMDB liability. The margin offset figures used are a little higher than those found from the arbitrage-free method of the section on pricing by deduction from the separate account in Chapter 8. We use 10 basis points (b.p.) for the fixed guarantee compared with 6 b.p. for the arbitrage-free rate, and 40 b.p. for the increasing guarantee compared with 38 b.p. for the arbitrage-free rate. Also, because we used 20 percent per year volatility in that calculation, which is somewhat higher than the true rate, there is substantial margin in the figures of 10 b.p. and 40 b.p. used in this example.

The contract details used in this section are as follows:

- A 30-year single premium contract.
- A 2.25 percent per year management charge, applied monthly.
- Guarantee: We consider two variants,

  1. One-hundred percent of premium paid on death with no guarantee increases and 10 b.p. per year margin offset.
  2. Guarantee starts at 100 percent of premium, increasing by 5 percent compounded at each year-end and 40 b.p. per year margin offset.

The simulation details for all projections are as follows:

- RSLN stock returns with TSE 300 parameters from Table 6.2.
- Mortality follows the tables in Appendix A.
- The same 5,000 simulations of the stock return process are used for all projections.
- All cash flows are discounted at the risk-free rate of interest of 6 percent per year.

In addition, for the dynamic-hedging risk management we assume as before:

- Black-Scholes-Merton hedging using 20 percent per year fixed volatility and 6 percent risk-free rate of interest.
- Monthly rebalancing of hedge.
- Transactions costs of 0.2 percent of change in stock holding at rebalancing dates.

Table 9.4 shows CTE and quantile risk measures for the two contracts. The results are shown separately for the actuarial and dynamic-hedging risk management strategies. The risk measures are illustrated in Figure 9.3.

The fixed GMDB carries relatively little risk, with more than a 95 percent estimated probability that the income is greater than the outgo. There is a slight tail risk from the fixed guarantee, with a 95 percent CTE of nearly 1 percent using actuarial risk management, but this is damped by using a hedging strategy, which virtually eliminates the risk.

TABLE 9.4 Risk measures for VA-type GMDB benefits, 30-year contract; percentage of initial fund value.

Guarantee	Risk Management Strategy	Quantile		CTE	
		90%	95%	90%	95%
Fixed	Actuarial	−0.350	−0.072	0.317	0.798
Fixed	Hedging	−0.294	−0.161	−0.119	−0.003
5% p.a. increasing	Actuarial	−0.086	1.452	1.857	3.044
5% p.a. increasing	Hedging	0.071	0.579	0.706	1.102

The increasing GMDB is a more substantial risk, with a 95 percent CTE of around 3 percent of the initial single premium using actuarial risk management. Again, the hedging strategy significantly reduces the tail risk.

The comparisons provided in Figures 9.2 and 9.3 between actuarial and dynamic-hedging strategies give rise to the question: Which is better? The CTE curves show that, on average (i.e., at $CTE_{0\%}$), the actuarial approach is substantially more profitable than the dynamic-hedging approach. On the other hand, at the right tail the risk associated with the actuarial approach is greater than the dynamic-hedging approach, in some cases very substantially so. If solvency capital is to be determined using, for example, the 95 percent

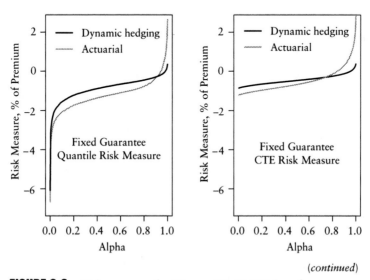

(continued)

FIGURE 9.3 Risk measures for 30-year VA-GMDB benefits, comparing actuarial and dynamic-hedging risk management.

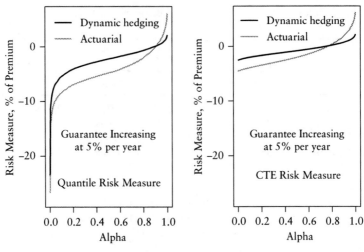

FIGURE 9.3   *(Continued)*

CTE, then the actuarial approach will require considerably more solvency capital to be maintained than the dynamic-hedging approach, and the cost of retaining this capital needs to be taken into consideration in determining whether to hedge or not. Indeed, it needs to be considered for all aspects of the management of equity-linked contracts, including decisions about commercial viability and pricing. Such decisions are the topic of the next chapter.

CHAPTER 10

Emerging Cost Analysis

DECISIONS

In this chapter, we show how to use the results of the analysis described in previous chapters to make strategic decisions about pricing and risk management for equity-linked contracts. The first decision is whether to sell the policy at all; if so, then at what price and with what benefits. If the contract has been sold, then the insurer must decide how much capital to hold in respect of the contract, and how that capital is to be managed. Market and competition issues are important in the decision process—for example, what are competitors charging for similar products? However, pure market considerations are not sufficient for actuarial pricing decisions. It is also essential to have some quantitative analysis available to ensure that business is sold with appropriate margins, to avoid following others on potentially ruinous paths.

Emerging cost analysis (also called *profit testing*) is a straightforward and intuitive approach to this analysis. It is very similar to the techniques of Chapters 6 and 8 in that it involves the projection of all the cash flows under the contract, according to the risk management strategy that the insurer proposes to adopt. The major difference between the projections in this chapter and those in earlier chapters is that here we take into account the capital requirements, so that the cash flows projected represent the loss or profit emerging each year after capital costs are taken into consideration. These cash flows are the returns to the shareholder funds and should be analyzed from the shareholders' perspective.

Emerging cost analysis has been part of the actuarial skill set for some time; it is a standard feature of most actuarial curricula. However, it is commonly presented as a deterministic technique. Deterministically, emerging costs are projected under a single scenario for stock returns. The scenario may be called "best estimate," and may be derived from a mean or median projection of a stochastic process. Although deterministic projections may be useful in traditional insurance, they provide very little insight for equity-linked insurance, for exactly the reasons that deterministic methods were discussed and rejected in Chapter 2. Given the systematic risk of equity-linked insurance, no single scenario can adequately capture the risk return relationship of the contracts. That is why, in this chapter, the emerging costs are random processes. The processes are generally too complex for analytic analysis, so stochastic simulation will be used to derive the distributions of interest.

In this chapter, we discuss and illustrate with examples the use of emerging cost analysis for separate account-type products. The worked example is a guaranteed minimum accumulation benefit (GMAB) contract with both death and survival benefits.

The formulation that we use for the cash flows and for defining the net present value of a contract adopts a traditional actuarial approach and ignores many factors that are important for practical implementation. In particular, we ignore the distinction between policy reserves and additional solvency capital. The total of reserves plus additional required solvency capital is the total balance sheet provision. In practice, the allocation of the total balance sheet provision to reserves and additional solvency capital may have a substantial impact on the financial management of the insurance portfolio, as a result of taxation and regulatory requirements. Hancock (2002) writes of finanacial projections that

> *If you are ignoring taxes, the distinction between reserves and capital is moot, but in practice there is a very significant difference—capital is "after tax" and hence a $1 provision in capital is generally more expensive than $1 in reserves. Also, on a going-concern basis, the company may need to hold some multiple (more than 100%) of solvency (regulatory) capital. This is another reason that holding $1 of provision in capital is more expensive than the $1 allocated to liabilities (all else being equal, including tax reserves).*

Emerging Costs Using Actuarial Risk Management

For the emerging cost analysis for the actuarially managed risk, we simulate the cash flows each month using the following:

- MO_t is the margin offset at t, conditional on the contract being in force at t.
- G_t^d is the guarantee in force if the policyholder dies in the month $t-1$ to t.
- G_t^s is the guarantee in force for any survival benefit due at t. In most months this would be zero, but it is required for the maturity benefit under a guaranteed minimum maturity benefit (GMMB) or for the rollover maturity benefits under a GMAB.

- F_t is the separate fund.
- $_tV$ is the required solvency capital at t given that the contract is still in force.
- Interest of i_t is assumed to be earned on the solvency capital, and it would be reasonable to take this to be the risk-free rate. This implicitly assumes that the solvency capital is invested in bonds.
- Mortality is treated deterministically, for the reasons discussed earlier in Chapter 6.

Then the outgo cash flow emerging at the end of month t is

$$
CF_t = \begin{cases}
{}_0V - MO_0 & t = 0 \\[6pt]
{}_{t-1|}q_x^d\,(G_t^d - F_t)^+ + {}_tp_x^\tau(G_t^s - F_t)^+ - {}_tp_x^\tau MO_t \\
\quad + ({}_tp_x^\tau\,{}_tV - {}_{t-1}p_x^\tau\,{}_{t-1}V(1 + i_t)) & t = 1, \ldots, n-1 \\[6pt]
{}_{n-1|}q_x^d\,(G_n^d - F_n)^+ + {}_np_x^\tau(G_n^s - F_n)^+ \\
\quad - {}_{n-1}p_x^\tau\,{}_{n-1}V(1 + i_n) & t = n
\end{cases}
$$

$$(10.1)$$

We are using cash flow in a broad sense. For example, the initial required solvency capital, $_0V - MO_0$, is not, of course, a cash flow out of the company, but may be considered as the cost of writing the contract. This equation just sums the outgo each month and deducts the income. Income comes from the margin offset; outgo is required for any death or maturity benefit, plus required increase in solvency capital.

It may be more realistic to assume annual revision of capital requirements, rather than monthly. It is easy to adapt equation 10.1 appropriately. In the equation, the only element of the cash-flow projection that has not been derived in previous chapters is the capital requirement $_tV$.

Emerging Costs Using Dynamic-Hedging Risk Management

For the dynamic-hedging approach we use again the cash flows defined in Chapter 8:

- HE_t is the hedging error emerging at t derived in the section on discrete hedging error in Chapter 8, allowing for survival and exit probabilities.
- TC_t is the transaction cost at t, derived in the section on transaction costs in Chapter 8, allowing for survival and exit probabilities.
- $H(t)$ is the market value of the hedge required at t, given that the contract is in force at the start of the projection.

Because in practice the hedge will not be self-financing, we need to carry some capital in addition to the hedge to meet the unhedged liability—that is, the hedging error and transactions costs.[3] Let $_tV^{T\&H}$ denote the capital required at t for the additional risks associated with hedging, given the contract is in force at t. Then the projected cash-flow outgo at each month end is

$$CF_t = \begin{cases} H(0) + \mathrm{TC}_0 + {_0}V^{T\&H} - \mathrm{MO}_0 & t = 0 \\[2mm] \mathrm{HE}_t + \mathrm{TC}_t + {_t}p_x^\tau {_t}V^{T\&H} - {_{t-1}}p_x^\tau {_{t-1}}V^{T\&H}(1 + i_t) - {_t}p_x^\tau \mathrm{MO}_t & \\ & t = 1, \ldots, n - 1 \\[2mm] \mathrm{HE}_n + \mathrm{TC}_n - {_{n-1}}p_x^\tau {_{n-1}}V^{T\&H}(1 + i_t) & t = n \end{cases} \tag{10.2}$$

Note that the hedging error term includes all actual payouts—so that, for example, the hedging error at maturity is the difference between the actual guarantee cost and the hedge carried forward from the previous month. The only element of the cash-flow projection in equation 10.2 that has not already been derived is the capital requirement for transaction costs and hedging error, $_tV^{T\&H}$. In the following sections, we discuss allowance for capital requirements using the actuarial and dynamic-hedging strategies.

CAPITAL REQUIREMENTS: ACTUARIAL RISK MANAGEMENT

The capital requirements for equity-linked insurance differ by jurisdiction. Although many contracts in the United States have minimum requirements based on simple deterministic projection, some actuaries have recognized the potential inadequacy of this method and have moved to stochastic simulation to determine the requirements. In Canada, regulations permitting the determination of capital requirements by stochastic simulation of the liabilities are due to come into full effect by 2004; the method is already in use for statement liabilities. In the United Kingdom also, valuation by stochastic simulation is required for unit-linked contracts with maturity guarantees.

Taking the Canadian regulations as an example, described in SFTF (2002), it is proposed that the total capital requirement should be determined by simulating the liabilities and taking the 95 percent conditional tail expectation ($\mathrm{CTE}_{95\%}$) risk measure of the output.[4] This seems like a

---

[3] Other risks, such as liquidity or basis risk, may also need to be allowed for in the additional capital requirement.

[4] This only applies if the office does not use a risk mitigation strategy such as dynamic hedging. Requirements are more complex and relatively more onerous for offices that use dynamic hedging.

reasonable approach and, with the techniques of the last few chapters, is perfectly feasible. For the example in Chapter 9, a GMAB contract with a 10-year initial term and one potential rollover, and with guarantee 100 percent of the premium or fund after rollover, managed without dynamic hedging, the 95 percent CTE capital requirement is $8.60% of the premium. However, that figure only applies to the contract at issue. At every subsequent revaluation the requirement will be different, depending on the relationship between the market value of the fund and the guarantee level and the remaining term. The relationship between the fund market value and the guarantee is summarized in the ratio of the fund value to the guarantee amount, denoted F/G.

In Table 10.1, 95 percent CTE values are given for a 10-year initial term GMAB (with mortality and survival benefits), with a single rollover option at the tenth policy anniversary. The contract details are the same as the section on risk measures for GMAB liability in Chapter 9. Each

TABLE 10.1   Ninety-five percent CTE for 20-Year GMAB contract maturing at age 70. Figures given as percentage of fund value.

Term to Maturity	Fund Value/Guarantee							
	0.7	0.8	1.0	1.2	1.4	1.6	1.8	2.0
20	19.14	14.69	8.60	4.99	3.01	1.92	1.32	0.99
19	22.21	17.11	10.11	5.95	3.69	2.52	1.93	1.59
18	26.03	20.17	12.12	7.37	4.88	3.62	2.97	2.61
17	30.42	23.70	14.44	8.81	5.72	4.12	3.30	2.83
16	36.01	28.30	17.59	10.92	7.20	5.29	4.26	3.74
15	40.62	31.75	19.42	11.94	7.97	6.02	5.11	4.68
14	47.28	37.19	22.95	14.05	9.14	6.71	5.59	5.05
13	52.69	41.11	24.75	14.59	9.55	7.36	6.50	6.16
12	57.92	44.45	25.67	14.25	9.23	7.53	6.95	6.80
11	62.44	46.92	25.33	13.31	9.32	8.16	7.82	7.73
Rollover								
10	20.06	15.37	8.92	4.82	2.05	0.39	−0.52	−1.01
9	23.57	18.22	10.85	6.17	2.96	0.96	−0.15	−0.79
8	27.39	21.29	12.87	7.48	3.76	1.40	0.10	−0.62
7	31.43	24.47	14.85	8.66	4.37	1.63	0.19	0.55
6	36.21	28.27	17.28	10.20	5.26	2.08	0.47	−0.40
5	42.01	32.93	20.34	12.19	6.49	2.69	0.78	−0.16
4	47.60	37.22	22.80	13.42	6.84	2.72	0.80	−0.10
3	53.72	41.85	25.33	14.54	6.94	2.54	0.68	−0.13
2	60.23	46.64	27.68	15.21	6.47	2.15	0.49	−0.13
1	62.63	48.07	26.29	11.89	3.05	0.46	−0.17	−0.34

number in the table is the CTE determined from 10,000 simulations for a contract with final maturity at age 70. The CTEs are given for a range of terms to maturity and F/G ratios. This table is quite extensive because we will use the entries later in this chapter for forward projection of capital requirements.

The table shows that the CTE requirements are substantial at all terms if the guarantee is at-the-money or in-the-money; or for out-of-the-money guarantees the requirements are substantial at all terms if there is a rollover remaining. The bold figure in the F/G = 1.0 column is particularly important. At the rollover date the F/G ratio returns to 1.0, which means that the value in bold is the capital requirement factor (per $100 fund value) immediately after the rollover, regardless of the starting F/G ratio. The contract illustrated has only one rollover.

The negative values in the final columns after the rollover indicate that even allowing for the extreme circumstances using the CTE risk measure, the possible outgo on guarantee is less than the income from margin offset. Because treating a negative reserve as an asset leads to withdrawal risk, the insurer may not take credit in these cases, so the actual solvency capital may have a minimum of zero. In fact, it does not seem very important whether there are one or two rollovers remaining; the main factor determining the CTE level for a rollover contract is the term until next rollover. The CTE requirements before a rollover are very similar whether there is one or more than one rollover remaining. The requirements between the final rollover and maturity do differ from the pre-rollover figures for the out-of-the-money guarantees. This is illustrated in Figure 10.1 where the 95 percent CTE estimates are plotted for a 30-year GMAB contract with two rollovers. The results are plotted for four different F/G ratios, and by term since the last rollover or inception. The 30-year contract is plotted in three separate lines, one for each 10-year period.

For contracts at-the-money or in-the-money, the term to the next rollover is the only important factor; it does not matter if, at the end of the 10-year period, the contract rolls over or terminates. For contracts out-of-the-money there is a difference; the bold line in each plot represents the final 10 years. The requirements are lower in the final 10 years for these contracts than in the earlier periods. This is because the ultimate liability in the final 10 years for an out-of-the-money contract is zero, whereas in the earlier periods the ultimate liability is the at-the-money CTE for a newly rolled over policy. Note that any contract will vary in its F/G ratio over the term, and so will not follow a particular column of this table but will jump from column to column as the fund changes value over time.

It is good practice to determine some estimate of the standard errors involved whenever stochastic simulation is used to estimate a measure.

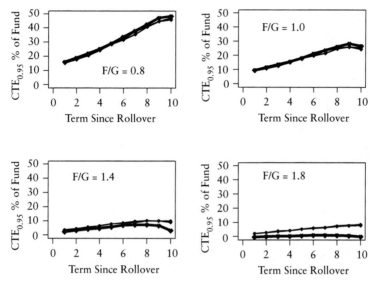

FIGURE 10.1 CTE contract, by year since last rollover. The bold line indicates the final 10 years to maturity; thin lines indicate periods prior to rollover.

For some of the numbers in Table 10.2 standard errors have been calculated for the F/G = 1 case by repeating the 10,000 simulations 50 times, each time with an independent set of random numbers. The 95 percent CTE is calculated for each set of simulations, and the estimated standard error is the standard deviation of these 50 estimates. The relative standard error is the ratio of the estimated standard error to the estimated CTE.

Standard errors vary by the "moneyness" of the guarantee, but not by very much. For example, for a contract with 15 years to final maturity,

TABLE 10.2 Estimated standard errors for 95 percent CTE for 20-year GMAB contract, F/G = 1.0.

	Term to Maturity					
	20	15	12	10	5	2
Estimated standard error	0.22	0.34	0.46	0.25	0.37	0.50
Relative standard error	2.5%	1.7%	1.8%	2.6%	1.8%	1.8%

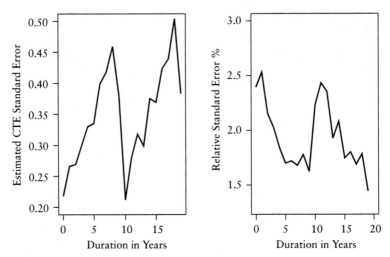

FIGURE 10.2   Estimated standard errors and relative standard errors for 95 percent CTE, 20-year GMAB, with F/G = 1.

renewal in 5 years, the estimated standard error for F/G = 0.8 is 0.350, for F/G = 1.0 is 0.340, and for F/G = 2.0 is 0.227.

The figures for F/G = 1.0 are also illustrated in Figure 10.2. In the left-hand plot, the estimated standard errors are plotted for a 10-year contract with a single rollover at time 10 (i.e., a maximum term of 20 years), showing increasing standard errors as the contract nears rollover or maturity. However, the right-hand plot shows the relative standard errors—that is, the ratio of the standard errors to the estimated CTEs, which indicates that the standard errors are increasing slower than the CTEs.

CAPITAL REQUIREMENTS: DYNAMIC-HEDGING RISK MANAGEMENT

The capital requirement under a dynamic-hedging strategy comprises the capital allocated to the hedge itself, plus an allowance for the additional costs that may be required to cover transactions costs and hedging error. The income from the margin offset is taken away from these costs. Treating these random liabilities in the same way as the random ultimate guarantee liability in the previous section, a reasonable capital requirement might be the 95 percent CTE for the present value of the projected net costs, discounted at the risk-free rate of interest.

As an example, the GMAB contract already examined in the previous section is reconsidered here, under the assumption of dynamic-hedging

TABLE 10.3 Ninety-five percent CTE for 20-Year GMAB; figures given as percentage of fund value and include hedge value.

Term to Final Maturity	Fund Value/Guarantee							
	0.7	0.8	1.0	1.2	1.4	1.6	1.8	2.0
20	8.67	5.79	2.32	0.61	−0.31	−0.82	−1.07	−1.20
19	10.53	7.00	2.96	0.99	−0.07	−0.62	−0.92	−1.06
18	12.38	8.21	3.61	1.38	0.17	−0.43	−0.76	−0.92
17	14.71	9.88	4.54	1.96	0.63	−0.06	−0.44	−0.64
16	17.03	11.55	5.48	2.53	1.10	0.32	−0.13	−0.36
15	20.19	13.57	6.46	3.18	1.58	0.66	0.12	−0.12
14	23.35	15.59	7.44	3.82	2.06	1.00	0.36	0.12
13	27.90	18.69	8.62	4.20	2.23	1.26	0.74	0.51
12	32.45	21.79	9.80	4.57	2.40	1.52	1.12	0.90
11	36.97	23.28	9.06	4.31	2.17	1.27	1.14	1.07
				Rollover				
10	9.50	6.03	2.13	0.24	−0.79	−1.31	−1.59	−1.75
9	11.33	7.15	2.87	0.71	−0.44	−1.07	−1.40	−1.58
8	13.16	8.27	3.62	1.18	−0.08	−0.83	−1.21	−1.41
7	15.25	9.95	4.45	1.75	0.26	−0.61	−1.05	−1.26
6	17.35	11.63	5.28	2.31	0.61	−0.39	−0.89	−1.11
5	20.51	13.72	6.08	2.72	0.93	−0.11	−0.68	−0.93
4	23.66	15.81	6.88	3.13	1.25	0.17	−0.47	−0.74
3	27.76	18.34	7.99	3.64	1.53	0.29	−0.33	−0.60
2	31.86	20.88	9.11	4.15	1.81	0.41	−0.19	−0.47
1	36.60	23.91	9.92	3.58	0.87	−0.11	−0.37	−0.42

risk management. Estimated values for the capital requirement figures for various terms to maturity, and for various starting F/G ratios, are given in Table 10.3. These figures are not definitive, they depend very strongly on the particular assumptions, and contract details that we have used that might not be appropriate for all contracts. The GMAB contract simulated is the same as we have used in previous examples. It is further assumed that the insurer holds a Black-Scholes hedge in respect of the liability, and rebalances the hedge monthly.[5] The volatility used to determine the hedge is 20 percent. This is higher than the average volatility assumed in the stock return model, which is a two-state regime switching lognormal (RSLN) model with TSE parameters from Table 6.2. Using a higher volatility in the hedge means that we are over-hedging; that is, the hedge error is generally

---

[5]In practice, the insurer would use futures in the underlying stocks or index to achieve the required position in the segregated fund.

negative because the true liability cost is less than that assumed with the higher volatility assumption.

The figures shown in Table 10.3 are for the total capital requirement. That includes the hedge cost plus the reserve in respect of future hedging errors and transactions costs. The reserve for the unhedged liability, $V^{T\&H}$, is given in Table 10.4. These are the figures from Table 10.3 minus the appropriate hedge cost for each entry. All entries are based on 1,000 scenarios.

Some interesting features of these two tables are:

▪ Most of the entries in the Table 10.4 are negative. As explained in the introduction to the example in this section, most hedging errors are negative, because we deliberately over-hedge by assuming a higher value for volatility than that in the model. It would also be possible to

TABLE 10.4   Ninety-five percent CTE (or unhedged liablility 20-year GMAB; figures given as percentage of fund value).

Term to Final Maturity	Fund Value/Guarantee							
	0.7	0.8	1.0	1.2	1.4	1.6	1.8	2.0
20	−2.98	−2.80	−2.78	−2.78	−2.80	−2.81	−2.78	−2.73
19	−2.84	−2.79	−2.74	−2.74	−2.79	−2.80	−2.78	−2.74
18	−2.71	−2.77	−2.70	−2.70	−2.79	−2.79	−2.79	−2.75
17	−2.64	−2.60	−2.45	−2.48	−2.55	−2.60	−2.64	−2.64
16	−2.58	−2.43	−2.21	−2.26	−2.31	−2.40	−2.49	−2.53
15	−2.44	−2.29	−1.93	−1.90	−2.00	−2.22	−2.42	−2.49
14	−2.30	−2.15	−1.65	−1.55	−1.69	−2.04	−2.36	−2.46
13	−1.94	−1.36	−0.89	−1.15	−1.54	−1.91	−2.19	−2.33
12	−1.58	−0.57	−0.14	−0.75	−1.38	−1.78	−2.03	−2.20
11	−2.96	−1.85	−0.41	−0.39	−1.50	−2.23	−2.33	−2.40
				Rollover				
10	−1.57	−1.69	−1.79	−1.88	−2.01	−2.04	−2.04	−2.04
9	−1.19	−1.52	−1.44	−1.57	−1.72	−1.82	−1.85	−1.86
8	−0.81	−1.35	−1.09	−1.27	−1.43	−1.60	−1.67	−1.68
7	−0.60	−0.86	−0.70	−0.84	−1.10	−1.36	−1.48	−1.51
6	−0.40	−0.37	−0.32	−0.41	−0.78	−1.12	−1.29	−1.33
5	0.22	0.23	0.08	−0.03	−0.38	−0.76	−1.01	−1.10
4	0.84	0.83	0.48	0.36	0.02	−0.39	−0.73	−0.86
3	1.36	1.53	1.51	1.19	0.58	−0.09	−0.49	−0.68
2	1.87	2.23	2.54	2.03	1.15	0.21	−0.25	−0.49
1	1.44	3.03	4.16	2.41	0.68	−0.14	−0.38	−0.42

use a lower value for volatility, which would decrease the hedge cost but increase the additional capital requirements. Also, these figures include future margin offset income. The outgo is on transactions costs.

■ The total capital figures from Table 10.3 behave similarly to those for the actuarial approach in Table 10.1, with less capital required for contract out-of-the-money, with requirements broadly increasing, and with the discontinuity immediately after the rollover at the end of the tenth year. However, the total capital requirements using dynamic hedging are lower at all points than those required for actuarial risk management, though for out-of-the-money options nearing maturity the figures are very similar for the two approaches.

■ The unhedged liability reserve table (Table 10.4) shows a slightly different pattern to the total requirement figures in Table 10.3: Requirements are broadly increasing with term without the sharp adjustment for the rollover, and with higher values for at-the-money guarantees than for in-the-money or out-of-the-money guarantees.

A graphical comparison of the difference between the capital requirements for the actuarial approach and the dynamic-hedging approach is given in Figure 10.3. In this figure, the total balance sheet requirements are plotted for various F/G ratios for both the actuarial risk management and (in broken line) dynamic-hedging risk management strategies. The x-axis represents the duration of a 20-year GMAB contract; the y-axis shows the 95 percent CTE, as a percentage of the fund value. The rollover is assumed to occur at duration 10 years, and final maturity at duration 20 years.

The figure shows that for lower values of F/G (near the money guarantees) the actuarial approach requires substantially more capital than the dynamic-hedging approach. This is also true even where the guarantee is well out-of-the-money before the rollover. Only for the final 10 years of the contract are the capital requirements under the two approaches similar.

However, this is not the whole story. Although the capital requirements are generally higher for the actuarial approach, the overall cost may be lower. It is important to remember that the solvency capital requirements under the actuarial approach are held in the event of an unfavorable investment experience. If an investment experience is favorable, then the capital is not required and it is released back to the insurer; the only cost here is the cost of carrying the capital for the period of the contract. For the dynamic-hedging approach only the unhedged liability reserve is available to the company if the experience is favorable; if the guarantee ends up out-of-the-money, then the hedge will end up with zero value and none of the hedge cost is returned to the company (except for that emerging in hedging error). One of the objectives of the cash-flow analysis described in this chapter is to provide a method of assessing the advantages and

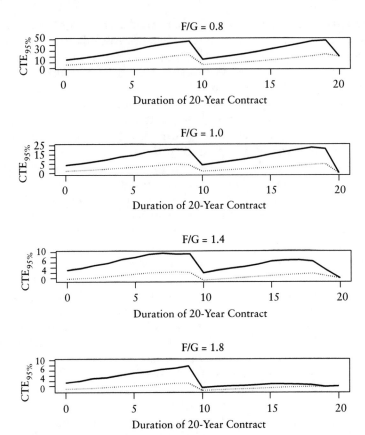

FIGURE 10.3 Comparison of capital requirements for a GMAB contract, actuarial risk management (unbroken lines) and dynamic-hedging risk management (broken lines).

disadvantages of the two approaches, taking the cost of additional solvency capital into account, where appropriate.

EMERGING COSTS WITH SOLVENCY CAPITAL

In the previous two sections, the capital requirements were explored in some detail for a GMAB contract with a 10-year nominal term and a 20-year actual term, for a range of F/G ratios. Each CTE value in the previous tables is a result of 1,000 or 10,000 simulations, and some of these projections take significant computer time. The objective in this section is to use stochastic simulation to project all the cash flows for a contract, including the capital requirements. To use the methods of the last two sections would require a two-tier simulation process—that is, within a single simulation of the emerging costs, we would need to rerun several thousand simulations every time the capital requirements are assumed to be recalculated. This means that if we want to run, say, just 1,000 projections of the emerging costs with a 20-year horizon and annual recalculation of capital requirements, and supposing that only 1,000 projections are used to determine the appropriate capital requirements each year, then in total we have 20 million simulations. Clearly this soon becomes impractical.

Several short cuts have been suggested to manage this problem:

- Use a much smaller number of simulations for the second-tier simulations (e.g., just 100); although the standard errors are large, this approach is much more accurate than reducing the number of first-tier simulations.

   The 95 percent CTE used would be simply the average of the five largest values from each second-tier simulation. The number of simulations required is reduced to 2 million, which is still a large number for a complex process.
- Use approximate analytic methods; for example, in the actuarial approach we can calculate the capital requirement for a simple GMMB analytically, provided management charge income is ignored. For a combined GMMB and guaranteed minimum death benefit (GMDB) it may be possible to make a simple adjustment to allow roughly for the income from margin offset and the outgo on death benefits. However, no analytic approach is available for the GMAB.
- Use a factor-based approach. Using the tables developed in the previous two sections, the capital requirements at each year end can be approximated by interpolating the table values for the projected F/G ratio. For complex products, this appears a reasonable compromise of computational efficiency and accuracy. This is the method adopted in the example that is used in the remainder of this chapter.

EXAMPLE: EMERGING COSTS FOR 20-YEAR GMAB

Net Present Value of Future Loss

In this section, we use a 20-year GMAB contract, with both death and survival benefits, to illustrate the information available from a stochastic emerging cost analysis. Adopting actuarial tradition, in the graphs in this section the random variable under consideration is the *loss* random variable (finance tradition uses profit; actuaries in finance tend to use either depending on the context). The net present value of future loss random variable is denoted NPVFL.

The 20-year GMAB that we use is assumed to have a rollover benefit after 10 years and to mature on the twentieth policy anniversary if the policyholder survives. The contract details and assumptions are identical to the example in the section on risk measures for GMAB liability in Chapter 9. Reserves are incorporated using the interpolated factor approach described in the preceding section. This means that prior to the emerging cost analysis we have calculated reserves for a range of F/G values and for all integer terms for the 20-year contract.

The value to the insurance company shareholders of the GMAB segregated fund portfolio should be calculated using an appropriate risk discount rate. The risk discount rate represents the return required by the shareholders; it is also known as a *hurdle rate*. Typical risk discount rates would vary from perhaps 10 percent to 20 percent, with higher values for riskier contracts.

In Figure 10.4 the mean values for the NPVFL are given for a range of risk discount rates for the actuarial and dynamic-hedging approaches. These values are calculated from 1,000 scenarios for the 20-year contract, generated using the RSLN stock return model. The same scenarios are used for the two strategies. Using the same investment scenarios gives more information, because it eliminates sampling error as a source of difference between the methods.

A negative mean NPVFL implies that the expected outcome is a profit, whereas positive indicates an expected loss. Figure 10.4 shows that the actuarial method is profitable, on average, at risk discount rates less than around 11 percent, and the dynamic-hedging approach is profitable, on average, for risk discount rates less than around 14.5 percent. If the

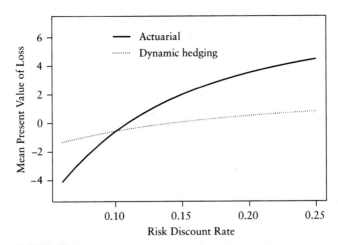

FIGURE 10.4   Mean NPVFL with actuarial and dynamic-hedging risk management.

shareholders' required return on capital is higher than these figures, it will be necessary to return to the contract design and adjust accordingly. Note that setting a higher margin offset rate will increase the management charge total, which will, in turn, increase the liability. Balancing income and outgo requires some experimentation with the contract design.

The graph also shows that at very low discount rates the actuarial approach results in a higher mean expected profit than dynamic hedging. However, the actuarial approach is much more sensitive to the risk discount rate, because the capital carried is so much higher than for the dynamic-hedging approach, and the analysis includes the allowance for the cost of higher capital requirements. So, for risk discount rates higher than around 10 percent per year, the dynamic-hedging approach is more profitable on average.

We can also use the simulations to investigate risk by looking at the whole distribution rather than just the mean. Using 3,000 simulations, and using a risk discount rate of 12 percent, we can derive the simulated density functions for the NPVFL random variable. These are plotted in Figure 10.5. The plot shows that both approaches have median and mode NPVFL of around zero—that is, either strategy will result, on average, at roughly breakeven using a 12 percent interest rate. This means that the company expects, on average, to return the hurdle rate of 12 percent to the shareholders for the use of their capital using either strategy. However, the two strategies are not equally risky. The actuarial strategy shows a substantially heavier right tail, indicating that there is a much greater

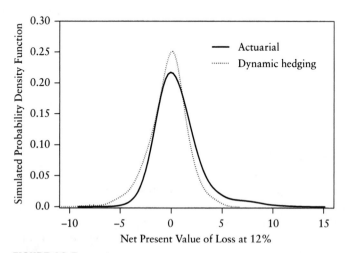

FIGURE 10.5 NPVFL probability density functions at 12 percent risk discount rate, with actuarial and dynamic-hedging risk management.

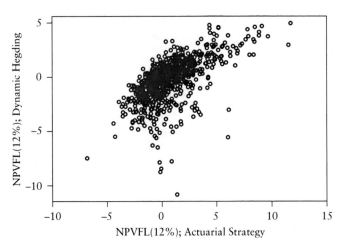

FIGURE 10.6 Simulated NPVFLs (12 percent); actuarial and dynamic-hedging risk management.

probability of a substantial loss experience on the contracts using the actuarial strategy. This is, incidentally, consistent with results using different contracts and assumptions in Hardy (1998).

Because we have used the same investment scenarios for the actuarial and dynamic-hedging results, it is possible to explore the relationship between the results. In Figure 10.6 the results of 1,000 simulations of the NPVFL are plotted, with the x-axis representing the NPVFL under the actuarial management strategy and the y-axis representing the NPVFL under the dynamic-hedging strategy. This shows broadly that the two methods are sensitive to the same scenarios, but the potential losses are substantially greater under the actuarial strategy. However, it is certainly not guaranteed that the hedging strategy will result in a lower future loss; there is approximately a 65 percent probability that the dynamic-hedging approach would be more profitable at the 12 percent risk discount rate.

Simulated Cash Flows

In all the results of the previous section the cash flows generated by the model have been summarized in a net present value. We can also look at the cash-flow patterns. Some sample cash flows are plotted in Figure 10.7. These are annual cash flows; intra-year income and outgo is accumulated to the year-end at the risk-free rate of interest. The broken lines are the cash flows using dynamic hedging, the regular lines are the cash flows for the same investment scenarios using the actuarial risk-management strategy. The initial cash flows for a contract with single premium of $100 are $8.55

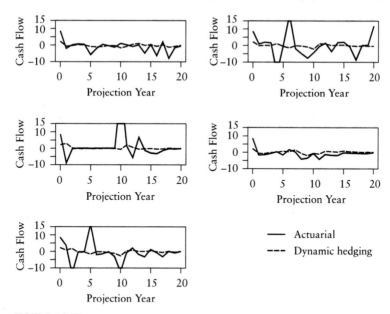

FIGURE 10.7 Sample cash flows for 20-year GMAB; actuarial and dynamic-hedging risk management.

using the actuarial method (which is the initial capital required less the initial margin offset income) and $2.35 for the dynamic-hedging strategy.

In each of these five sample simulations the cash flows using the actuarial approach are more variable than the cash flows under the dynamic-hedging strategy, though in one case not by very much. In the top right plot, the final cash flow using the actuarial strategy is relatively large. In this scenario there was a substantial final payment under the guarantee, which exceeded the capital held using the actuarial approach. However, the payment does not show up under the dynamic-hedging strategy because the hedge has done the job of meeting the guarantee. The middle left example demonstrates the same situation for the rollover guarantee liability in the tenth projection year: A large payout drastically affects the payouts using the actuarial risk-management approach, but is absorbed by the hedge and, therefore, does not register any shock to the dynamic-hedging cash flows. This is actually a dramatic demonstration of the hedge achieving its objective. The bottom left plot shows a scenario where a substantial capital requirement was held until the tenth year, indicating that the F/G ratio was low. However, the capital was not actually required, because there was no rollover payment, so it was released at the end of the tenth year. This release resulted in a large negative cash flow under the actuarial approach; again, no major effect was registered under the dynamic-hedging strategy.

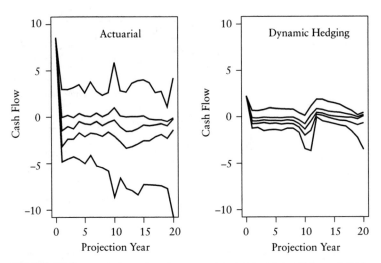

FIGURE 10.8   Cash flow distributions: 5th, 25th, 50th, 75th, and 95th percentiles of cash flow distributions; actuarial and dynamic-hedging risk management.

The range of outcomes of the annual cash flows are shown again in Figure 10.8. Here we have plotted some quantiles for the cash flows in each year; the left hand plot shows the cash flow 5th, 25th, 50th, 75th, and 95th percentiles using the actuarial approach, and the right plot gives the same percentiles for the dynamic-hedging approach, on the same axes. The quantiles are calculated using 1,000 scenarios.

The difference in range is very striking. As we showed more informally in Figure 10.7, it is clear that the cash flows under the dynamic-hedging strategy are much less variable than those under the actuarial strategy. The perturbations around the tenth projection year result from the additional variation from the rollover payment at that time.

Decisions

For this example the pricing, at 50 basis points margin offset, only breaks even at around 11 percent (actuarial strategy) or 14.5 percent (dynamic hedging). The figure for the actuarial strategy is a relatively low hurdle rate for a fairly risky contract, so the pricing or benefit design might need reevaluating.

All of the results indicate that the dynamic-hedging approach to risk management is preferred to the actuarial approach except at very low-risk discount rates. Note, however, that this is just an example. For different contracts or for different investment assumptions, a different conclusion may be appropriate. The important message is that stochastic emerging costs analysis provides solid evidence to support the decision-making process.

CHAPTER 11

Forecast Uncertainty

SOURCES OF UNCERTAINTY

With straightforward stochastic simulation, we assume that the model used accurately mimics the true process, and that the parameters adopted are correct. Under these assumptions, forecast error is entirely due to *random effects* or sampling error, which is readily subject to statistical analysis. Quantifying this potential error is the first topic of this chapter. We also discuss practical methods of reducing the potential for sampling error by using variance reduction techniques.

However, despite the efforts outlined in Chapter 3, the model that provides the best fit historically may not be the best model prospectively, and the error from using a model that is not an accurate predictor of the equity price path distribution must be considered. We discuss *model uncertainty* in the last section of this chapter.

Even if we have the best model structure, the parameters derived from the historical data may not be accurate for prediction. The parameters used for the results in previous chapters are those emerging from the maximum likelihood exercise described in Chapter 3. However, estimating parameters involves some uncertainty, and although the maximum likelihood parameter set may be optimal in the sense of the overall fit to historic data, many other parameter combinations provide a fit almost equally good and may be more accurate for future forecasts. One source of *parameter uncertainty* is pure random error in the estimation procedure. Another is that shifts in parameter values have occurred over the term of the historic data, and we need to consider carefully the period of observation used for estimation purposes. Parameter uncertainty is discussed later in the chapter. In this chapter we consider parameter uncertainty using Bayesian and stress-testing methods.

Finally, there are sources of forecast error that are not susceptible to statistical analysis. Economic shocks that change the whole econometric structure may strike at some time in the forecast period, rendering useless the historical evidence used to determine the model and parameters. Those involved in econometric forecasting must be aware of this possibility. It has been used as a reason not to attempt to forecast economic variables at all. This was certainly the view of early economists such as Morganstern and Persons in the early twentieth century; their views are described in Morgan (1990). However, this view was gradually replaced by an acceptance of time series modeling of econometric data, using the standard theory of statistical inference, but with an awareness that econometric and social time series are more susceptible to structural shifts than physical time series.

The nihilistic view that there is no point in using the past to forecast the future is still espoused by some, so we should consider the alternatives. One is pure guesswork. This has no advantages over statistical methods. In fact, resorting to guessing or "actuarial judgment" without technical analysis is likely to be very dangerous. A second conclusion drawn by some actuaries is that stochastic models should be rejected in favor of old-fashioned deterministic methods. But deterministic modeling misses so much of the point with financial guarantees—especially the tail risks— that it is certain to provide more inaccurate or inadequate results than stochastic modeling, however uncertain the models and parameters. As long as insurers issue contracts involving financial guarantees, stochastic models are required for any useful guidance as to how to manage the risks involved.

RANDOM SAMPLING ERROR

All the analysis of the liabilities discussed in previous chapters relied on stochastic simulation. This starts with a random number generator that is used to generate random paths for fund values, which in turn are used to determine the contract cash flows. In this section we address the question of how much the original random sample affected the results. In other words, how might the results change if we repeated the projections using a different set of random numbers with the same probability distribution as the first, and can we reduce the effect of sampling variability?

The answer depends on what particular results we are interested in and, crucially, on how many scenarios are used in the projection. For example, the answer will differ if the output of interest is the mean future loss compared with a tail measure such as the 95 percent conditional tail expectation (CTE) of the future loss, and the uncertainty arising from a sample of 1,000 projections will clearly be greater than if we use 100,000 projections. In fact, a simple method of reducing the effects of sampling error from simulation is to increase the number of projections. This is not always practical if the simulation is very complex.

Expected Values

It is simplest to consider the effect of sampling error on expected values, using elementary statistical theory. Ordinary stochastic simulation provides a random, independent sample from the distribution in which we are interested. Suppose, for example, that we generate N values for the present value of future loss under an equity-linked contract, labeled l_i for $i = 1, 2, \ldots, N$. Let L represent the random variable. Obviously, the estimated value of $E[L]$ is the mean loss:

$$\bar{l} = \frac{\sum_{i=1}^{N} l_i}{N}$$

Because the individual L_i are independent and identically distributed, the central limit theorem tells us that $\bar{l}$ is unbiased, that is, $E[\bar{l}] = E[L]$, and that for sufficiently large N, $\bar{l}$ is approximately normally distributed with a standard deviation of $\sigma_L/\sqrt{N}$, where σ_L is the standard deviation of the L. So, the standard error of $\bar{l}$ as an estimator of $E[L]$ is of the order of $1/\sqrt{N}$. A 95 percent confidence interval for the true mean is

$$\bar{l} \pm 1.96 \frac{\sigma_L}{\sqrt{N}}$$

which, using $N = 100$ projections, would have width of approximately 39 percent of the distribution standard deviation, decreasing to 3.9 percent with 10,000 scenarios.

As an example, in Figure 11.1 we show the results of a simulation comprising 10,000 projections of the net present value of liabilities under a 20-year guaranteed minimum accumulation benefit (GMAB) contract, with actuarial risk management. The graph shows the mean as well as the upper and lower 95 percent confidence intervals, all estimated from different numbers of projections. The contract is identical to that in Chapter 10 in the section on emerging costs for a 20-year GMAB. This is a 20-year GMAB with initial fund value and guarantee value both equal to $100, and with a single rollover due on the tenth anniversary of the valuation date. There is no allowance for cost of capital requirement, and we discount at the risk-free rate of interest, as we did in Chapter 9 to determine capital requirements.

In Figure 11.2 we show the relative error in the estimated mean for different numbers of scenarios, that is

$$\text{Relative error for } k \text{ scenarios} = \frac{\sum_{i=1}^{k} l_i/k}{\sum_{i=1}^{10,000} l_i/10,000} - 1.0$$

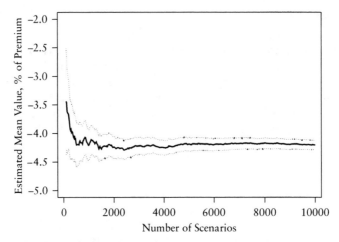

FIGURE 11.1   Estimated mean and 95 percent confidence interval for E[L], based on different numbers of scenarios.

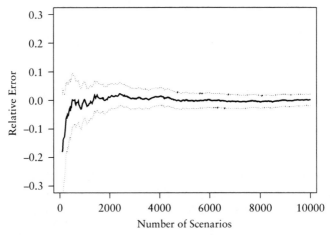

FIGURE 11.2   Relative error for E[L] estimation for GMAB contract.

For both Figures 11.1 and 11.2, the curve starts from 100 scenarios. Note that estimates based on fewer than 1,000 scenarios are very unreliable.

Quantile Risk Measure

When we are concerned with the more extreme parts of the distribution, the relative errors tend to increase. The quantile risk measure is described in Chapter 9, and, in the section on simulation in Chapter 9, a method is given for constructing a nonparametric confidence interval for the quantile risk measure.

The quantile risk measure is estimated by ordering the simulated quantities, so let $l_{(i)}$ represent the ith smallest simulated value from the N scenarios. The estimated α-quantile is $l_{(N\alpha)}$. The 100β percent confidence interval from Chapter 9 is:

$$(l_{(N\alpha - A)}, \; l_{(N\alpha + A)})$$

where

$$A = \Phi^{-1}\left(\frac{1 + \beta}{2}\right) \sqrt{N\alpha(1 - \alpha)} \tag{11.1}$$

and the width of this interval depends on how heavy-tailed the simulated distribution is. In Figure 11.3 the 95 percent quantile estimates for the 20-year GMAB are plotted for 100 to 10,000 simulations, together with the binomial confidence intervals. The scale is changed from Figure 11.2. The path is very much more volatile than that of the mean, and the confidence intervals at lower scenario numbers are very wide. Even after 10,000 simulations, the 95 percent confidence interval for the 95 percent quantile risk measure is six times wider than that for the mean.

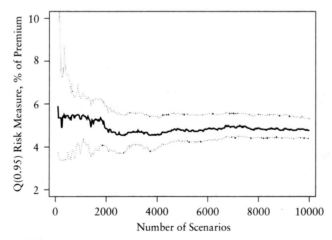

FIGURE 11.3 Estimated 95 percent quantile risk measure and 95 percent confidence interval for the loss random variable, based on different numbers of scenarios.

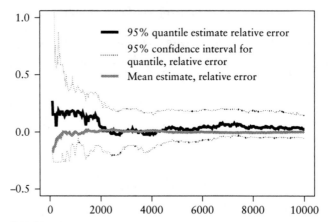

FIGURE 11.4 Relative errors for the 95 percent quantile risk measure and its 95 percent confidence interval, based on different numbers of scenarios.

Figure 11.4 shows the relative error for the quantile and the confidence limits. The error is relative to the value from 100,000 scenarios. At the start of the simulation, after 100 to 200 scenarios, the relative error of 0.5 means that the estimated value using, say, 200 scenarios is 50 percent higher than the ultimate estimate, taken from 100,000 scenarios. The 95 percent confidence interval ranges from 75 percent to 120 percent of the estimated value after 10,000 simulations, compared with a confidence interval of 98 percent to 102 percent for the mean. The grey line on the plot is the relative error for the mean from Figure 11.1, shown to the same scale to demonstrate how much faster it converges. In fact, continuing the simulation to 100,000 scenarios gives an estimated quantile of 4.635, compared with 4.681 after 10,000 scenarios. Even after 100,000 scenarios the quantile risk measure is only accurate to within around 1 percent of the value to which it converges after 1,000,000 scenarios. Of course, convergence would be even slower for higher values of α in the quantile risk measure.

The CTE Risk Measure

The CTE(α) risk measure is defined in the section on the CTE risk measure in Chapter 9, the broad explanation being that it is the expected loss given that the loss is in the upper $(1 - \alpha)$ quantile of the loss distribution. Using simulation, the CTE(α) is estimated from averaging the upper $100(1 - \alpha)$ percent of the simulations. One of the justifications given in Chapter 9 for using the CTE rather than the quantile risk measure was that, in averaging the upper part of the distribution, we expect less sampling error than the quantile approach of picking out a single value. On the other hand, it

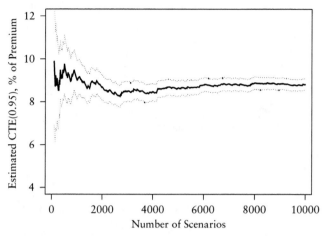

FIGURE 11.5 Estimated 95 percent CTE risk measure with 95 percent confidence interval, based on different numbers of scenarios.

was also noted that the calculation of confidence intervals is more difficult, with no straightforward analytic calculation available unless the quantile measure V_α is known rather than estimated from the simulation. We can estimate the 95 percent confidence interval using the standard deviation of the upper $100(1 - \alpha)$ percent of the sample, dividing by $\sqrt{N(1 - \alpha)}$ for the standard error, and although this is biased low, because it ignores the uncertainty around the use of the $(N\alpha)$th value as an estimate of V_α, it appears from experiments to be reasonably accurate. Also, as mentioned in Chapter 9, the work by Hancock and Manistre (2002) provides a good analytic approximation.

In Figure 11.5 we show the CTE values for different scenario numbers. In Figure 11.6 we show the estimated relative errors for both the quantile and CTE risk measures, both using $\alpha = 95$ percent. Although both measures are substantially more volatile than the mean, the CTE does prove to be more stable than the quantile measure. In fact, the 95 percent CTE is a more extreme risk measure than the 95 percent quantile, the CTE being closer to the 98 percent quantile.

VARIANCE REDUCTION

Introduction

In the previous section, we demonstrated that uncertainty can be reduced by increasing the number of scenarios, but that it may take a large number

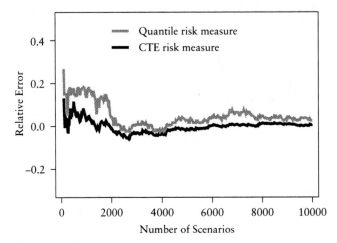

FIGURE 11.6   Relative errors for the 95 percent CTE(0.95) risk measure and for quantile(0.95) risk measure, based on different numbers of scenarios.

of extra scenarios to achieve the desired increase in accuracy. *Variance reduction* is used to improve the accuracy of an estimate more efficiently than just ploughing through larger and larger numbers of simulations.

The standard error of an estimate of a mean value from a distribution with standard deviation σ is $\sigma/\sqrt{N}$. Recall that both the CTE and quantile risk measures can be rewritten as mean values of a transformed distribution,[1] so the standard error formulation applies to other risk measures as well as mean values. By using an increased number of simulations, we are reducing the standard error by increasing the denominator of the standard error. With variance reduction our aim is to decrease σ. The complication is that where we are interested in a risk measure other than the mean, σ represents the variance of a transformed distribution, so variance reduction methods depend on the output variable (e.g., the risk measure) of interest in a way that straightforward stochastic simulation does not.

Variance reduction is discussed in general terms in simulation textbooks, such as Ross (1996). Boyle, Broadie, and Glasserman (1997) survey applications of variance reduction in option pricing, and this section draws from that paper. Boyle and Tan (2003) also give a very accessible introduction.

Most of the applications for variance reduction focus on the use of simulation to estimate a mean value, and some do not adapt well where the concern is around the tail of a distribution rather than a central location measure. Some also are not readily applicable to problems involving a

---

[1]See Wirch and Hardy (1999).

series of (dependent) cash flows. Importantly, some variance reduction techniques designed for estimation of quantities dependent on the center of the distribution will give worse estimates of tail measures than ordinary simulation. Using standard simulation, the output variable need not affect the simulation process; that is, we can use the same set of projections to estimate both the mean loss and the 95 percent CTE, though we need fewer scenarios to get an accurate estimate of the mean than for the CTE. Variance reduction techniques do depend on the output variable, so different output objectives may need to be simulated in separate exercises.

In the following sections we describe some of the variance reduction techniques in common use. Even though not all are useful for the particular applications of interest here, and some will actually make things worse, they are all listed for ease of reference, and because readers may find other uses.

Moment Matching

Very simple in concept, moment matching involves ensuring that the underlying random variables used in a simulation exercise have moments that exactly match the distributions from which they are drawn. For example, generating N random variates from a lognormal distribution with parameters μ and σ requires drawing N normal random numbers with mean μ and variance σ, denoted $x_1, x_2, \ldots, x_N$, say. Because of sampling error, the mean and variance of the sample, $\bar{x}$ and s_x^2, will differ a little from the distribution mean and variance μ and σ. So we might translate the random variables x_i to

$$x_i' = \left(\frac{x_i - \bar{x}}{s}\right)\sigma + \mu$$

and we know, then, that the x_i' are a sample having mean and variance of exactly μ and σ. In fact, the translated sample is no longer independent, since each x_i' depends on all the original sample through $\bar{x}$. This is a slight technical drawback.

Moment matching is very simple to implement and can dramatically improve estimation in certain circumstances. It works well, for example, for simple contracts, including options that are in-the-money. For typical financial guarantees attached to variable-annuity (VA), segregated fund, or unit-linked contracts, the risk is in the tail and the option is usually well out-of-the-money. The expense of moment matching is large storage requirements in the computing; for a single set of, say, 5,000 scenarios with a 20-year contract, and monthly time units, there are over 10^7 random variables with a regime-switching lognormal (RSLN) investment model.

These would have to be generated, suitably translated, and stored for use in generating the investment returns. For typical segregated fund or VA-type contracts, the improvements in accuracy are not sufficiently large or reliable to warrant this additional computational burden.

As an illustration, we have repeated the example used earlier in this chapter using moment matching. The example is a 20-year GMAB contract with a rollover after 10 years and a 3 percent per year expense charge, of which 0.5 percent is margin offset income. The single premium is $100, and the guarantee before the rollover is also $100. Mortality and withdrawal experience follows the table in Appendix A.

The output variables are the 95 percent quantile and the 95 percent CTE of the net present value of liability, discounted at the risk-free rate of interest, without cost of capital. The contract is projected out to maturity for between 100 and 10,000 scenarios. The investment model is, as usual, the RSLN model. Simulating investment returns using this model involves two random variates for each time unit. The first is uniformly distributed and determines which regime the process is in. The second has the standard Normal(0,1) distribution. The accumulation factor for the month is, then, $\exp(z\,\sigma_\rho + \mu_\rho)$, where $\rho = 1$ or 2 is the regime indicator. We have used moment matching on the Normal(0,1) sample, matching the mean and standard distribution. Table 11.1 shows some results from this exercise. We have given the relative error, relative to the estimated value from 10^6 scenarios of 4.635 for the 95 percent quantile and 8.692 for the 95 percent CTE .

Moment matching appears to help for the quantile measure until 2,000 scenarios, when it gives a substantially worse estimate than that from the unmatched scenarios. The CTE estimate without moment matching is better than with moment matching at 100 and 2,000 scenarios. This result is typical for the out-of-the-money type of option. The result is intuitive because the effect of matching moments is to concentrate on getting accuracy in the center of the distribution, but with most investment guarantee problems we are more interested in the extremes.

Antithetic Variates

The method of antithetic variates is a common and simple variance reduction technique that is related to moment matching. It is important to understand the circumstances in which the method works, particularly because it can actually decrease the accuracy of the estimate if used inappropriately.

The antithetic variate method is commonly used where the underlying random variates are generated from a uniform or normal distribution. Suppose we wish to estimate the mean cost under a guarantee liability, arising in T months, using a lognormal distribution for stock returns. Let μ and σ be parameters for the lognormal model, let G be the guarantee, and

TABLE 11.1 Example of moment matching for quantile and CTE calculation.

Number of Scenarios		Estimated 95% Quantile Relative Error	Estimated 95% CTE Relative Error
100	No moment matching	0.272	0.139
	Matching mean and standard deviation	−0.116	−0.238
500	No moment matching	0.176	0.124
	Matching mean and standard deviation	0.092	0.059
1,000	No moment matching	0.142	0.042
	Matching mean and standard deviation	−0.067	−0.023
2,000	No moment matching	0.046	0.000
	Matching mean and standard deviation	0.092	0.025

let F_0 be the starting fund. For the sake of simplicity, ignore management charges and exits. Then a single scenario can be generated with a single standard random normal deviate Z. That is, having generated N standard random variates Z_i, the estimated cost from the ith scenario is E_i, say, where

$$E_i = (G - F_0 \exp(T\mu + \sqrt{T}\sigma Z_i))^+$$

Now, clearly $-Z_i$ has the same distribution as Z_i, so we can calculate the estimated cost again with $-Z_i$ in place of Z_i; denote this estimate E_i', say. Then the average of these two estimates is

$$E_i^* = \frac{E_i + E_i'}{2}$$

and the mean of the E_i^*'s is a more efficient estimate of the mean guarantee cost than the mean of the E_i's. That is, if we use N scenarios, each doubled up by using Z_i and $-Z_i$, then the estimated mean cost

$$\bar{E}_N^* = \frac{1}{N} \sum_{i=1}^{N} E_i^* = \frac{\bar{E}_N + \bar{E}_N'}{2N}$$

is a more efficient estimator of the mean cost than generating $2N$ values, of E_i.

The intuition is that because Z_i and $-Z_i$ are negatively correlated, errors will be, to some extent, evened out. The theory comes from considering the variances, noting that E_i and E_i' have the same variance, so

$$V[E_i^*] = \frac{1}{4}\left(V[E_i] + V[E_i'] + 2\,\text{Cov}[E_i, E_i']\right) \qquad (11.2)$$

$$= \frac{1}{2}\left(V[E_i] + \text{Cov}[E_i, E_i']\right) \qquad (11.3)$$

The variance of the mean of N values of E_i^* is $V[E_i^*]/N$; the variance of the mean of $2N$ values of E_i is $V[E_i]/2N$. For the antithetic variates to improve the efficiency of the estimator, we require then:

$$V[E_i^*]/N < V[E_i]/2N \;\Leftrightarrow\; \text{Cov}[E_i, E_i'] < 0 \qquad (11.4)$$

That is, that the antithetic estimates have negative covariance. Another common application of antithetic pairs is where the underlying random deviates are drawn from a Uniform(0,1) distribution, where if U_i is drawn from the uniform distribution, its antithetic variate is $1 - U_i$.

Boyle, Broadie, and Glasserman (1997) prove that for antithetic variates to improve the forecast accuracy for some output, the output must be a monotonic function of the random variates used. This is very important—the method may make the forecast less accurate for non-monotonic functions.

An example where the output is not monotonic would be the 20-year, one-rollover GMAB contract. Assume, for example, that a separate fund account follows the lognormal model, and ignore death and survival, management charges, and margin offset. We start with a fund and guarantee, both with a value of \$100. Let the lognormal parameters for the annualized lognormal model be $\mu = 0.08$ and $\sigma = 0.2$. The liability under the ith scenario at time 10, at the first rollover is

$$(100 - 100\exp(\sqrt{10}\sigma\, Z_{i,1} + 10\mu))^+$$

and at the second rollover the liability is

$$(F_{10} - F_{10}\exp(\sqrt{10}\sigma\, Z_{i,2} + 10\mu))^+$$

where

$$F_{10} = \max(100, 100\exp(\sqrt{10}\sigma\, Z_{i,1} + 10\mu))$$

If F_t is the fund before any GMAB benefit due at t, we have for the antithetic variate pairs:

$(Z_{i,1}, Z_{i,2})$	F_{10}	F_{20}	Time 10 Liability	Time 20 Liability
$(3, -3)$	$1,484	$495	0	$989
$(0, 0)$	$222	$495	0	0
$(-3, 3)$	$33	$1,484	$67	0

So we have a positive liability for variates $(3, -3)$ and $(-3, 3)$ and a zero liability for variates $(0, 0)$. Clearly the payoff is not a monotonic function of the normal random variates.

For contracts without rollover or reset features, the payoff may be a monotonic function of the input normal deviates. However, Boyle and Tan (2003) suggest that the method does not work well for deep out-of-the-money options, nor for tail measures. Antithetic variates work best where the output is clearly a monotonic function of the underlying random numbers, and where the focus is the middle of the distribution.

Control Variate

In contrast with antithetic variates and the method of moments, the control variate method has been used successfully for GMMB- and GMAB-type options.

The control variate is a function of the projected scenarios with the following two characteristics:

1. The value of the control variate can be calculated analytically (that is, accurately without simulation).
2. The value of the control variate is highly correlated with the value of the output variable of interest.

The control variate acts to calibrate the simulation.

A simple example would be the net present value of a simple fixed guarantee on death or maturity type contract—that is, a joint GMDB and GMMB contract. The major factor in the calculation is the payoff at maturity and, if the equity index is assumed to follow a lognormal or RSLN or similarly tractable model, the expected value of that payoff (or quantile or CTE measure) can be calculated analytically. This can then be used as a control variate. Then under the simulation we compare the simulated value of the control variate with the known, true value. Provided the control variate is closely correlated with the output we are calculating, it will help the accuracy of the output to adjust by the difference between the known and estimated values of the control variate.

For example, for the joint GMMB and GMDB contract the future loss random variable is

$$L = \text{PV of GMMB} + \text{PV of GMDB} - \text{PV of margin offset}$$

And, because the death benefit, maturity benefit, and margin offset are highly co-dependent, even with a simple process for the fund F_t it is generally not possible to calculate moments of L analytically.

However, consider just the first term, PV of GMMB $= L^*$, say. If we use a suitably tractable distribution for the fund at maturity, F_n, the quantiles, CTEs, and moments of L^* can be calculated analytically. For example, assume a fixed guarantee, G, and let $f_F(x)$ denote the density function for the fund value, and $Q_\alpha(F_n)$ denote the α-quantile of the distribution of F_n,

$$\text{CTE}_\alpha(L^*) = {}_np_x^\tau \int_0^{Q_{1-\alpha}(F_n)} (G - x)^+ f_F(x)dx \qquad (11.5)$$

Clearly, if we are interested in the CTE of L, a major part will come from the distribution of L^* and the CTE of L^* can be used to calibrate the simulation estimate of the CTE of L. So, say a set of 1,000 scenarios gives an estimated 95 percent CTE for L of \$5.00 and for L^* of \$4.15; and we know from the analytic calculation that the true CTE for L^* is \$4.35. This indicates that the scenario sample we are using is valuing a little low; a simple adjustment is to add the difference of \$0.20 back to the original CTE for L, giving a control variate adjusted value of \$5.20.

The simplest algorithm for estimating a value E using a control variate is:

1. Choose your control variate and calculate the true value E_{CV}.
2. Generate the scenarios for the simulation, and use them to estimate both the control variate $\hat{E}_{CV}$ and the required output $\hat{E}$.
3. Then the control variate adjusted estimate of E is

$$E^* = \hat{E} + (E_{CV} - \hat{E}_{CV})$$

We will use the GMAB example from earlier in this chapter to demonstrate the benefits from the control variate method with a fuller numerical example. To repeat the critical features, this is a 20-year GMAB with a single rollover at time 10. The fund and guarantee are both \$100 at the start of the contract.

Suppose we are interested in, for example, the 95 percent CTE of the net present value of the liability for the contract. The liability includes payoffs at both the rollover and final maturity dates, as well as death benefits. Income from margin offset is also allowed for.

The control variate that we use is the 95 percent CTE of the liability under the first rollover, allowing for management charges and survival appropriately. This is highly correlated with the liability present value. The rollover liability depends on the random accumulation factor from $t = 0$ to $t = 10$, which we denote S_{10}. We will assume this comes from the RSLN distribution with parameters from Table 6.2. To determine the present value of the liability at the first rollover, we assume

* Monthly time steps.
* A management charge of 25 basis points per month.
* Discount at the risk-free force of interest of $r = 0.005$ per month.
* A survival probability of $_{120}p_x^\tau = 0.422467$.

These assumptions give

$$L^* = \max(100 - 100\, S_{10}(0.9975)^{120}, \; 0)e^{-120r}\,_{120}p_x^\tau$$

The accurate CTE for L^* can be calculated by conditioning on R, the total sojourn in regime 1, which we used in the section on RSLN in Chapter 2. The detailed derivation is given in the section on exact calculation in Chapter 9.

For the first rollover of a 20-year contract using the RSLN model as before, with initial fund and guarantee both equal to $100 the 95 percent CTE of the present value of the first rollover liability is $10.959. This is our control variate E_{CV}.

Now we simulate the full net present value of the liability for, say $N = 1,000$ scenarios. At the same time we pull out the simulated liability for the first rollover. We find that the simulated CTE for the control variate is $\hat{E}_{CV} = \$11.265$, indicating that this set of scenarios has slightly overvalued the control variate. The same scenarios give a CTE of $E = \$9.006$. This gives an estimate of

$$E^* = 9.006 + (10.959 - 11.265) = 8.700$$

which compares well with the estimate of $8.727 from 10^6 simulations. This is not a coincidence; the control variate method actually converges much more quickly than the straight simulation method for the CTE for these contracts. This is demonstrated in Figure 11.7, which shows the convergence of the CTE for 100 to 20,000 simulations, both with and without the control variate; notice the fast convergence with the control variate, and in particular the much greater accuracy around 1,000 scenarios. This is very important because it is quite rare for actuaries to use more than 1,000 simulations, but the CTE accuracy without variance reduction is actually quite poor in that range.

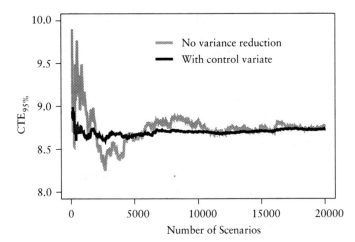

FIGURE 11.7 Estimated 95 percent CTE risk measure with and without control variate.

The control variate method appears to work well with other distributions for the stock price and for other contract designs. The additional computation is small, and the payoff with a good control variate is high.

The more general form of the control variate method is to use

$$E^* = \hat{E} + \beta(E_{CV} - \hat{E}_{CV}) \qquad (11.6)$$

so that the variance of the estimate is

$$V[E^*] = V[\hat{E}] + \beta^2 V[\hat{E}_{CV}] - 2\beta \text{Cov}[\hat{E}, \hat{E}_{CV}] \qquad (11.7)$$

The variance is minimized when the parameter β is

$$\beta^* = \frac{\text{Cov}[\hat{E}, \hat{E}_{CV}]}{V[\hat{E}_{CV}]} \qquad (11.8)$$

In general, we will not know β^* to get the minimum variance estimator, but some experimentation with different simulated pairs $\{\hat{E}, \hat{E}_{CV}\}$ can provide an estimate using regression. For the GMAB example used in this section, the parameter is around 1.0, so the estimate we have used is roughly optimal.

The control variate method is straightforward to apply, with little additional computation over ordinary simulation, and, as we have seen, using a control variate provides dramatic improvements in accuracy in some cases. It works well for estimating the mean or the CTEs of the net present value of the liability for investment guarantees. The use of guarantee liabilities for estimating tail quantile measures has not achieved such good

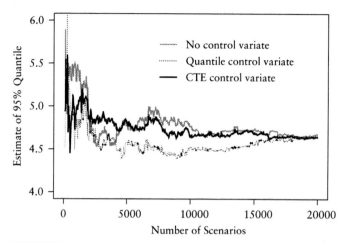

FIGURE 11.8 Estimated 95 percent quantile risk measure with CTE and quantile control variates, and without control variate.

results. The quantile estimate comes from a specific simulation value, the one that happens to be in the correct place in the ordered sample, and it is not clear what control variate might be useful. In Figure 11.8 the estimated 95 percent quantile for the 20-year GMAB is plotted with control variates again based on the rollover cost at time 10 years. The grey line indicates the estimate without variance reduction. The broken line uses the 95 percent quantile of the year 10 living benefit as a control variate, and it does not improve accuracy substantially. The unbroken line does provide some improvement. The control variate for that line is the CTE of the year 10 liability, which is the same control variate that we used for the CTE simulation.

Importance Sampling

Suppose we are interested in estimating $E_f[A]$, where the subscript denotes the model density function. Standard stochastic simulation uses N values of A generated from the model distribution $f(\ )$, say $A_1, \ldots, A_N$, giving an estimate for $E_f[A]$ of $\sum A_i/N$. With importance sampling, we generate N values of A from a different distribution, $f^*(\ )$, say. It can be chosen to cover the important parts of the sample space with higher probability than the model distribution. Let these values of A be denoted $A_i^*, \ldots, A_N^*$. For each value generated we also calculate the likelihood ratio[2] for that value, $\mathscr{L}$:

$$\mathscr{L}(\mathscr{A}_i^*) = \frac{f(A_i^*)}{f^*(A_i^*)} \tag{11.9}$$

---

[2]Also known as the Radon-Nikodym derivative.

Then, provided the likelihood ratio is well defined for all possible values of A^*, the importance sampling estimate of the mean is

$$E[A] \approx \frac{1}{N} \sum_{i=1}^{N} A_i^* \mathcal{L}(A_i^*)$$

For the likelihood ratio to exist, the support of $f^*(\,)$ must contain the support of $f(\,)$, meaning that if $f^*(A_i^*) = 0$, then $f(A_i^*)$ must also equal zero, so that the likelihood ratio is defined.

A simple example of importance sampling might be to use a distribution with higher variance to sample the output variable where the important part of the distribution is in the tails. This can ensure that the tail is sampled sufficiently. What we are doing is dropping the usual Monte Carlo assumption that each output is equally weighted; instead we weight with the likelihood ratio. That way we can sample rare events with higher probability, then reduce their weighting in the calculation appropriately.

Boyle, Broadie, and Glasserman (1997) explain the use of importance sampling in more detail, for example, for valuation of deep out-of-the-money options. It may be usefully applied to GMMB liabilities therefore, which are essentially out-of-the-money options. However, the net liability—that is, taking the income from margin offset and guarantee liability together—is less conducive to importance sampling because of the path dependence, and the different timing of the cash flows. Research continues in how to adapt the method to actuarial cash-flow modeling.

Low Discrepancy Sequences

A relatively recent innovation in stochastic simulation techniques is the use of low discrepancy (LD) sequences, also called quasi Monte Carlo or QMC, methods. Standard Monte Carlo simulation uses a pseudo-random number generator, which is a deterministic function that produces numbers that appear to behave as if they are random. Often, we use Uniform(0,1) numbers as the basis for generating random variates of other distributions. We hope that our sample of $U(0,1)$ variates are dispersed roughly evenly over $(0,1)$; we know the results will be inaccurate if, say, all the variates fall in $(0,0.5)$, though this is theoretically possible. We also use the fact that the numbers are effectively serially independent. In contrast, LD sequences are known deterministic sequences, which are selected to cover the sample space evenly. LD methods are not random or even pseudo-random.

Suppose, for example, the problem was to estimate $\int_0^1 h(x)dx$ using a sample size n. We could simulate n values for x from a $U(0,1)$ distribution, $x_1, \ldots, x_n$, say, and estimate $\int_0^1 h(x)dx$ from the mean value of $h(x_i)$. However, it would be more accurate to pick n evenly spaced values for x_i

between zero and one—for example, to use the trapezium rule. The random nature of the first method is a disadvantage rather than an advantage, and given a choice between stochastic simulation and numerical integration we would always select the latter for accuracy where it is feasible.

Picking evenly spaced values is more difficult where the problem is more complex. Modern LD sequences allow the use of nonrandom, evenly dispersed sequences in higher dimension simulations. Dramatic improvements in accuracy have been achieved in some complex financial applications using LD methods. Examples of applications are given in Boyle, Broadie, and Glasserman (1997) and in Boyle and Tan (2002).

The problems surrounding equity-linked insurance tend to be very high-dimensional, meaning many separate sequences of random numbers are required. For a simple model of a 20-year GMMB contract with monthly timesteps, we have a model with at least 240 dimensions, more if the investment model is at all complex. At this level of complexity, the LD methods tend to lose their advantage over ordinary Monte Carlo methods. However, research in combining traditional Monte Carlo methods with the new LD sequences is ongoing, and it seems likely that this approach will prove to be very useful for a range of actuarial applications.

PARAMETER UNCERTAINTY

The effect of parameter uncertainty on forecast accuracy is often unexplored. Having determined a parameter set for a model, by maximum likelihood or by other means, that set is then deemed to be fixed and known, and we draw all inference relying entirely without margin on that best-fit parameter vector. In fact, parameter estimation, however sophisticated the method, is subject to uncertainty. Even if the model itself is the best possible model of the equity process, if the parameters used are inaccurate then the results may not be reliable.

It is useful, then, to have some idea of the effect of parameter uncertainty. In fact, this is part of the actuarial risk management responsibility. This is quite specific in the context of Canadian valuation, where allowance for parameter uncertainty in policy liabilities is a normal part of the required *provision for adverse deviation* or PAD. This allowance currently tends to be rather ad hoc. In this section we demonstrate a more rigorous approach.

Bayesian Methods for Parameter Uncertainty

Bayesian methods were introduced in Chapter 5, where Markov chain Monte Carlo (MCMC) techniques were applied to parameter estimation for the RSLN for equity returns. We give a very brief recap here. The Bayesian approach to parameter uncertainty is to treat the parameters as random variables, with a distribution that models not intrinsic variability, but rather intrinsic uncertainty. Thus, the mean of the parameter distribution represents the best point estimate of the parameter (technically, minimizing quadratic loss). The variance of the parameter distribution represents the uncertainty associated with that estimate.

We assign a *prior* distribution to the parameters even before we start working with data. We can then combine the information from the data together with our prior distribution to determine a revised distribution for the parameters, the *posterior* distribution. Using MCMC, the joint posterior distribution for the entire parameter set is found by generating a sample from that distribution; that is, the output from the MCMC calculations is a sample of parameter vectors, the sample having the posterior distribution.

In our work in Chapter 5, the prior distributions used are very disperse, and have negligible influence on the posterior distributions. We use the same approach in this section. With disperse prior distributions the Bayesian approach is connected to the frequentist approach to parameter uncertainty through extensive reliance on the likelihood function, considered as a function of the parameters. The posterior distribution of parameter vectors is roughly proportional to the likelihood functions for the vectors.

The advantage of the MCMC method is that it leads very naturally to a method of forecasting taking parameter uncertainty into consideration, as we have already demonstrated in the final section of Chapter 5. We are not interested so much in the distribution of the parameter vector, rather, our goal is to quantify the effect of parameter uncertainty on the distribution of equity-linked liabilities.

The predictive distribution for, say, the net present value of the guarantee liability under a separate account product is the expected value of the distribution taken over the posterior distribution of the parameters. That is, if the parameter vector is θ, with posterior distribution $\pi(\theta)$, and our output random variable is X, then the predictive density function of X is:

$$f(x) = \int_\theta f(x|\theta)\pi(\theta)\,d\theta \qquad (11.10)$$

In terms of stochastic simulation, this formula means that we simulate from the predictive distribution by drawing a new parameter vector from the MCMC output for each scenario used to generate the distribution of guarantee costs. For example, if we want to generate the distribution of the net present value of the liability (without cost of capital) for the GMMB contracts studied in Chapter 9, we first generate a sample from the posterior distribution for the parameters. We will use 5,000 simulations to examine the GMMB liability. We need more projections of the posterior distribution because (a) the first one-hundred values are discarded as "run-in" and (b) successive values are highly dependent. Recall that each individual parameter only changes with probability according to an *acceptance probability*, which means that the probability of changing at each point is generally between 30 percent and 50 percent. To reduce the influence of this serial dependence, the GMMB liability is calculated using every tenth parameter set generated from the MCMC procedure.

Two of the contracts studied in Chapter 9 were VA-style death benefit guarantees (GMDBs). The first example has a fixed death benefit of 100 percent of the single premium, paid for by a margin offset of 10 basis points per year. The second has a guaranteed death benefit that increases monthly at an annual effective rate of 5 percent. The benefit in the first month is equal to the $100 single premium, and the margin offset is 40 basis points per year.

In Figure 11.9, we show the simulated probability density functions for the net liability present value for the two contracts, separately for the actuarial and the dynamic-hedging risk management approaches. These plots show that the effect of parameter uncertainty is small in the mean values, but does affect the spread of results, giving more extreme outcomes in both tails. Although the effect appears more noticeable in the dynamic-hedging plots, the effect on the tail of allowing for parameter uncertainty is more expensive in the actuarial case, in terms of the percentage of fund required for a tail measure capital requirement. For example, for the level death benefit contract with a $100 premium, in the actuarial case allowing for parameter uncertainty increases the 95 percent CTE from $0.79 to $1.13 premium. If we use dynamic hedging for the same contract, allowing for parameter, uncertainty increases the 95 percent CTE from $0.00 to $0.08, an increase of only 8 cents per $100 dollars of premium.

In Figure 11.10, we show the addition to the CTE risk measure resulting from this approach to parameter uncertainty for the GMDB contract. This shows that the dynamic-hedging approach appears to be less vulnerable to parameter uncertainty than the actuarial approach. We get similar results for GMMB and GMAB contracts. In some cases, the addition to the risk measure can be significant. In Table 11.2 we give the 95 percent quantile and 95 percent CTE risk measures for a 20-year GMAB contract. This is the same contract that was described and used as an example in the sections on risk measures for GMAB liability in Chapter 9 and capital requirements in Chapter 10.

The influence of parameter uncertainty is very significant using actuarial risk management, resulting in an addition of $2.27 to the 95 percent CTE for a $100 single premium. On the other hand, using dynamic hedging, the 95 percent CTE is increased by only $0.31. In fact, in all of the separate-fund cases that were examined in preparation for this book the actuarial approach was substantially more vulnerable to parameter error than the dynamic-hedging approach.

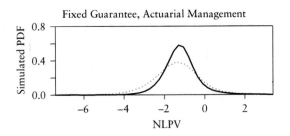

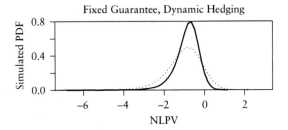

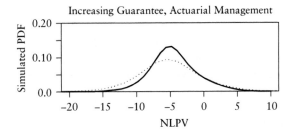

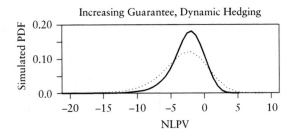

———— Without parameter uncertainty

·········· With parameter uncertainty

FIGURE 11.9 Simulated probability density function for net liability present value and GMDB, with and without allowance for parameter uncertainty.

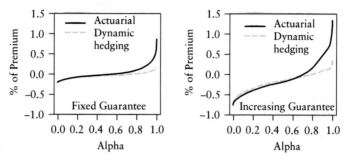

FIGURE 11.10 Addition to CTE risk measure from parameter uncertainty; GMDB; percentage of single premium.

TABLE 11.2 The effect of parameter uncertainty; risk measures for 20-year GMAB contract, per $100 single premium.

Risk Management	Without Parameter Uncertainty		With Parameter Uncertainty	
	$Q_{95\%}$	$CTE_{95\%}$	$Q_{95\%}$	$CTE_{95\%}$
Actuarial	$5.06	$8.85	$6.37	$11.12
Dynamic hedging	$1.58	$2.36	$1.84	$2.67

Stress Testing for Parameter Uncertainty

To use the *stress-testing* technique for parameter uncertainty, simulations are repeated using different parameter sets to see the effect of different assumptions on the output. The parameters for the stress test may be chosen arbitrarily, or may be imposed by regulators. These "what if ...?" scenarios will give some qualitative information about the sensitivity of results to parameter error, but will generally not be helpful quantitatively, particularly if the stress test parameter sets are not equally likely. Stress testing provides additional information on sensitivity to parameter uncertainty, but is very subjective and tends to be difficult to interpret.

However, stress testing can provide some useful insight into the vulnerability of the results to parameter error, or even structural changes in parameters. Structural changes arise when parameters or the model itself appears to undergo a permanent and significant alteration. Under the regime-switching model framework, one-off structural changes in parameters that have occurred in the past may be indicated in the estimation process if there is sufficient evidence. If the change is recent, or has yet to occur, then our results are highly speculative, though they may still be useful.

To explore parameter error, we may return to the data to consider how vulnerable the parameter estimates are to the period chosen for the data, and how that parameter vulnerability affects the results of the simulation exercises. For example, we have estimated the parameters for the stock return distributions by looking at stock index data back to 1956. It seems reasonable to look back 45 years when we are projecting forward 20 years or more. However, it is also useful to use only the more recent data, in case structural changes are indicated, making the older data less relevant. In Table 11.3 we give parameter estimates for the TSE 300 index split for the periods 1956 to 1978 and 1979 to 2001.

Table 11.3 shows that the more recent data indicates a lower chance of moving to the high-volatility regime than is generated using the full range of data, and a slightly longer average period in the high-volatility regime once it does change. Also, the volatility in the high-volatility regime is higher for the 1979 to 2001 data. Note that the parameter estimates for the later period are all within two standard errors of the estimates for the full period. This is not true for the first 22 years, where the estimates of σ_1, σ_2, and p_{12} are quite different to those for the full 46-year period.

We might be concerned to see the effect on the estimates of using only more recent data to estimate the parameters. This comparison is given in Table 11.4, where we show right-tail CTE values for the 20-year GMAB contract (as in the sections on risk measures for GMAB liability in Chapter 9, capital requirements in Chapter 10, and Bayesian methods in this chapter). The table is interesting, in demonstrating that the different risk management strategies show quite different sensitivities to the different parameter sets. The actuarial approach shows a difference of $3.00 to $4.00 for the tail measures, per $100 single premium; the difference for the dynamic-hedging strategy is no more than $1.1 per $100. The worst parameter set for the actuarial approach comes from the figures for the years 1990 to 2001. The worst parameter set for the dynamic-hedging strategy is the set from 1978 to 2001.

TABLE 11.3 Maximum likelihood estimates for RSLN parameters, using TSE data.

Data Period	$\hat{\mu}_1$	$\hat{\mu}_2$	$\hat{\sigma}_1$	$\hat{\sigma}_2$	$\hat{p}_{12}$	$\hat{p}_{21}$
1956–1999	0.012	−0.016	0.035	0.078	0.037	0.210
(These are the parameters used in examples)						
1956–2001	0.013	−0.016	0.035	0.075	0.040	0.190
St. Errors (approx)	(0.002)	(0.010)	(0.001)	(0.007)	(0.013)	(0.064)
1956–1978	0.016	−0.006	0.027	0.051	0.176	0.221
1979–2001	0.014	−0.016	0.037	0.085	0.034	0.152
1990–2001	0.012	−0.034	0.037	0.077	0.028	0.207

TABLE 11.4 Stress testing; risk measures for 20-year GMAB contract, per $100 single premium.

Risk Management	Data Period	CTE$_{90\%}$	CTE$_{95\%}$	CTE$_{99\%}$
Actuarial	1956–1999	5.93	8.85	14.11
	1979–2001	7.85	11.03	16.52
	1990–2001	9.79	12.72	17.06
Dynamic hedging	1956–1999	1.75	2.36	3.28
	1979–2001	2.87	3.45	4.33
	1990–2001	2.36	2.76	3.54

The reason for the difference in sensitivity to parameters is that the hedging costs are most vulnerable to large movements in the stock price, and are not very sensitive to the μ values. The worst parameter set is the 1979 to 2001 set, because this has the highest overall volatility. The actuarial approach is sensitive to the μ values, in particular the very low value for μ_2 under the parameter set for the years 1990 to 2001.

Other methods of selecting parameters for stress are possible. Often an actuary will test the effect of changing one factor only. However, it is important to remember that the parameters are all connected; a higher value for p_{12} generates a higher likelihood if the mean and standard deviation of regime 2 are closer to those of regime 1, for example.

MODEL UNCERTAINTY

In Chapter 2 several models for stock returns are described, and in Chapter 3 we used likelihood measures to compare the fit of these models. Based on the data and measures used there, the RSLN model seemed to provide the best fit. However, it is important to understand that there is no one "correct" model. Different data sets might require different models, and, subject to the sort of left-tail calibration described in Chapter 4, many models may provide adequate forecasts of distributions.

Cairns (2000) proposes an integrated approach to model and parameter uncertainty, broadly using likelihoods to weight the results from different models, similar to the approach to parameter uncertainty in the section on Bayesian methods for parameter uncertainty. A simpler approach, similar to the parameter stress testing of the previous section, is to reproduce the results of the simulations using different models to assess the vulnerability to model error. For example, in Table 11.5 we show the right-tail measures for the 20-year GMAB contract used in the previous sections. This table is similar to Table 11.4, but instead of looking at robustness of tail measures with respect to parameter uncertainty, here we look at robustness with

TABLE 11.5   Model uncertainty; risk measures for 20-year GMAB contract, per $100 single premium.

Actuarial Risk Management	$CTE_{90\%}$	$CTE_{95\%}$	$CTE_{99\%}$
Lognormal (Uncalibrated)	3.08	5.77	10.60
GARCH (Uncalibrated)	1.35	4.07	8.89
Lognormal (Calibrated)	5.85	8.75	13.49
GARCH (Calibrated)	6.85	9.88	14.19
RSLN	5.93	8.85	14.11
Dynamic-Hedging Risk Management			
Lognormal (Uncalibrated)	0.77	1.14	1.81
GARCH (Uncalibrated)	1.11	1.65	2.88
Lognormal (Calibrated)	2.25	2.58	3.16
GARCH (Calibrated)	3.44	4.04	5.56
RSLN	1.75	2.36	3.28

respect to model uncertainty. We consider three models: the lognormal model, the GARCH model, and the RSLN model. We also consider two sets of parameters. The first are the maximum likelihood parameters; the second are the calibrated parameters, using the Canadian Institute of Actuaries (CIA) calibration criteria described in Chapter 4. The objective of the left-tail calibration was to try to reduce discrepancies in results caused by model selection; we can see if that has worked for this contract. Note that because the RSLN with maximum likelihood parameter meets the calibration criteria without adjustment, only one set of results is given for that model.

Without calibration, the figures are fairly varied between the three models, with the 95 percent CTE ranging from $4.07 to $8.85 per $100 single premium for actuarial risk management, and $1.14 to $2.36 per $100 single premium for dynamic-hedging risk management. As with parameter uncertainty, the dynamic-hedging approach appears more robust. However, once we allow for right-tail calibration, the figures for the actuarial approach are much closer, with the 95 percent CTE ranging from $8.75 to $9.88 per $100 single premium. The calibration appears to have done the job of bringing the results closer together, reducing model error effect. However, calibration is not so useful in the dynamic-hedging approach, where the calibrated lognormal figures and RSLN figures are reasonably consistent, but the GARCH figures are substantially higher.

Further, case studies demonstrating the effects of both model and parameter uncertainty for segregated fund contracts are given in Hancock (2001).

CHAPTER 12

Guaranteed Annuity Options

INTRODUCTION

I n this chapter, we apply the techniques of Chapters 6 and 8 to the liability from annuitization options within an equity-linked contract. A guaranteed annuity option (GAO) or guaranteed minimum income benefit (GMIB) is a maturity guarantee in the form of a guaranteed minimum income on annuitization of the maturity payout. GAO is the term used for the options offered in the United Kingdom, and GMIB for the options offered in the United States. In this chapter we will explore simple models and methods for these benefits, with emphasis on the U.K. GAO associated with a unit-linked contract. A more detailed exploration is available in, for example, Yang (2001). Other relevant papers for the U.K. contract are Pelsser (2002) and Annuity Guarantee Working Party (AGWP)(1997).

Although this is a more complex guarantee than the fixed-sum guarantee payable at contract expiry, the basic modeling process is similar. We start by assessing appropriate models. In this chapter it is very important to incorporate the risk from stochastic movements in interest rates; in previous chapters we have not allowed for the interest rate risk because it has a relatively small effect on the liability. With annuitization guarantees, the interest rate has a crucial role, and relatively small movements can substantially change the liability. In the section on interest rate and annuity modeling, we look at models for the interest rate and annuity processes. In the section on actuarial modeling, we use the models for interest rates and stock returns to generate a distribution for the liabilities, using the actuarial approach; in the section on dynamic hedging, we consider a dynamic-hedging model and assess how well it succeeds in reducing risks.

In the United Kingdom, the GAO associated with both fixed- and variable-sum insured contracts guarantees a minimum conversion rate of lump sum to annuity. Typically, guarantees of £111 annual annuity per £1000 maturity lump sum have been offered for male policyholders, and around £91 annuity per £1000 maturity lump sum for females. The conversion rate is known as the guaranteed annuity rate or GAR.

Under this framework, let g be the guaranteed annuity rate (e.g., $g = 1/9$ for a rate of 111 annuity per 1000 lump sum), and let $a_x(t)$ be the market price at t of a whole-life annuity of £1 per year payable immediately to a life aged x. As before, the value of the separate fund at t is F_t. Then the payoff under the GAO at the maturity of the separate fund account, say $t = n$ (which is the annuity vesting date), for a life age 65 at vesting, is

$$\max(g\, F_n\, a_{65}(n) - F_n, 0) \tag{12.1}$$

This option is, then, in-the-money when $a_{65}(t)$ is greater than $1/g$ and out-of-the-money otherwise.

In North America there is a plethora of guarantee designs associated with annuitization. Policyholders may have an option of fixed or variable annuitization: Fixed means that the annuity amount is fixed, as in the United Kingdom; variable means that the amount depends on investment performance after annuitization. Also, the policyholder may choose between an annuity certain or a life annuity. In this chapter we discuss only fixed, whole life annuitization. That is, it is assumed that the annuity amount is level and payable for life. Within this category, guarantees offered may be in the same form as the GAO used in the United Kingdom, though usually with much lower guarantees. An alternative is to guarantee a fixed minimum income per year at the start of the contract, so that the liability at maturity of the variable-annuity account is, for guaranteed income X per year:

$$\max(X\, a_{65}(n) - F_n, 0) \tag{12.2}$$

The value of X may be determined at the start of the contract with reference to the annuity rates in force at that time. For example, an insurer may guarantee an income of at least $(1.05)^n/a_{65}(0)$ times the single premium paid at time $t = 0$; that is, the guarantee is the annuity available assuming the fund grows at 5 percent per year and that the annuity rates in force at maturity are the same as those in force at inception. Whatever the calculation, the actual annual rate of payment guaranteed is fixed at inception, unlike the United Kingdom contract, which depends on the fund growth.

Adding guaranteed income benefits to variable benefit contracts has proved to be somewhat perilous. The problems caused in the United Kingdom have been described in Chapter 1. In the United States, too, there has been some concern. In California, GMIBs were banned (along with other guaranteed living benefits) for a few months amid concern about a lack of consensus on a methodology for determining capital requirements.

In previous chapters we have treated the rate of interest as a fixed and known quantity. In practice, of course, the interest rate varies randomly, though with very much lower volatility than the stock indices we have considered. The valuation of annuity options requires us to consider this interest rate risk, because the cost of annuitizing the benefit from an equity-linked insurance contract is sensitive to quite small changes in the interest rate. Using Canadian annuitants' mortality, for example, the liability for a UK-style GAO on a separate fund contract is around 24 percent of the fund at maturity if the long-term interest rate is then 5 percent per year, 15 percent of the fund at 6 percent per year interest, 7 percent of the fund at 7 percent per year interest, and 0 percent of the fund at 8 percent per year interest, for a continuous whole-life annuity issued to a male aged 65.

Interest rate modeling is rather more complex than stock price modeling. The main reason is that the term structure of interest rates requires modeling a curve rather than a single variable, and the no-arbitrage principle constrains the possible outcomes. It is outside the scope of this work to consider interest rate models in detail, so we will adopt some simplifications here for illustrative purposes that would not necessarily be appropriate in practice. For a more detailed consideration of interest rate econometrics and interest rate options, a very useful book is Webber and James (2000).

The nature of the interest rate term structure is that short-term rates are more volatile than long-term rates. Market annuity prices are much more influenced by long-term interest rates than by short-term, because an annuity issued to a life aged, say, 65, has an expected term of around 17 years. Because the term structure of interest rates usually levels off between five and 10 years, the long-term rates are most critical in annuity pricing. This is demonstrated more fully in Yang (2001). In this chapter, we keep things simple by generally assuming a flat yield curve for valuing the life annuity and bonds. The long-term yields are modeled using the same econometric analysis we used for stocks in Chapters 2 and 3.

In practice, the term structure effect may have a significant influence on the risk measures, and more sophisticated modeling is recommended than what is described here if the annuity option offered affects a material proportion of the portfolio of contracts. For a more sophisticated approach, it is necessary to use a term structure model that is appropriate for real-world modeling (*P*-measure) rather than (or in addition to) risk-neutral modeling (*Q*-measure). Most term structure models used in financial engineering are market models—that is, designed for risk-neutral application. One of the most popular models suitable for both *P*- and *Q*-measure is the Cox-Ingersoll-Ross model, described in Cox, Ingersoll, and Ross (1985).

INTEREST RATE AND ANNUITY MODELING

Annuity Prices

We will estimate approximate prices for an immediate annuity of £1 per year for a male annuitant aged 65, payable continuously through life, using current Canadian annuitants' mortality[1] from Appendix A, and using historic U.K. interest rates. Because guaranteed annuity options have proved most troublesome in the United Kingdom, in this chapter we will use parameters for simulation appropriate for U.K. data. In Figure 12.1 the estimated values of a whole-life annuity are plotted based on historic interest rates. For simplicity, the term structure has been assumed to follow a straight line between the three-month rate and the 2.5 percent consols rate, which is assumed to apply for all terms of greater than five years. The 2.5 percent consols used for the long-term rate are effectively irredeemable U.K. government bonds. The horizontal line on the plot gives the threshold for a nonzero liability for a guaranteed annuity option with a guaranteed annuity conversion rate of £1 for £9 lump sum.

The GAOs were a feature of contracts sold in the late 1970s and early 1980s, when annuity rates for male 65-year-old annuitants were substantially less than £9. In fact, they would have appeared even cheaper, because the mortality rates used for valuation purposes did not sufficiently

FIGURE 12.1   Estimated annuity costs, based on modern mortality rates and historic U.K. Government bond yields.

---

[1]The use of Canadian mortality rather than U.K. mortality will make very little difference here.

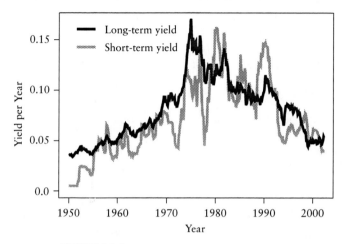

FIGURE 12.2 U.K. government bond yields.

allow for improvement before or after vesting. Many offices used mortality appropriate to annuitants in 1955 (the a(55) table). With this mortality, the threshold for the liability occurred when interest rates fell below around 6.5 percent. With more contemporary mortality, that threshold has increased to over 7 percent. However, even considering the lower threshold, in 1980 one did not have to look too far into history for dangerously low interest rates. The assumption of many actuaries that interest rates would never again fall below the approximate 6.5 percent per year threshold seems very odd given that rates only around 10 to 15 years earlier were lower.

The correlation with the stock price yield (in this case the FTSE[2] All Share Total Return Index) is quite small.

Long-Term Yields and Stock Returns

The annuity cost graph is close to a mirror image of the long-term bond yields shown in Figure 12.2, so most of the comments made in the previous section also apply here. In this figure, we also show the short (three-month) interest rates, demonstrating the low volatility of the long rates compared with the short rates.

The long-term yields are very highly autocorrelated, with first-order autocorrelation of around 99.5 percent. The best models of those listed in Chapter 2 are the autoregressive, or AR(1), model and the regime-switching-

---

[2]Financial Times Stock Exchange.

AR(1) model with two regimes, fitted to the logarithm of $(1 +$ long-term annual yield rate). The latter model is called the RSAR(1,2) model in this chapter. For this model, let i_t be the annual yield in the month t to $t + 1$, then i_t depends on the Markov regime-switching process $\rho_t^y = 1, 2$ as:

$$\log(1 + i_t) \mid \rho_t^y = \mu_{\rho_t^y}^y + \phi_{\rho_t^y}^y (\log(1 + i_{t-1}) - \mu_{\rho_t^y}^y) + \sigma_{\rho_t^y}^y \varepsilon_t$$

$$\varepsilon_t \text{ independent and identically distributed (iid)} \sim N(0,1) \qquad (12.3)$$

Parameters have been estimated using yields on 2.5 percent consols from 1956 to 2001. This gives maximum likelihood parameters for the RSAR(1, 2) model of:

$$\mu_1^y = 0.066 \qquad \sigma_1^y = 0.0014 \qquad \phi_1^y = 0.9895 \qquad p_{12}^y = 0.0279$$
$$\mu_2^y = 0.109 \qquad \sigma_2^y = 0.0038 \qquad \phi_2^y = 0.9895 \qquad p_{21}^y = 0.0440$$

The correlation of log-long-term bond yields with log-FTSE All Share total return yields is approximately 6 percent. However, this understates the connection. The correlation of the monthly log-returns of an investment in consols with the monthly log-returns on the FTSE All Share Index is around 30 percent.

The FTSE data best fit is provided by the RSLN model with two regimes. The maximum likelihood parameter estimates found using data from the U.K. FTSE All Share Total Return Index from 1956 to 2001 are:

$$\mu_1 = 0.012 \qquad \sigma_1 = 0.043 \qquad p_{12} = 0.012$$
$$\mu_2 = -0.014 \qquad \sigma_2 = 0.133 \qquad p_{21} = 0.165$$

These parameters are for the monthly log-returns on stocks. The parameters show higher volatility in both regimes than the North American data, but a much smaller probability of transition from the low-volatility to the high-volatility regime. The overall effect is a thinner-tailed distribution than the Canadian (TSE 300) experience, and a fatter-tailed distribution than the U.S. (S&P 500) experience.

Annual equivalent figures for the regime-switching lognormal (RSLN) model are around 15 percent and 46 percent for the standard deviation parameters in regimes 1 and 2, respectively. These compare with unconditional standard deviations of around 1 percent and 2.7 percent for the bond yield model. The relatively low variance of the bond yields is the reason why, in many cases, it is sufficient to treat them as constant, but not for the GAO liability where we have seen that a 2 percent change in bond yields can have a dramatic effect on the liabilities.

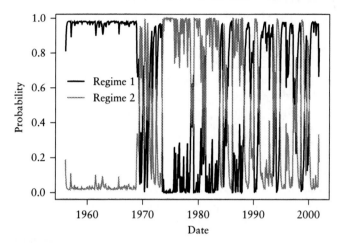

FIGURE 12.3 U.K. long-term bond yield data regime probabilities for RSAR model.

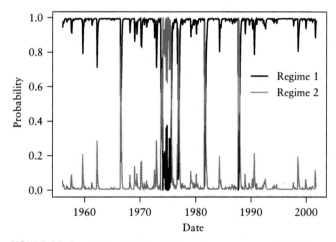

FIGURE 12.4 FTSE All-Share Index data regime probabilities for RSLN model.

We can compare the timing of regime switches for the interest rates and stock yields. For interest rates, using the two-regime model, we find both regimes are quite persistent. The probabilities associated with the regimes for the historic data are given in Figures 12.3 (bond yield data) and 12.4 (stock yield data). Looking at the historic data for bond yields, the first regime appears to describe the series through the 1950s and 1960s, and the second for most of the period to 1990; since then, the two regimes have switched at intervals of between 12 and 36 months. Even in the period where switches of regime are more frequent, both regimes display approximately the same persistence. This is quite different from the stock return model, which has one persistent and one nonpersistent regime. Although there is some connection between the timing of regime switches in the interest rate and stock return regime-switching models, it is not straightforward to model, and we will ignore it in this chapter.

ACTUARIAL MODELING

In this section we consider using the actuarial approach to assess capital requirements for the GAO-type option. Using the actuarial approach we project the liability under the contract, net of any management charge income, and then discount the net liability to the start of the projection period.

The Contract and Simulation Details

We consider a single-premium contract with premium £100 issued to a policyholder aged 50. The death benefit is a return of the fund at the time of death, with no guarantee. The fund is assumed to be invested in a U.K. broad-based equity fund. We have modeled the fund using the RSLN-2 model, with parameters from the section on long-term yields and stock returns. A management charge of 2 percent per year is deducted monthly. There is no margin offset income to fund the guarantee.

At maturity, at age 65, the funds are annuitized to a level whole-life annuity. The minimum amount of annual income is guaranteed at $g = 1/9$ of the fund value at that time. The annuity price in force at maturity, $a_{65}(15)$, is determined using annuitants' mortality and an interest rate corresponding to the long-term bond yield generated using the RSAR(1, 2) model (for $\log(1+\text{yield})$), with parameters from the section on long-term yields and stock returns.

The contract is similar to a standard guaranteed minimum maturity benefit (GMMB), with $g F_n a_{65}(n)$ replacing the guarantee, G. This guarantee, however, is substantially more complex than the fixed GMMB because the guarantee itself depends on the separate fund value, and because of the introduction of the stochastic annuity cost process.

We have assumed that the long-term yields are independent of the stock returns.

In principle, the yield model can generate negative yields, which, of course, are impossible in practice. In this event, we have set a minimum yield of 0.5 percent. This minimum was rarely required in the 10,000 sets of projection used below. It was not needed at all when the starting value for the yield was 8 percent per year and was needed for just one projection where the starting value for the yield was 5 percent per year.

We have assumed that mortality before the annuity vesting date follows Canadian annuitants' mortality, given in Appendix A, and we show results with and without that table's lapse assumption; after vesting there are no lapses, of course. The mortality after vesting is from the same table as used for prevesting.

Results

In considering the fixed GMMB in previous chapters we have assumed that solvency capital is invested in risk-free instruments. For the standard separate fund account (unit-linked, variable-annuity, or segregated fund) with maturity guarantee, the liability is highest when the fund accumulation is smallest, so it makes sense to keep the solvency capital in bonds. However, for the GAO the liability is proportional to the fund (for a given annuity interest rate)—good fund performance means a higher liability. It makes more sense with the GAO liability to invest the solvency capital in the same assets as the separate fund. In this case, there is no need to simulate the fund itself, because we discount by applying a factor F_0/F_n, where n is the time to vesting, so that the liability per $\pounds F_0$ premium is

$$(F_n(g\,a_{65}(n) - 1)^+)\frac{F_0}{F_n} = F_0(g\,a_{65}(n) - 1)^+$$

In Table 12.1 we show some risk measures for the GAO liability, using both the bond and stocks assumption for solvency capital accumulation. The risk measures are expressed per £100 single premium. We show the figures assuming 8 percent per year lapses before vesting, which is identical to

TABLE 12.1 Solvency capital using actuarial risk management, percentage of single premium, for 15-year GAO, with guaranteed annuity rate $1/9$.

Solvency Capital Invested in:	Yield per Year at Start	CTE$_{90\%}$ %	CTE$_{95\%}$ %	CTE$_{99\%}$ %
Bonds, with lapses	8%	12.88	19.29	39.16
Stocks, with lapses	8%	4.41	5.89	9.45
Stocks, no lapses	8%	14.73	19.67	31.56
Stocks, no lapses	5%	18.67	23.90	36.38

the assumption used for separate fund GMMBs and guaranteed minimum death benefits (GMDBs) in previous chapters. We also give the figures for capital invested in stocks, assuming no lapses. Another variable is the starting value for the yield. With such a large autocorrelation coefficient, this will have significant influence. We show the figures for starting long-term yields of 8 percent and 5 percent, with the starting regime randomly selected.

Clearly, looking at the top two rows of the table, it makes sense to invest the solvency capital in the same assets as the fund, as the tail risk is significantly reduced.

Even with the stock assumption for the invested solvency capital, and even allowing for substantial lapses, around 5 percent to 7 percent of the premium is required as solvency capital. With no lapses this has increased to nearly 20 percent for the 95 percent conditional tail expectation (CTE), even if interest rates are relatively high in the beginning. Where the GAO is in-the-money at the outset, with a long-term rate of interest of 5 percent at the valuation date, the 95 percent CTE is nearly 24 percent of the single premium. We would not expect a high rate of lapse, because the funds are associated with pensions contracts, and there are strong tax disincentives to cashing the contract in, even where this is permitted. Transfers to other pensions arrangements may be possible.

It is interesting to note that this kind of analysis does not require modern techniques. Yang (2001) has shown that, given the models and data available at the time these contracts were written in the 1980s, a similar, substantial liability would have been revealed. This is not surprising given the plots in Figures 12.1 and 12.2. And yet, according to the survey conducted in 1997 by the AGWP of the Faculty of Actuaries and the Institute of Actuaries (AGWP 1997), roughly one-half of the companies offering GAO benefits held no reserve; the other half used a deterministic method based on fixed, current long-term yields. From the 10,000 simulations used here, the estimated probability of a nonzero liability is around 44 percent, too big to ignore, but undetectable by deterministic methods when the contracts were issued.

DYNAMIC HEDGING

The Hedge

As with the standard GMMB contracts, we may explore the possibility of using financial economics to develop a replicating hedging strategy for this option. Interest rate options require an entire book of their own to describe and derive valuation methods. In the equity-linked GAO case we also have the stock process involved, and the theory required to value the option is beyond the scope of this book. Instead, we will describe the basic principles and adopt some highly simplifying assumptions to see how far they will take us.[3]

Because the option critically depends on interest rates, it is no longer sufficient to treat the risk-free rate as a fixed parameter. Instead, we use the stochastic discount factor $B(t_1, t_2)$, which is the value at t_1 of a unit sum payable at t_2, where there is no default risk. For $t_2 > t_1$, this can be thought of as the price at t_1 of a unit zero coupon bond maturing at t_2. We assume that at the start of the projection $t_1 = 0$, and all values of $B(0, t)$ are known. Then, analogously with the Black-Scholes-Merton framework, we have the value at $t = 0$ of a GAO maturing at n:

$$H_0 = B(0, n)E_Q[F_n(g\, a_{65}(n) - 1)^+] \qquad (12.4)$$

If we assume F_n is independent of the annuity value $a_{65}(n)$, this becomes more tractable because we can separate the expectation for F_n from the option part $(g\, a_{65}(n) - 1)^+$. Just as $F_t e^{-rt} = F_0$ in the constant interest rate model of the preceding chapters (ignoring management charges), with stochastic discount we have $F_t\, B(0, t) = F_0$.

We also define the (random) discounted annuity:

$$a_{65}^d(t_1, t_2) = B(t_1, t_2)a_{65}(t_2)$$

Then

$$H_0 = F_0 E_Q\left[\left(\frac{g\, a_{65}^d(0, n)}{B(0, n)} - 1\right)^+\right] \qquad (12.5)$$

Now if, further, we assume that $a_{65}^d(0, n)$ has a lognormal distribution, with annual variance σ_y^2, then this looks like a call option. The hedge at time $t = 0$ is

$$H_0 = F_0\{g\, a_{65}(0)\,\Phi(d_1(0)) - \Phi(d_2(0))\} \qquad (12.6)$$

More generally, the hedge at $t < n$ is

$$H_t = F_t\{g\, a_{65}(t)\,\Phi(d_1(t)) - \Phi(d_2(t))\} \qquad (12.7)$$

---

[3]This section draws heavily on Yang (2001).

where

$$d_1(t) = \frac{\log(g\, a_{65}(t)) + \sigma_y^2\,(n - t)/2}{\sigma_y\,\sqrt{n - t}}$$

and

$$d_2(t) = d_1(t) - \sigma_y\,\sqrt{n - t}$$

This assumption of lognormality for the discounted annuity is rather courageous, perhaps even foolhardy. It is quite plain that the discounted annuity process does not nearly follow the geometric Brownian motion underlying the Black-Scholes analysis. It is, in fact, very strongly autocorrelated. Nevertheless, we will follow this hedge through to see how it performs; if the hedge does not prove adequate under the projection with a more realistic autoregressive model for interest rates, that will emerge in large hedging errors when the hedge is projected under stochastic simulation.

It is not obvious from equation 12.7 how the hedge portfolio is constituted. Yang (2001) shows how to derive the constituent parts, using the three random processes, $a_{65}(t)$, $B(t, n)$, and F_t. The hedge comprises investments in each of these, that is $H_t = H_t^a + H_t^B + H_t^F$ where the first part is invested in a forward annuity with term $n - t$, the second part in bonds, and the third part in the fund. A forward annuity contract at t, maturing at n, is an annuity where the price is determined at t but is not paid until the annuity vests at n. With a flat yield curve, the forward annuity and immediate annuity prices are identical, both $a_{65}(t)$ at t, but of course the contracts are different. The hedge components at time t are

$$H_t^a = F_t\, g\, a_{65}(t)\, \Phi(d_1(t)) \tag{12.8}$$

$$H_t^B = -F_t\, g\, a_{65}(t)\, \Phi(d_1(t)) \tag{12.9}$$

$$H_t^F = F_t\{g\, a_{65}(t)\, \Phi(d_1(t)) - \Phi(d_2(t))\} \tag{12.10}$$

It should be said that this is not the only way to approach the hedge for this contract, but it is consistent with delta-hedging principles. One technical drawback is that the forward annuity is not in itself a traded instrument, though it can easily be replicated with bonds, allowing for deterministic mortality, provided the mortality risk is sufficiently diversified.

Because we will want to assess hedging error using this hedge strategy, we will note here how these constituent parts of the hedge develop to time

$t + 1^-$ assuming no rebalancing between t and $t + 1^-$:

$$H^a_{t+1^-} = F_t \, g \, a_{65}(t + 1) \, \Phi(d_1(t)) \tag{12.11}$$

$$H^B_{t+1^-} = -F_t \, g \, a_{65}(t) \, \Phi(d_1(t)) \, \frac{B(t + 1, n)}{B(t, n)} \tag{12.12}$$

$$H^F_{t+1^-} = F_{t+1} \{ g \, a_{65}(t) \, \Phi(d_1(t)) - \Phi(d_2(t)) \} \tag{12.13}$$

and the hedging error at $t + 1$ is then $H_{t+1} - H_{t+1^-}$. The second part of hedging expenses is transactions costs, and we assume here transactions costs of 0.2 percent of equities transactions, with no costs for transactions involving bonds and annuities.

Initial Hedge Value

Assuming $a_{65}(0) = 9.0$ and $\sigma_y = 0.015$ gives an initial hedge of £2.32 per £100 single premium, for each life in force at maturity. Allowing for mortality before vesting reduces this figure to £2.05. However, the constituent parts of the hedge at the start of the projection under these assumptions are

$$H^a_0 = 51.16; \quad H^B_0 = -51.16; \quad H^F_0 = 2.32$$

and there is clearly room for substantial hedging errors with these relatively large holdings in bonds and forward annuities.

The initial hedge cost is very sensitive to the current annuity price. Some examples are given in Table 12.2.

If we look further at the costs under this form of dynamic hedging, using the techniques described in Chapter 8 to determine the costs arising from

TABLE 12.2 Hedge and annuity part of hedge, GAO with $1/9$ guarantee rate, 15-year deferred period, vesting at age 65; with mortality allowance prevesting, no lapses.

Long-Term Yield at $t = 0$	$a_{65}(0)$	$\sigma_y = 0.015$		$\sigma_y = 0.025$	
		H_0	H^a_0	H_0	H^a_0
5%	10.61	15.88	104.23	16.04	100.27
6%	9.77	7.81	89.13	8.60	78.53
7%	9.04	2.27	48.41	3.64	47.95
8%	8.40	0.29	10.19	1.16	20.93
9%	7.83	0.01	0.70	0.27	6.38
10%	7.33	0.00	0.02	0.05	1.38

TABLE 12.3 Solvency capital using dynamic hedging, percentage of single premium, for 15-year GAO; with guaranteed annuity rate $1/9$, no lapses.

Nonhedge Solvency Capital Invested in:	Yield per Year at $t = 0$	$CTE_{90\%}$ %	$CTE_{95\%}$ %	$CTE_{99\%}$ %	Hedge Cost %
Bonds	8%	32.20	41.04	66.73	1.16
Stocks	8%	13.51	15.39	19.43	1.16
Stocks	5%	25.34	28.30	32.62	16.04

discrete hedging error and transactions costs, then dynamic hedging appears even more expensive. The hedge is very sensitive to movements in interest rates, so there tend to be occasional, substantial additional costs when the interest rate model moves regimes. Also, the hedge assumes a lognormal process with independent increments for interest rates and annuity prices. In fact, the P-measure model uses a very high autocorrelation factor.

As with the actuarial approach, it makes sense to hold the hedging error and transactions costs reserves in the separate fund rather than in bonds. The comparison is given in Table 12.3, which gives CTE figures for the dynamic-hedging approach. The figures include the initial hedge cost, which is also given in the table. The balance of the CTE over the hedge cost is the reserve for hedging error and transactions costs. To generate these numbers, we have used the hedge described above, with volatility $\sigma_y = 2.5$ percent. This is higher than the model volatility and means that we are *overhedging* somewhat, so that the average hedging error is negative.

A comparison of Table 12.3 with the actuarial approach in Table 12.1 shows that where the risk management is arranged while the option is out-of-the-money, with initial yield of 8 percent, the dynamic-hedging approach requires less capital than the actuarial approach for any of the CTE values specified. In fact, in common with the comparison of actuarial and dynamic-hedging risk measures for separate fund death and maturity guarantees in Chapter 9, the mean cost is less using the actuarial approach, but there is a heavy tail that pulls up the CTE risk measures. The CTE measures are plotted in Figure 12.5 for the two approaches, assuming starting long-term yields of 5 percent and 8 percent and assuming all solvency capital is held in the same assets as the separate fund.

The CTE risk measure is greater for the actuarial approach than for the dynamic-hedging approach for values of α greater than 83 percent for the out-of-the-money option in the right side graph in Figure 12.5. However, the "moneyness" of the option has a much greater effect on the dynamic-hedging costs than on the actuarial approach, and the CTE tail measure

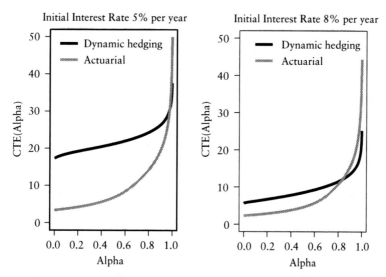

FIGURE 12.5 CTE risk measure for GAO with actuarial and dynamic-hedging risk management; starting yield in-the-money and out-of-the-money.

for the in-the-money projection (i.e., starting with a long-term yield of 5 percent per year) is greater for the dynamic-hedge approach for values of α up to around 97 percent.

The methods of Chapter 10 could usefully be applied to assess which risk management strategy is preferred here. As of June 2002, these options are quite deeply in-the-money. It is at least noteworthy that, even so, the hedging approach limits the right-tail liability risk.

STATIC REPLICATION

Rather than use a dynamic-hedge approach for the option, we may be able to replicate the annuity payments with readily available traded options. This effectively means reinsuring the risk with the option providers. This is called static replication because once the options are purchased there is no requirement (in principle) to make any other arrangement for the GAO liability.

Pelsser (2002) describes how to use traded swaption contracts to match the liabilities under a GAO with a fixed sum insured. A swaption is an option to swap—in this case, to swap the variable rate annuity for a fixed rate annuity based on the guaranteed annuity rate. Swaptions are very actively traded option contracts, readily available for a variety of terms. The usual swaption contract would offer an option to swap a bond paying variable interest (e.g., LIBOR) for a bond paying a fixed rate. This is similar to the liability under the GAO benefit, with the following exceptions:

- The payments required are level payments rather than coupon- and redemption-type payments typical for the standard swap.
- The payments are life contingent.
- The payments depend on the separate account value at maturity (or on the bonuses declared for with profit contracts).

The first two of these complications do not cause grievous problems; it is simple to combine bond-type payments to make up a level annuity, and the life contingency problems can be managed by assuming payments at age $x + t$ reduced by a factor $_tp_x$, exactly analogously to the deterministic treatment of mortality in the guaranteed minimum death benefit. This is justifiable if the portfolio is sufficiently large to ensure that mortality variation is not significant.

Pelsser shows that in the case of a fixed sum insured the purchase of swaptions requires less capital than the actuarial approach (using Yang (2001) for the comparable cost under the actuarial approach). He does not discuss how to deal with variable maturity values for the option.

It should be noted that an added complication that needs to be taken into consideration is the risk that the option provider will default. This is called the counterparty risk. For such long terms, this risk is substantial, and insurers purchasing options for any guarantee liability should consider using credit insurance as a second tier. At the very least, the credit rating of potential option providers is a critical factor in deciding whether to use this approach.

CHAPTER 13

Equity-Indexed Annuities

INTRODUCTION

An equity-indexed annuity (EIA) contract provides the policyholder with a guaranteed accumulation rate on their premium, and also, at maturity, benefits from an additional return based on the increase in an equity index over the term of the contract. This latter part is the equity-linking benefit, often called the *indexation* benefit. How this indexation is calculated varies among contracts, and some different policy designs are described later in this chapter. Although this sounds very similar to the variable-annuity (VA) contract with guaranteed minimum maturity benefit (GMMB), it is really quite a different contract. There is no separate fund invested in the underlying equities; the premium net of an expense allowance is essentially invested in risk-free bonds, and the contract up to maturity most closely resembles the fixed-interest contracts also available in the U.S. market, such as a fixed-interest deferred annuity or a certificate of deposit. At maturity, the contract benefits partially from the increase in a stock index—usually the S&P 500 price index—even though the assets of the contract are not directly invested in the index or underlying equities.

EIAs are popular contracts in the United States, though somewhat less so than the VA contracts of the previous chapters. Whereas U.S. sales of VA contracts exceeded $100 billion in 2001, sales of EIAs were less than $10 billion. In the section on contract design, we describe the most common forms of EIA contracts: the point-to-point, the annual ratchet (which comes in compound and simple versions), and the high water mark. In the section on valuing the embedded options, we show how the indexation benefit may be viewed as a call option on the equity index, and we describe how to value that option, using Black-Scholes-Merton principles from Chapter 7. In the section on dynamic hedging for the PTP option, we show further how to project the replicating portfolio under the real-world measure to derive the additional expenses of dynamic hedging. This section relies on material from

Chapter 8. The actuarial approach that we used in previous chapters, under which liabilities are projected under the real-world probability distribution without using the replicating-hedge approach to manage the risk, is not used for this contract. Finally, in the last section of this chapter, we give some suggestions for further reading.

In previous chapters the focus has been on separate fund contracts such as variable annuities and segregated fund policies. One reason for the emphasis on these contracts is that in North America these probably provide the greatest risk management challenge currently. EIAs are very different contracts, with somewhat simpler risk management issues than for the separate account products.

The major differences between the VA and the EIA are the following:

- EIA contracts are relatively short-term, compared with VA and segregated fund contracts. Terms between five and ten years are common, with seven years being typical.
- The EIA guarantee is in the form of a call option on the underlying equity index, rather than the put option of the VA contract.
- The EIA guarantee is usually in-the-money at maturity. The VA guarantee is rarely in-the-money at maturity.
- Because the EIA is written in the expectation that the guarantee would mature in-the-money, the contracts were designed with a view to passing the equity risk on to a third party, by buying appropriate call options. This is in contrast with the separate fund guarantees, which are rarely in-the-money, resulting (in the past) in a more lax approach to policy design, pricing, and risk management. The range of EIA contract designs resembles the range of call option designs available on the market. The option sellers are providing full reinsurance for the equity-linking risk.
- The equity indices used to link these contracts are not total return indices, as used for separate account products, but are price indices, which do not allow for dividend reinvestment and, therefore, accumulate rather more slowly than the total return versions of the indices.

Although a seven-year contract is a lot shorter than the 20 to 30 years typical for a separate account product, it is still a long term for an option. An option vendor would allow for the additional uncertainty involved with such a long contract by using a higher margin in the volatility assumption used to determine the price. The insurer must ensure that the option vendor has minimal default risk, and may wish to purchase additional credit insurance to cover the possibility of the default of the option vendor, which would leave the insurer very dangerously exposed.

CONTRACT DESIGN

There are many different contract designs and modifications. An introduction to the indexation methods and other policy features is given in Streiff and DiBiase (1999). We describe here the major contract types in force. The contract may be designed as a single premium or flexible premium contract. We will consider the single premium case only.

Given a single premium P, a proportion (95 percent is common) is invested in fixed-interest securities, earning a guaranteed rate of interest for the investor. This is commonly set at around 3 percent but may vary with more or less generous equity linking. So, the guaranteed amount at maturity is matched by the fixed-interest investments, and is typically equal to

$$G = (0.95) P (1.03)^n$$

where n is the term of the contract. We will use this guarantee throughout this chapter.

The equity linking provides an extra payoff on top of the guaranteed fund value, and it is in the method of determining this extra payoff that the contracts mostly vary.

Point-to-Point (PTP)

The simplest method of indexation for the equity-linked benefit is point-to-point, or PTP, indexing. Let S_t represent the value at t of the equity index used. Given a participation rate α, greater than zero and invariably (but not essentially) less than one, the additional maturity benefit at $t = n$ is[1]:

$$\left(P \left(1 + \alpha \left(\frac{S_n}{S_0} - 1 \right) \right) - G \right)^+ \tag{13.1}$$

So, for example, take a seven-year contract, indexed by reference to the S&P 500 index, sold on January 1, 1995, maturing on December 31, 2001. The increase in the S&P 500 index over the seven-year term was $S_7/S_0 = 2.501$. Assume a single premium of \$100, and that the guaranteed payout is found by accumulating 95 percent of the premium at 3 percent per year interest, so that $G = 116.84$. If we assume a participation rate of $\alpha = 0.6$, then the payoff under the equity indexation is

$$100(1 + (0.6)(2.501 - 1)) = 190.060$$

---

[1]Recall that $(X)^+ = \max(X, 0)$.

Because this amount is greater than the minimum, the benefit is set at $190.06. Had the policyholder invested in the equities that make up the index directly, the maturity value would have been $250.10; in addition, the policyholder would have received the dividends paid on the stocks. However, the EIA eliminates the risk that the index does not rise by more than around 3 percent per year.

Annual Ratchet

Under the annual ratchet method, the index participation is evaluated year by year. Each year the payout figure is increased by the greater of the *floor* rate—usually 0 percent—and the increase in the underlying index, multiplied by the participation rate. The increases may compound, or may not.

For example, take a three-year contract with a $100 premium. If the index grows in subsequent years by 5 percent, 15 percent, and –5 percent, then the payout under the compound annual ratchet (CAR), assuming a 0 percent floor rate and a participation rate of α, is

$$100\,(1 + 0.05\,\alpha)\,(1 + 0.15\,\alpha)$$

with no contribution from the final year as the –5 percent is replaced by the floor value of 0 percent.

The version without compounding, which we refer to as the simple annual ratchet, or SAR, would give a payout of

$$100(1 + .05\,\alpha + .15\,\alpha)$$

These payouts are subject to a fixed minimum of, say, 95 percent of the premium accumulated at 3 percent for three years.

More realistically, we return to the seven-year contract used to illustrate the PTP design, sold on January 1, 1995, maturing on December 31, 2001. Assume now that the indexing method used is the annual ratchet method, with floor rate 0 percent, all else being as before.

The annual increases in the S&P 500 index since January 1, 1995, have been:

1995	1996	1997	1998	1999	2000	2001
35.2%	18.7%	31.0%	26.2%	19.4%	−11.8%	−11.9%

So the payout under the compounded annual ratchet method is the greater of the minimum of $116.838 and the compounded ratcheted amount:

$$100\,(1 + (0.6)(0.352))(1 + (0.6)(0.187)) \cdots (1 + (0.6)(0.194)) = 206.401$$

And under the simple (that is, non-compound) annual ratchet the payout is the greater of $116.838 and

$$1000 \left\{ 1 + (0.6)(0.352) + (0.6)(0.187) + \cdots + (0.6)(0.194) \right\} = 178.300$$

Note that the difference is very significant. Under the compound version of the annual ratchet, the payout cannot be less than the PTP payout. Under the simple version, it certainly can, and the comforting impression given of year-to-year ratcheting belies the true, substantially detrimental (to the policyholder) effect of replacing the compounded index returns with simple returns. In much of the information available on annual ratchet contracts[2] it is not stated whether the ratcheting is simple or compound, and it seems very likely, therefore, that it is not well understood by policyholders. This may explain the rise in popularity of the annual ratchet design.

It is useful to express the guarantee symbolically; let S_t represent the stock index value at t; P is the premium and α is the participation rate. Then the CAR indexation pays the greater of the *ratcheted premium*

$$P \prod_{t=1}^{n} \left\{ 1 + \max\left(\alpha \left(\frac{S_t}{S_{t-1}} - 1 \right), 0 \right) \right\}$$

and the guarantee $G = 0.95 \, P(1.03)^n$ where 3 percent interest on 95 percent of the premium is guaranteed, and the term is n years. For the SAR, the guarantee is the greater of the ratcheted premium

$$P \left\{ 1 + \sum_{t=1}^{n} \max\left(\alpha \left(\frac{S_t}{S_{t-1}} - 1 \right), 0 \right) \right\}$$

and the accumulated premium $0.95 \, P(1.03)^n$.

An extra complication of some annual ratchet contracts is a *cap* rate. This is the maximum rate applying in any year. Assume a floor rate of 0 percent, and a cap rate of $100c$ percent; then the guarantee in the compound case is

$$P \prod_{t=1}^{n} \left\{ 1 + \min\left[\max\left(\alpha \left(\frac{S_t}{S_{t-1}} - 1 \right), 0 \right), c \right] \right\}$$

and similarly for the simple ratchet. In years when the equity index is increasing, the cap may have a significant effect. A 10 percent cap on the

---

[2]For example, see www.annuityratewatch.com.

1995 to 2001 contract, above, would affect each of the first five years, reducing the payout in the compound case to:

$$100(1 + \min(0.2112, 0.1))(1 + \min(0.1122, 0.1)) \cdots (1 + \min(0, 0.1))$$
$$= 161.05$$

which is still greater than the guaranteed minimum payout of $116.84. Note that over the full seven years of the contract, we use five years at the cap rate (10 percent) and two years at the floor rate (0 percent) in determining the ratcheted premium, and the benefit would be the same for a wide range of participation rates—in fact, for all $\alpha > 53$ percent. Thus, the use of a cap rate reduces the influence of the participation rate, a fact that will be born out in the results later in this chapter.

Under the simple annual ratchet with 10 percent cap, the payout under the equity indexing is

$$100(1 + 5(0.1)) = 150.$$

Together, the PTP and annual ratchet are by far the most common EIA designs.

High Water Mark

This indexing is very similar to the PTP design except that the payout under the indexation uses the maximum equity index value over the term, taking policy anniversary values only, in place of the index at maturity. That is, the payout is the greater of the guarantee G and

$$P\left(1 + \alpha\left(\frac{S^{\max}}{S_0} - 1\right)\right)$$

where $S^{\max} = \max(S_0, S_1, S_2, S_3, \ldots, S_n)$.

Consider the example contract written in 1995, and assume now that it is indexed using the high water mark method, all else unchanged. With a starting S&P 500 value of 459.11, the highest anniversary value is at the start of 2000, when the index reached 1455.22. So the payout for a $100 premium with a 60 percent participation rate is the greater of the guarantee of $116.84 and the indexed amount:

$$100\left\{1 + (0.6)\left(\frac{1455.22}{459.11} - 1\right)\right\} = 230.180$$

Clearly, the high water mark method of indexation will give a higher base for equity linking than the PTP. This would generally be reflected in a lower participation rate.

VALUING THE EMBEDDED OPTIONS

In the following sections, we derive valuation formulae for the benefits under different indexation schemes. The most common approach to risk management for EIA contracts is to purchase options from an external vendor matching the payout in excess of the minimum guarantee, and these valuation formulae will give the price for the option benefit. The minimum guarantee of (usually) 3 percent per year accumulation is easily matched by the insurer with fixed-interest instruments; if the risk-free rate is 6 percent, then guaranteeing 3 percent can be completely managed by investing in the risk-free instruments. So the insurer will only purchase the option cost in excess of this guarantee from the third party.

For a premium of $P, the guarantee only requires 95 percent invested, leaving 5 percent of the premium available to fund the necessary options. In addition, there are funds available from the *interest spread* on the invested premium. The interest spread loosely refers to the difference between the interest used to fund the policyholder's guarantee and the interest actually earned on the premium. If the long-term rate of interest available for such investments is around 6 percent per year, and the guaranteed interest rate on the contract is 3 percent, then the difference of 3 percent per year provides funds for the insurer to use for expenses, to purchase the necessary options, or for profit and contingencies.

Some, but not all, of this interest spread of around 3 percent per year is available to fund the option; the interest spread must also be sufficient to fund other expenses and contingencies. The guaranteed rates of interest on contracts such as certificates of deposit (CDs) run at approximately 2 percent higher than the guarantees available on EIA contracts. Since the CD contract is similar to the EIA with a guaranteed interest rate to maturity, and with no equity participation, we might infer that the 2 percent spread between the guaranteed rates is used to pay for the equity participation, and the remaining 1 percent spread between the CD rate and the risk-free rate is used for general expenses.

If this is a reasonable assumption, then for a premium of $P we have the cost of guarantee plus non-option expenses associated with a 3 percent guarantee of approximately 4 percent per year. In this case, there is 2 percent per year interest spread available from the invested premium to fund the equity indexation benefit.

It is convenient to work with the force of interest. Say the risk-free force of interest is 6 percent; the cost of the guaranteed premium plus additional expenses accounts for 4 percent per year on the premium less the 5 percent front-end expense deduction (remember, the guarantee only applies to

95 percent of the premium). So the cost of guarantee plus expenses is estimated at:

$$0.95 \, P \, e^{(.04-r)\,(7)} = 0.8259 \, P \tag{13.2}$$

leaving 17.41 percent of the premium available to pay for the indexation benefit.

In the sections that follow we give results assuming that the interest spread available for funding indexation benefits is 1 percent, 2 percent (as in equation 13.2), and 3 percent, which give funds available for the equity indexation benefit of $11.42 percent, $17.41 percent, and $22.99 percent of the single premium, respectively.

PTP OPTION VALUATION

Having said that we can manage the risk by purchasing options, in this section we delve a little deeper into how to use standard option formulae to value the option benefits for a simple PTP contract.

Now, recall from Chapter 7 that the payoff under a standard call option on S_t with strike price K and term n is $\max(S_n - K, 0) = (S_n - K)^+$. If we rearrange the payoff under the PTP indexation method given in equation 13.1 we have payoff H, say, where

$$H = \left(P \left(1 + \alpha \left(\frac{S_n}{S_0} - 1 \right) \right) - G \right)^+ \tag{13.3}$$

$$= \frac{\alpha P}{S_0} \left\{ S_n - \frac{S_0}{\alpha} \left(\frac{G}{P} - (1 - \alpha) \right) \right\}^+ \tag{13.4}$$

which is just the payoff under a plain vanilla call option, multiplied by $\alpha P / S_0$, and where the strike price is

$$K^{ptp} = \frac{S_0}{\alpha} \left(\frac{G}{P} - (1 - \alpha) \right)$$

So, to precisely match the equity indexation with options purchased from an external provider, the insurer should buy $P\alpha / S_0$ options on the stock S_t, with term corresponding to the term of the option and strike price K^{ptp}.

An important difference between the equity linking of EIA contracts and the equity linking of the separate fund contracts, such as variable annuities, arises from the fact that equity linking for the EIA contract is invariably by reference to a price index, which does not allow for reinvested dividends. This makes call options cheaper, because the replicating portfolio can use the incoming dividends to increase the stock part of the replicating portfolio. This is described in Chapter 7, with the formula given in equation 7.36 for an option on the stock with price S_t at t, where dividends are paid continuously on the stock at a rate of d per year.

Using the standard Black-Scholes call option formula, with allowance for dividend income, the cost of the option at the inception of the contract, using PTP indexation, assuming index linking to a regular index without reinvested dividends, and where dividends are received continuously at a rate of d per year, is

$$H_0 = \frac{\alpha P}{S_0} \left\{ S_0 e^{-dn} \Phi(d_1) - K^{ptp} e^{-rn} \Phi(d_2) \right\} \qquad (13.5)$$

$$= P \left(e^{-dn} \alpha \Phi(d_1) - \left(\frac{G}{P} - (1 - \alpha) \right) e^{-rn} \Phi(d_2) \right) \qquad (13.6)$$

$$= \alpha P e^{-dn} \Phi(d_1) - (G - P(1 - \alpha)) e^{-rn} \Phi(d_2) \qquad (13.7)$$

where

$$d_1 = \frac{\log(S_0/K^{ptp}) + (r - d + \sigma^2/2)n}{\sigma\sqrt{n}} \qquad (13.8)$$

$$= \frac{\log(\alpha P/(G - P(1 - \alpha))) + (r - d + \sigma^2/2)n}{\sigma\sqrt{n}} \qquad (13.9)$$

and

$$d_2 = d_1 - \sigma\sqrt{n}$$

We can use the formula to value the option cost of equity indexation for a standard PTP EIA contract. The details are as follows:

- Seven-year contract with PTP indexation.
- Sixty percent participation rate.
- A single premium of $100.
- Three percent per year minimum return guarantee, applied to 95 percent of the premium.

In addition, we need parameters for the Black-Scholes call option value; say, a risk-free force of interest of $r = 6$ percent per year, a dividend rate of $d = 2$ percent, and a volatility of $\sigma = 20$ percent. The cost of the call option for the contract is $11.567. Using a 2 percent interest spread, the

TABLE 13.1 Break-even participation rates for seven-year PTP EIA.

Interest Spread Available*	Volatility, σ		
	0.20	0.25	0.30
1%	59.5%	51.1%	44.6%
2%	81.3%	70.5%	62.1%
3%	101.3%	88.4%	78.2%

*Net of non-option expenses.

funds available to fund the option are $17.41, which is substantially on the profitable side of the break-even point.

Most authors treat the participation rate as the variable controlling the cost of the embedded option. The guaranteed minimum benefit is generally not used to adjust costs. If the insurer approaches an external option vendor to provide a static hedge for the contract, the option price quoted may be based on a high volatility value, because option vendors use volatility margin for profit and contingencies. In Table 13.1 we show the break-even participation rates for the seven-year PTP contract described in this section, assuming a $100 premium, of which the interest spread available to fund the option is between 1 percent and 3 percent, where an available interest spread of δ implies funds available of $P - (0.95)Pe^{-\delta n}$.

There is no allowance in these figures for lapses or deaths; incorporating these assumptions would reduce the cost of the option and increase the break-even participation rates. As a relatively new contract, there is little lapse experience available. Because the market offers a range of terms, and the standard contract is relatively short compared with most variable annuity contracts, it is expected that lower lapse rates will apply. The participation rates in the middle row of Table 13.1 do correspond approximately to those offered in the market; particularly for values of σ of around 25 percent.

Tiong (2001)

Tiong (2001) is a well-known paper in U.S. actuarial circles giving valuation formulae for some options, including PTP and CAR. The break-even participation rates in Tiong's work for the PTP option are somewhat different from those in Table 13.1, as is her valuation formula, and it is worth exploring briefly why.

Tiong values embedded options in EIAs by a more circuitous route than we have used, using Esscher transforms. This is a device to find the market price. For the PTP and CAR contracts there does not appear to be any advantage over the usual method of expectation under Q-measure for these contracts, although there may be for others. Within the regular Black-Scholes-Merton framework, where stock prices follow a geometric Brownian motion process, the Esscher transform method must give the same results as the standard methodology of taking the Q-measure expectation of the discounted payoff. So this is not a source of difference in the results.

The first difference between the results in this chapter and Tiong's results is that Tiong assumes that the guaranteed minimum interest rate applies to 90 percent of the premium, where we have assumed 95 percent, so that the guarantee appears more expensive here. Second, Tiong assumes that the entire difference between the risk-free rate and the guaranteed rate is available to fund the option, so that her figures correspond to the bottom row of the table. The third difference—and this is the reason for the difference in the final valuation formulae—is that Tiong is valuing a different option in her section on PTP contracts. The participation rate is applied to the $\log_e$ of the stock index appreciation; that is, she values the payoff:

$$\left(P\left(\frac{S_n}{S_0}\right)^{\alpha} - G \right)^{+}$$

The first term can be expanded using the binomial theorem, showing that the standard payoff under the equity indexation, given in equation 13.1, corresponds to the first two terms in the power series. The contract valued by Tiong is generally smaller than the true EIA payoff for $\alpha < 1$, because the third term in the binomial expansion of $(S_n/S_0)^{\alpha}$ is

$$\frac{\alpha(\alpha - 1)}{2!}\left(\frac{S_n}{S_0} - 1\right)^{2}$$

which is negative for $\alpha < 1$.

All of these differences work the same way, so that the break-even participation rates in Tiong's work are rather higher than those found in this section.

COMPOUND ANNUAL RATCHET VALUATION

Viewed as a derivative security, the annual ratchet benefit is an option on an option. That is, the payout is the greater of the ratcheted premium, in the compound case:

$$P\prod_{t=1}^{n}\left\{ 1 + \max\left(\alpha\left(\frac{S_t}{S_{t-1}} - 1\right), 0\right)\right\} = RP \quad \text{(say)}$$

and the fixed interest guarantee $G = 0.95\,P(1.03)^n$. So we can write the option benefit, which is the payout required in addition to the fixed interest guarantee, as

$$H = \max(\text{RP} - G, 0)$$

which is clearly a call option on the benefit RP, which is a function of the stock index S_t. However, the payout RP itself involves an option, referred to as a ratchet or ladder option in the exotic derivatives literature.

In the compound case, we can calculate the value of the ratcheted premium as an option, even with the cap applied. The simple ratcheted premium option cannot be valued analytically. The difference is that multiplying lognormal random variables in the compound case gives another lognormal random variable, but adding them in the simple case requires the distribution of the sum of dependent lognormal random variables, which has no manageable analytic form. However, even in the compound form, the additional guarantee of G, called the *life-of-contract* guarantee by Boyle and Tan (2002), means that no analytic form for the replicating portfolio is available.

In this section, we will derive the formula for the compound ratchet and explore whether this may be used as an approximation for the CAR with life-of-contract guarantee, which is the most common form of annual ratchet EIA.

CAR without Life-of-Contract Guarantee

Without the life-of-contract guarantee, the benefit under the CAR contract is the ratcheted premium RP, which can be written:

$$\text{RP} = P \prod_{t=1}^{n} \left\{ 1 + \max\left(\alpha\left(\frac{S_t}{S_{t-1}} - 1 \right), 0 \right) \right\} \tag{13.10}$$

To find the value of the ratcheted premium using Black-Scholes principles we take expectation under the risk-neutral distribution of the discounted payout. The only result we need is the standard Black-Scholes call option formula.

Under the normal Black-Scholes assumptions, S_t/S_{t-1} are independent and identically distributed for $t = 1, 2, \ldots$ under the unique Q-measure. This means that we can replace each term in the product in equation 13.10 with its expectation, using independence, and that all the expectations are the same, because the annual accumulations S_t/S_{t-1} are identically distributed. So the value of the RP option is

$$H = E_Q\left[e^{-rn}(\text{RP})\right] \tag{13.11}$$

$$= P\,E_Q\left[\prod_{t=1}^{n} e^{-r}\left\{1 + \max\left(\alpha\left(\frac{S_t}{S_{t-1}} - 1\right), 0\right)\right\}\right] \tag{13.12}$$

$$= P\prod_{t=1}^{n}\left\{e^{-r} + E_Q\left[e^{-r}\max\left(\alpha\left(\frac{S_t}{S_{t-1}} - 1\right), 0\right)\right]\right\} \tag{13.13}$$

Now $\quad E_Q\left[e^{-r}\max\left(\left(\frac{S_t}{S_{t-1}} - 1\right), 0\right)\right]$

is the value of a one-year call option on the stock S_t, with initial stock value and strike price both equal to 1.0. This comes from the fact that S_t/S_{t-1} has the same distribution as S_1/S_0, and if we assume (without losing generality because it is an index) that $S_0 = 1$, the expectation becomes

$$E_Q\left[e^{-r}\max(S_1 - 1, 0)\right] \tag{13.14}$$

which is clearly the one-year call option value, with unit strike and unit current stock price. Using the Black-Scholes call-option formula, allowing for dividends of d per year, we have

$$\alpha E_Q\left[e^{-r}\max(S_1 - 1, 0)\right] = \alpha\left\{e^{-d}\Phi(d_1) - e^{-r}\Phi(d_2)\right\} \tag{13.15}$$

where

$$d_1 = \frac{r - d + \sigma^2/2}{\sigma} \quad \text{and} \quad d_2 = d_1 - \sigma$$

So the value of the ratcheted premium option is

$$H = P\left\{e^{-r} + \alpha\left(e^{-d}\Phi(d_1) - e^{-r}\Phi(d_2)\right)\right\}^{n} \tag{13.16}$$

In Table 13.2, we show the results for an initial premium of $P = 100$, using the following parameters: $r = 0.06$; $d = 0.02$; the term n is 7 years; the volatility is $\sigma = 0.2, 0.25,$ and 0.3; and we show a range of participation rates. The value given is the market value of the entire ratcheted premium payout. What these figures show is how much it would cost to provide the

TABLE 13.2 Ratchet premium option values, $100 initial premium.

		RP Value	
Participation Rate	$\sigma = 0.20$	$\sigma = 0.25$	$\sigma = 0.30$
0.4	87.24	92.01	97.02
0.5	93.48	99.84	106.60
0.6	100.10	108.24	116.97
0.7	107.11	117.24	128.20

ratcheted premium payout, under the standard Black-Scholes assumptions. So, if an insurer is purchasing option coverage for the benefit from an external vendor that uses a 25 percent volatility assumption in pricing the contract, it would cost them $99.84 for 50 percent participation; that is, leaving $0.16 of the premium for the insurer. The insurer has no remaining liability unless the option vendor defaults. Clearly, the insurer cannot afford a participation rate higher than around 60 percent, because this would cost more than the premium received for $\sigma \geq 20$ percent.

It is really quite straightforward to adapt the RP formula to allow for slightly more complicated products. For example, under the scheme above, the ratcheted premium is guaranteed to increase each year by the lesser of 1.0 and $1 + \alpha(S_t/S_{t-1} - 1)$. Suppose that instead of a minimum accumulation factor of 1.0 we applied a minimum accumulation factor of, say, e^g for some g. Then in place of

$$E_Q\left[e^{-r}\left\{1 + \alpha\,\max\left(\frac{S_t}{S_{t-1}} - 1, 0\right)\right\}\right]$$

we have

$$E_Q\left[e^{-r}\left\{1 + \max\left(\alpha\left(\frac{S_t}{S_{t-1}} - 1\right), e^g - 1\right)\right\}\right] \tag{13.17}$$

$$= E_Q\left[e^{-r}\left\{1 + \max\left(\alpha(S_1 - 1), e^g - 1\right)\right\}\right] \tag{13.18}$$

$$= E_Q\left[e^{-r}\left\{1 + (e^g - 1) + \alpha\,\max\left(S_1 - \left(\frac{e^g - (1 - \alpha)}{\alpha}\right), 0\right)\right\}\right] \tag{13.19}$$

$$= e^{g-r} + \alpha\,\mathrm{BSC}\left(K = \frac{e^g - (1 - \alpha)}{\alpha}, n = 1\right) \tag{13.20}$$

where $\mathrm{BSC}(K, n)$ is the Black-Scholes call-option price with strike K, starting stock price 1.0, and term n years. Substituting the appropriate Black-Scholes option formula gives equation 13.22, below:

$$H = P\left\{ e^{g-r} + \alpha\left(e^{-d}\Phi(d_1) - e^{-r}\left(\frac{e^g - (1-\alpha)}{\alpha}\right)\Phi(d_2)\right)\right\}^n \quad (13.21)$$

$$= P\left\{ \alpha e^{-d}\Phi(d_1) + e^{g-r}\Phi(-d_2) + e^{-r}(1-\alpha)\Phi(d_2)\right\}^n \quad (13.22)$$

where

$$K_1 = \frac{e^g - (1-\alpha)}{\alpha} \quad (13.23)$$

and

$$d_1 = \frac{\log(1/K_1) + r - d + \sigma^2/2}{\sigma} \quad \text{and} \quad d_2 = d_1 - \sigma \quad (13.24)$$

Substituting some numbers gives a table of results comparable with Table 13.2, but with a 3 percent annual ratchet guarantee, that is $e^g = 1.03$. The results are given in Table 13.3. We can see that if the option is priced at a volatility rate of 25 percent, then the participation rate must be less than 40 percent for the contract to break even. A participation rate of 36.8 percent will exactly break even.

Now if we add an annual cap rate—that is, a maximum amount by which the premium is ratcheted up each year of $e^c - 1$—the valuation formula becomes:

$$P\left\{ \alpha e^{-d}\left(\Phi(d_1) - \Phi(d_3)\right) + (1-\alpha)e^{-r}\left(\Phi(d_2) - \Phi(d_4)\right)\right.$$
$$\left. + e^{g-r}\Phi(-d_2) + e^{c-r}\Phi(d_4)\right\}^n \quad (13.25)$$

TABLE 13.3 Ratchet premium option values with 3 percent annual minimum ratchet, $100 initial premium.

	RP Value		
Participation Rate	$\sigma = 0.20$	$\sigma = 0.25$	$\sigma = 0.30$
0.3	91.03	94.05	98.83
0.4	97.05	103.60	108.86
0.5	103.60	110.86	118.53
0.6	110.62	119.86	129.73

where d_1 and d_2 are defined in equation 1 and

$$K_2 = \frac{e^c - (1 - \alpha)}{\alpha} \qquad (13.26)$$

$$d_3 = \frac{\log(1/K_2) + r - d + \sigma^2/2}{\sigma} \quad \text{and} \quad d_4 = d_3 - \sigma \qquad (13.27)$$

With a cap of c where $e^c = 1.1$, all the values in Table 13.3 are reduced to between \$90 and \$96. The vulnerability to both the stock price volatility and the participation rate are very much reduced because the process is constrained at both ends, with a 3 percent floor and a 10 percent ceiling. This was demonstrated earlier in this chapter, where we showed that a seven-year CAR contract purchased on January 1, 1995, would have an RP benefit that is the same for any participation rate above 53 percent, because the returns in each year are either negative (so that the floor applies) or greater than 18.7 percent (so that the ceiling applies provided the participation rate is greater than $0.1/0.187 = 53$ percent).

The break-even participation rate for the CAR using 25 percent volatility is 180 percent, a dramatic increase on the rate of less than 40 percent without a cap. Increasing the cap quickly reduces the break-even participation rate; using 14 percent in place of 10 percent reduces the break-even participation rate from 180 percent to 52 percent. Even this relatively high cap is a very effective way of reducing the guarantee costs, compared with offering unlimited upside annual ratchet.

Some readers will notice that the participation rates quoted here are lower than some of those quoted in the market. For example, a selection of annual ratchet contracts from a few different companies featured on www.annuityratewatch.com currently (as at June 2002) shows:

Contract	Participation Rate	Annual Cap
A	75%	12%
B	70%	11%
C	55%	none
D	100%	none

All of these companies offer an annual floor rate of $g = 0$ percent as well as a life-of-contract minimum guarantee of 3 percent per year. Without the life-of-contract guarantee, and assuming 25 percent volatility and a compound ratchet benefit, the break-even participation rates for these contracts are greater than 100 percent for contracts A and B, and 50.1 percent for contracts C and D. So it appears that contracts A and B are comfortably profitable, at least before the life-of-contract guarantee cost is added, whereas contracts C and D are not. Clearly contract D stands out here—how can the insurer offer such generous terms? One answer is in the use of simple rather than compound annual ratcheting. We saw earlier in this chapter that the simple annual ratchet is cheaper than the compound version. Also, contract D uses *averaging* in determining the indexation. This means that the index value for determining the annual reset is averaged, either on a monthly or a daily basis, over the year prior to maturity. This decreases the volatility of returns greatly and makes the option cheaper, although it does not necessarily reduce payouts to policyholders, providing lower returns in rising markets and higher returns in falling markets.

CAR with Life-of-Contract Guarantee

The simple annual ratchet contract and the addition of a life-of-contract guarantee are not amenable to the analytic approach. A simple method of valuing the option in these cases is by stochastic simulation, also called the Monte Carlo method. Recall that the Black-Scholes valuation of any derivative contract is the expected value of the discounted payoff under the risk-neutral distribution. In the standard Black-Scholes context that we are using in this chapter, the risk-neutral distribution is lognormal, with independent and identically distributed increments, and with parameters for the annual log-return distribution of $r - d - \sigma^2/2$ and σ^2, where the d is the continuously compounded dividend yield rate.

We will simulate the payoff under the option for, say, 100,000 projections of the stock price process, and discount using the risk-free rate of interest. The mean value is the estimated Black-Scholes price of the option.

We will use the Monte Carlo method in this section for the compound ratchet option with life-of-contract guarantee, as well as in the next section for the simple annual ratchet with life-of-contract guarantee. Following the earlier results of this chapter, we ignore mortality and lapses.

We have used a control variate to improve the accuracy of the Monte Carlo simulation. This calibrates the simulation by using the same random variables for the option and for some related value, which can also be calculated exactly by analytic methods. This value is the control variate. The simulated value of the option is adjusted by the difference between the actual and estimated values of the control variate. The method is described in detail with examples and in Chapter 11. It is an obvious method to use here because the value of the compound annual ratchet benefit option with life-of-contract guarantee will be very close to the value of the annual ratchet benefit without life-of-contract guarantee, since in the great majority of cases the option will mature in-the-money.

For an example, we look at the simulated value of a compound annual ratchet option with life-of-contract guarantee as follows:

- One-hundred dollar single-premium contract.
- Seven-year term.
- Sixty percent participation rate.
- Zero percent annual floor.
- Ten percent annual cap.
- Life-of-contract guarantee of 3 percent per year on 95 percent of the premium.

We use the following assumptions:

- Risk-free rate of return of 6 percent per year continuously compounded.
- Volatility $\sigma = 0.25$.
- Dividend yield of 2 percent per year continuously compounded.
- Lapses and mortality ignored.

Then, using 100,000 simulations, the estimated value of the option before allowing for the control variate is $86.630; the estimated value of the ratcheted premium using the same simulations is $85.912. The true value of the ratcheted premium is $85.937, using equation 13.25. So the stochastic simulation appears to be valuing the option a little low, and we adjust by adding the difference $(85.937 - 85.912)$ back to the original estimated option value, to give a value of $86.655 for the option including the life-of-contract part.

The value of the complete benefit is estimated at, say, $86.66. The value of the ratchet-only part, without the life-of-contract benefit, is $85.94, so the additional cost of the life-of-contract benefit is around $0.72, relatively small as we would expect. It is worth noting that the ratchet-only part with a 3 percent annual floor costs $95.48 for a $100 premium, considerably more than the 0 percent annual floor and 3 percent per year life-of-contract minimum benefit; therefore it is not possible to use the ratchet floor in place of the life-of-contract guarantee.

The reason for this conclusion is quite clear from an example; suppose that returns in three successive years are 25 percent, −5 percent, and 15 percent. Consider a three-year contract with $100 premium, 10 percent cap, 0 percent floor, 60 percent participation rate, and a 3 percent life-of-contract benefit with no initial expense deduction (just to make things simpler). The ratchet hits the ceiling in the first year, hits the floor in the second, and falls in between in the third, giving the ratcheted premium value of

$$100(1.1)(1.0)(1 + 0.6(0.15)) = 1.199$$

This value is greater than the 3 percent per year minimum accumulation, and the 3 percent minimum interest rate does not enter the calculation. On the other hand, an annual floor of 3 percent in place of the life-of-contract benefit offers

$$100(1.1)(1.03)(1 + 0.6(0.15)) = 1.235$$

and the 3 percent minimum enters the calculation every year that the return falls below that rate. Some authors have used the annual floor as a proxy for the life-of-contract guarantee, but it will give poor results.

The benefit cost of $86.66 for the annual ratchet with life-of-contract guarantee includes the minimum payment of $0.95P(1.03)^7$, which will be met by the office; so the cost of the option net of the guaranteed minimum is the cost of the benefit as a whole less the discounted value of the guaranteed payment, that is, for a $100 premium,

$$86.66 - 95(1.03)^7 e^{-7r} = 9.89$$

Now this is the option to be funded by the excess of the premium over the cost of the guarantee and other expenses. In an earlier section we assumed that the amount available for funding the option could be taken as $P(1 - .95e^{-(\delta)n})$. This was referred to as an available spread of δ for funding the option. Recall that with an available spread of 1 percent the amount is $11.42 percent of the premium, with 2 percent (which seems close to industry values) it is $17.41 percent, and with 3 percent it is $22.99 percent. So, a 1 percent interest spread would be sufficient to fund the option valued above. On the other hand, if we increase the cap to 15 percent, the price becomes $93.53 gross of the guaranteed minimum and $16.76 net, which requires the 2 percent interest spread.

The participation rates implied by the three interest rate spreads are given in Table 13.4 for cap rates of 10 percent and 15 percent, and for no cap rate. We assume volatility of 25 percent per year and all other assumptions

TABLE 13.4 Break-even participation rates for capped compound annual ratchet contract with life-of-contract guarantee.

Interest Spread Available	10% Cap	15% Cap	No Cap
1%	81%	40%	33%
2%	*	63%	41%
3%	*	104%	49%

as before. The entries for 10 percent cap in the lower two rows are missing because there is no break-even rate. This is because the contracts are always profitable.

A Trinomial Lattice Approximation for CAR with Life-of-Contract Guarantee

It may be convenient to have an approximate formula for the annual ratchet with life-of-contract guarantee that avoids the need for repeated Monte Carlo simulation for a large portfolio of contracts. Boyle and Tan (2002) show the results of applying an annual trinomial lattice approach for the compound ratchet option with life-of-contract guarantee, where an annual cap applies.

With both a floor and a cap applying, the interest applied to the premium each year to make up the equity indexation benefit has a probability mass at the floor and at the cap, and a continuous density between these points. The trinomial approximation uses a three-point discrete distribution to approximate the mixed Q-measure distribution. Where the cap is c and the floor is g (generally $g = 0$), then the probability that the premium is increased by e^c is

$$\Pr\left[\alpha\left(\frac{S_t}{S_{t-1}} - 1\right) > e^c - 1\right] = \Pr\left[\frac{S_t}{S_{t-1}} > \frac{e^c - (1 - \alpha)}{\alpha}\right]$$

Now, under the Q-measure, and allowing for dividend income, S_t/S_{t-1} is lognormally distributed with parameters $r - d - \sigma^2/2$ and σ, so, from equation 13.27, this probability is

$$1 - \Phi\left\{\frac{\log(K_2) - (r - d - \sigma^2/2)}{\sigma}\right\} = 1 - \Phi(-d_4) = \Phi(d_4) \qquad (13.28)$$

Similarly, the probability that the equity-linking benefit is increased by g in a year is simply the probability that $\alpha(S_t/S_{t-1} - 1)$ is less than $e^g - 1$, which is $\Phi(-d_2)$, where d_2 is given in equation 1.

The remaining probability is $1 - \Phi(d_4) - \Phi(-d_2) = \Phi(d_2) - \Phi(d_4)$, and this is spread over the values between the floor and the cap. We approximate the annual accumulation factor by assigning this probability to the accumulation factor $e^{(c+g)/2}$. This is actually a little smaller in general than the expected value of the return, given that the return falls between the floor and ceiling, but allows the use of a recombining trinomial lattice. The symmetry allows us to combine, for example, a floor value followed by a ceiling value with two middle values, to arrive after two time units at an accumulation of e^{c+g} in either case.

The recombining trinomial tree with seven stages representing the seven years of the contract ends with 15 nodes. The first node represents seven years of floor accumulation factors, giving a final ratchet factor of e^{7g}; the second node represents six years of floor values and one year of the middle value, giving final ratchet factor $e^{6.5g+.5c}$; the third node represents both six floor plus one ceiling and five floor plus two middle values, giving final ratchet factor e^{6g+c} in both cases, and so on. It is straightforward to calculate the probabilities for each terminal node from the multinomial distribution. Hence, we can estimate the probabilities associated with each outcome for the ratchet factors.

We can then apply the life-of-contract minimum payment by replacing the ratchet premium payout with the guaranteed minimum for all nodes with ratchet payouts less than the guarantee. For example, if $e^c = 0.1, g = 0.0$, and the guarantee is 1.1684 times the premium (using 95 percent of the premium accumulated at 3 percent per year, as before), then the first four nodes out of 15 would be replaced by the minimum payment, because the first five ratchet factors are: $e^{7g} = 1.0, e^{6.5g+.5c} = 1.0488, e^{6g+c} = 1.105$, $e^{5.5g+1.5c} = 1.1618$, and $e^{5g+2c} = 1.2214$.

Boyle and Tan (2002) achieve accuracy of around 0.06 percent using this method, with a 10 percent cap. It should be noted, though, that the estimates are biased low, because the middle value used for the recombining lattice is less than the expected value of the ratchet factor, given that it falls between the two values. Using the notation of equations 1 and 13.27, this expected value is

$$1 + \alpha \left(e^r \frac{\Phi(d_1) - \Phi(d_3)}{\Phi(d_2) - \Phi(d_4)} - 1 \right)$$

In the case where $g = 0.0, e^c = 0.1, r = .06, \sigma = 0.25$, and $\alpha = 0.60$, the assumption of middle ratchet factor for the trinomial method is $e^{c/2} = 1.0488$. The true expected ratchet factor, given that it falls between the floor and the ceiling, is 1.0627. A non-recombining trinomial tree with the middle value equal to this expectation would be computationally slightly more complex, with 36 separate outcomes representing all the possible numerical combinations of high, middle, and low outcomes, over seven time steps. However, the results should be more accurate, particularly for higher cap rates.

THE SIMPLE ANNUAL RATCHET OPTION VALUATION

The SAR contract with life-of-contract guarantee, with no cap, pays at maturity the greater of the ratcheted premium:

$$P \left\{ 1 + \sum_{t=1}^{n} \alpha \left(\frac{S_t}{S_{t-1}} - 1 \right)^+ \right\} \tag{13.29}$$

TABLE 13.5 Break-even participation rates for capped
SAR contract with life-of-contract guarantee.

Interest Spread Available	10% Cap	15% Cap	No Cap
1%	> 200%	52%	38%
2%	*	107%	49%
3%	*	>200%	59%

and the accumulated premium minimum guarantee, usually $G = (0.95) \times P(1.03)^n$. If the contract includes a cap c, then the contribution to the ratchet function from the tth year is $\min(c, \alpha(S_t/S_{t-1} - 1)^+)$.

As we have mentioned, even without the life-of-contract guarantee, the simple ratchet is not amenable to analytic calculation. We shall therefore use the Monte Carlo method again.

The compound ratchet used in the previous section also provides a useful control variate for the SAR contract and has been used for the results of this section. We expect the simple ratchet to provide a cheaper benefit than the compound. With a volatility of 25 percent, and all other factors as in the example of the previous section, a 10 percent cap with a 60 percent participation rate cost an estimated \$86.66 under the CAR, and is estimated at \$84.44 under the simple ratchet.

The two rates are not very different, but under the risk-neutral distribution the expected value of $\min(c, \alpha(S_t/S_{t-1} - 1)^+)$ is relatively small for the values of c and α considered here—at approximately 2 percent—so the effect of compounding is not as pronounced as it would be under the true probabilities.

In Table 13.5 participation rates are given using the same assumptions as in Table 13.4, showing that the change from the compound to the simple version of the annual ratchet allows a substantial increase in the participation rates funded by the available part of the interest rate spread.

THE HIGH WATER MARK OPTION VALUATION

The high water mark, or HWM, contract pays the greater of the guarantee, typically, as used previously, 95 percent of the premium with 3 percent per year interest, and the equity participation:

$$P\left(1 + \alpha\left(\frac{S^{max}}{S_0} - 1\right)\right)$$

where $S^{max} = \max(S_0, S_1, S_2, S_3, \ldots, S_n)$.

TABLE 13.6 Break-even participation rates for HWM indexed EIA; percentage of premium.

Interest Spread Available	Volatility		
	$\sigma = 0.20$	$\sigma = 0.25$	$\sigma = 0.30$
1%	33%	25%	20%
2%	43%	33%	23%
3%	51%	40%	33%

This is an unusual form of *lookback* option. Lookback options, in general, are well documented in the derivatives literature. In the standard Black-Scholes framework, the lookback can be managed analytically if the maximum is taken over the continuous time process $\{S_t\}_{0 < t \le n}$. Where the process is monitored over discrete periods only, the analytic approach is no longer tractable. The analytic results for the continuous time process do not even give a particularly useful approximation for the discrete time liability, because the volatility of the stock price process means that the maximum of the continuously monitored process may be very much greater than the maximum of the discretely monitored process.

So, for an idea of the price of the option we use simulation once again. Results for the same contract as in the previous tables, but with HWM indexation, are given in Table 13.6.

In Table 13.7 we compare the break-even participation rates for all four indexing systems; we assume 20 percent and 25 percent volatility and 2 percent interest spread available to fund the equity participation. This table shows that the HWM indexation is the most expensive, with the PTP the least expensive. In fact, using a 10 percent cap with the compound

TABLE 13.7 Comparison of break-even participation rates for different indexation methods; 2 percent interest spread available to fund guarantee liability.

Indexation Method	$\sigma = 0.20$	$\sigma = 0.25$
PTP	81.3%	70.8%
CAR		
No Cap	50.0%	41.8%
15% Cap	68.9%	63.2%
SAR, no cap	58.7%	49.0%
HWM	42.6%	33.3%

annual ratchet method is even cheaper than the PTP method, with a break-even participation rate of more than 100 percent. The sensitivity to the volatility is similar for all methods except the CAR with cap, where it is smaller. This is because the added volatility is absorbed in the cap and floor rates.

DYNAMIC HEDGING FOR THE PTP OPTION

The valuations in the previous section are sufficient for calculating prices to pay a third party to take on the equity indexation liability of an EIA contract. An insurer who wishes to manage the risk internally should extend the analysis to allow for the additional costs of hedging, beyond the initial expense of establishing the replicating portfolio. Although, in theory, the hedge is self-financing, as we discussed for the separate fund contracts, there will be additional costs from discrete hedging error, from model error (because we use a regime-switching model), and from transactions costs.

The assessment of the unhedged liability has been described in detail in previous chapters, particularly in Chapter 8. In this section, we show how capital requirements beyond the hedge costs may be assessed using stochastic simulation for the EIA contract. The idea, as before, is that we project the hedge forward, using a realistic real-world distribution (that is, the P-measure, not the Q-measure, which is a pricing device), and rebalance the hedge each month. The hedging error and model error are captured in the difference between the hedge required at each month end and the hedge brought forward at each month end. The transactions costs are based on the absolute change in value of the equity part of the hedge; it is assumed that transactions in bonds are virtually free.

We will illustrate this with a PTP benefit. We showed in the section on PTP option valuation in this chapter that the hedge at inception of a contract for a PTP option is

$$H = \frac{\alpha P}{S_0} \left\{ S_0 e^{-dn} \Phi(d_1) - K^{ptp} e^{-rn} \Phi(d_2) \right\}$$

and if we assume a premium of \$100, and assume that $S_0 = 100$, then we can generalize this hedge from the amount required at inception to the amount required at any duration t of the contract, where $0 \leq t \leq n$:

$$H_t = \alpha \left\{ S_t e^{-d(n-t)} \Phi(d_1(t)) - K^{ptp} e^{-r(n-t)} \Phi(d_2(t)) \right\} \tag{13.30}$$

where

$$d_1(t) = \frac{\log(S_t/K^{ptp}) + (r - d + \sigma^2/2)(n - t)}{\sigma\sqrt{n - t}}$$

and

$$d_2(t) = d_1(t) - \sigma\sqrt{n - t}$$

To simulate the hedging error distribution, we use the P-measure to simulate a projection of S_t monthly from inception to maturity. At time $t + 1$ (in months), the hedge brought forward from the previous month has accumulated to

$$H_{t+1} = \alpha\left\{S_{t+1}e^{-d(n-t-1)}\Phi(d_1(t)) - K^{ptp}e^{-r(n-t-1)}\Phi(d_2(t))\right\} \quad (13.31)$$

and the hedge required is

$$H_{t+1} = \alpha\left\{S_{t+1}e^{-d(n-t-1)}\Phi(d_1(t+1)) - K^{ptp}e^{-r(n-t-1)}\Phi(d_2(t+1))\right\}$$

$$(13.32)$$

The difference is the hedging error. Transactions costs at rate $100tc$ percent of the cost of equity transactions amount at time $t + 1$ to

$$tc\,\alpha\,S_{t+1}\,e^{-d(n-t-1)}\left|\Phi(d_1(t+1)) - \Phi(d_1(t))\right| \quad (13.33)$$

We show results for the PTP contract described in the section on PTP option valuation. We have assumed a regime-switching lognormal (RSLN) model for the real-world distribution for stock returns, with parameters fitted using the S&P 500 total return index. Hedging is assumed to be rebalanced monthly, using a volatility of $\sigma = 0.20$. The transactions cost rate used is 0.2 percent of the equity transactions each month. All costs are discounted at the risk-free rate of interest of 6 percent per year compounded continuously.

The hedge cost for this contract is $11.567. The average total present value of hedging error is estimated at –$0.01 for the $100 premium, based on 10,000 simulations. The distribution of additional hedging costs—that is, the capital requirements indicated by the simulation over and above the initial hedge costs—are shown in Figure 13.1. When compared with the contracts of previous chapters, the variability of costs is much smaller. This is reasonable because the contract is shorter and being in-the-money most of

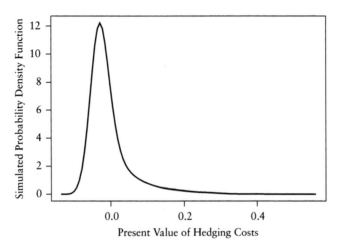

FIGURE 13.1 Simulated density function for hedging costs for seven-year PTP EIA contract with $100 premium.

the time reduces the variability of results, since we are working closer to the middle of the distribution of outcomes. From 10,000 simulated values of the additional expenses of hedging, the maximum cost for a $100 premium was $0.50.

In Chapter 9, we introduced some risk measures, including the quantile (or value at risk) measure and the conditional tail expectation (CTE) measure, which is the average loss given that the loss falls in the tail of the distribution. We also showed why the CTE is a superior measure to the quantile. Applying the CTE risk measure, we find that for the seven-year contract the total costs, including the initial hedge portfolio, have the capital requirements given in Table 13.8. The additional costs are really relatively small, even at the 99 percent CTE level. If the insurer chooses to pass the liability to a third party that uses a volatility of 25 percent for the risk, the cost would be $14.154 for a participation rate of 60 percent, very much

TABLE 13.8 Hedge cost and total capital requirements for seven-year PTP EIA with $100 premium.

Participation Rate	Initial Hedge	$CTE_{90\%}$	$CTE_{95\%}$	$CTE_{99\%}$
60%	11.567	11.709	11.755	11.864
70%	14.290	14.444	14.505	14.629
80%	17.047	17.220	17.288	17.427

greater than the hedge plus additional capital required for the in-house approach, making the in-house option appear attractive (particularly for the PTP, which is a tractable benefit from the option hedging viewpoint).

CONCLUSIONS AND FURTHER READING

In this chapter, we have shown that many EIA contracts can be valued by using basic results from the Black-Scholes-Merton theory of Chapter 7. Using this approach to option valuation is only appropriate if the insurer is calculating the price to purchase the option cover from a third party, or is planning to use a dynamic hedging approach themselves. In the latter case, all the issues surrounding dynamic hedging discussed in Chapter 8 and in subsequent chapters should be considered. In particular, additional capital should be held to allow for hedging error arising from discrete hedging, and from possible variations from the lognormal model of stock prices assumed in the Black-Scholes-Merton framework. For the PTP contract, we have shown that the additional hedging costs are not very onerous.

This chapter has only skimmed the surface of the valuation and management of EIA contracts. The options used are often complex derivatives requiring valuation and management techniques that fall outside the scope of this book. Issues such as averaging require more advanced techniques in financial engineering. The exotic derivatives, such as those embedded in EIA contracts, form the subject matter of a number of books; one that is recommended is Zhang (1998). Tiong (2001) and Lee (2002) value some exotic options that are not precisely those used in EIA contracts, but are similar. However, there is no difference between valuing the option within an EIA contract or outwith the EIA contract, particularly when mortality and lapse issues are not considered. Thus, the key to fully understanding the issues of in-house risk management for EIA contracts is to study the financial engineering of the appropriate exotic derivatives.

Lin and Tan (2002) explore additional issues from annuitization of EIAs, as well as looking at the effect of using stochastic interest rates.

Mortality and Survival Probabilities

In this appendix we give the mortality and survival rates used in the examples in the book. At $t = 0$, the life is assumed to be age 50; time t is in months. Independent withdrawal rates assumed 0.667 percent per month at all ages. Independent mortality rates are from the Canadian Institute of Actuaries male annuitants' mortality rates.

t	$p_{x,t}^\tau$	$_tp_x^\tau$	$_{t|1}q_x^d$	t	$p_{x,t}^\tau$	$_tp_x^\tau$	$_{t|1}q_x^d$
0	0.99307	1.00000	0.00029				
1	0.99307	0.99307	0.00029	45	0.99293	0.72911	0.00031
2	0.99306	0.98618	0.00029	46	0.99292	0.72396	0.00031
3	0.99306	0.97934	0.00029	47	0.99292	0.71883	0.00031
4	0.99306	0.97255	0.00029	48	0.99292	0.71374	0.00031
5	0.99306	0.96580	0.00029	49	0.99291	0.70869	0.00032
6	0.99305	0.95909	0.00029	50	0.99291	0.70366	0.00032
7	0.99305	0.95243	0.00029	51	0.99290	0.69867	0.00032
8	0.99305	0.94581	0.00029	52	0.99290	0.69372	0.00032
9	0.99304	0.93923	0.00029	53	0.99290	0.68879	0.00032
10	0.99304	0.93270	0.00029	54	0.99289	0.68390	0.00032
11	0.99304	0.92621	0.00029	55	0.99289	0.67903	0.00032
12	0.99304	0.91976	0.00029	56	0.99288	0.67420	0.00032
13	0.99303	0.91336	0.00029	57	0.99288	0.66941	0.00032
14	0.99303	0.90700	0.00030	58	0.99287	0.66464	0.00032
15	0.99303	0.90067	0.00030	59	0.99287	0.65990	0.00032
16	0.99302	0.89439	0.00030	60	0.99287	0.65520	0.00032
17	0.99302	0.88816	0.00030	61	0.99286	0.65052	0.00032
18	0.99302	0.88196	0.00030	62	0.99286	0.64588	0.00032
19	0.99302	0.87580	0.00030	63	0.99285	0.64127	0.00032
20	0.99301	0.86968	0.00030	64	0.99285	0.63668	0.00032
21	0.99301	0.86361	0.00030	65	0.99284	0.63213	0.00032
22	0.99301	0.85757	0.00030	66	0.99284	0.62761	0.00033
23	0.99300	0.85157	0.00030	67	0.99283	0.62311	0.00033
24	0.99300	0.84561	0.00030	68	0.99283	0.61865	0.00033
25	0.99300	0.83970	0.00030	69	0.99282	0.61421	0.00033
26	0.99299	0.83382	0.00030	70	0.99282	0.60980	0.00033
27	0.99299	0.82797	0.00030	71	0.99282	0.60542	0.00033
28	0.99299	0.82217	0.00030	72	0.99281	0.60107	0.00033
29	0.99298	0.81640	0.00030	73	0.99281	0.59675	0.00033
30	0.99298	0.81067	0.00031	74	0.99280	0.59246	0.00033
31	0.99298	0.80498	0.00031	75	0.99280	0.58820	0.00033
32	0.99297	0.79933	0.00031	76	0.99279	0.58396	0.00033
33	0.99297	0.79371	0.00031	77	0.99279	0.57975	0.00033
34	0.99297	0.78813	0.00031	78	0.99278	0.57557	0.00033
35	0.99296	0.78259	0.00031	79	0.99278	0.57141	0.00033
36	0.99296	0.77708	0.00031	80	0.99277	0.56728	0.00033
37	0.99296	0.77161	0.00031	81	0.99277	0.56318	0.00033
38	0.99295	0.76618	0.00031	82	0.99276	0.55911	0.00033
39	0.99295	0.76078	0.00031	83	0.99276	0.55506	0.00033
40	0.99295	0.75541	0.00031	84	0.99275	0.55104	0.00033
41	0.99294	0.75008	0.00031	85	0.99274	0.54704	0.00034
42	0.99294	0.74479	0.00031	86	0.99274	0.54307	0.00034
43	0.99293	0.73953	0.00031	87	0.99273	0.53913	0.00034
44	0.99293	0.73430	0.00031	88	0.99273	0.53521	0.00034

t	$p_{x,t}^{\tau}$	$_tp_x^{\tau}$	$_{t|1}q_x^d$	t	$p_{x,t}^{\tau}$	$_tp_x^{\tau}$	$_{t|1}q_x^d$
89	0.99272	0.53132	0.00034	134	0.99242	0.38009	0.00036
90	0.99272	0.52745	0.00034	135	0.99241	0.37721	0.00036
91	0.99271	0.52361	0.00034	136	0.99240	0.37435	0.00036
92	0.99271	0.51980	0.00034	137	0.99240	0.37151	0.00036
93	0.99270	0.51600	0.00034	138	0.99239	0.36868	0.00036
94	0.99269	0.51224	0.00034	139	0.99238	0.36588	0.00036
95	0.99269	0.50850	0.00034	140	0.99237	0.36309	0.00036
96	0.99268	0.50478	0.00034	141	0.99236	0.36032	0.00036
97	0.99268	0.50108	0.00034	142	0.99235	0.35757	0.00036
98	0.99267	0.49742	0.00034	143	0.99235	0.35483	0.00036
99	0.99266	0.49377	0.00034	144	0.99234	0.35212	0.00036
100	0.99266	0.49015	0.00034	145	0.99233	0.34942	0.00036
101	0.99265	0.48655	0.00034	146	0.99232	0.34674	0.00036
102	0.99265	0.48297	0.00034	147	0.99231	0.34407	0.00036
103	0.99264	0.47942	0.00034	148	0.99230	0.34143	0.00036
104	0.99263	0.47589	0.00034	149	0.99229	0.33880	0.00036
105	0.99263	0.47239	0.00035	150	0.99228	0.33619	0.00036
106	0.99262	0.46891	0.00035	151	0.99227	0.33360	0.00036
107	0.99262	0.46545	0.00035	152	0.99227	0.33102	0.00036
108	0.99261	0.46201	0.00035	153	0.99226	0.32846	0.00036
109	0.99260	0.45859	0.00035	154	0.99225	0.32591	0.00036
110	0.99260	0.45520	0.00035	155	0.99224	0.32339	0.00036
111	0.99259	0.45183	0.00035	156	0.99223	0.32088	0.00036
112	0.99258	0.44848	0.00035	157	0.99222	0.31838	0.00036
113	0.99258	0.44515	0.00035	158	0.99221	0.31591	0.00036
114	0.99257	0.44185	0.00035	159	0.99220	0.31345	0.00036
115	0.99256	0.43857	0.00035	160	0.99219	0.31100	0.00036
116	0.99255	0.43530	0.00035	161	0.99218	0.30857	0.00036
117	0.99255	0.43206	0.00035	162	0.99217	0.30616	0.00036
118	0.99254	0.42884	0.00035	163	0.99216	0.30376	0.00036
119	0.99253	0.42564	0.00035	164	0.99215	0.30138	0.00036
120	0.99253	0.42247	0.00035	165	0.99214	0.29901	0.00037
121	0.99252	0.41931	0.00035	166	0.99213	0.29666	0.00037
122	0.99251	0.41617	0.00035	167	0.99212	0.29433	0.00037
123	0.99251	0.41306	0.00035	168	0.99211	0.29201	0.00037
124	0.99250	0.40996	0.00035	169	0.99210	0.28970	0.00037
125	0.99249	0.40689	0.00035	170	0.99209	0.28741	0.00037
126	0.99248	0.40383	0.00035	171	0.99208	0.28514	0.00037
127	0.99248	0.40079	0.00035	172	0.99206	0.28288	0.00037
128	0.99247	0.39778	0.00035	173	0.99205	0.28063	0.00037
129	0.99246	0.39478	0.00035	174	0.99204	0.27840	0.00037
130	0.99245	0.39181	0.00035	175	0.99203	0.27619	0.00037
131	0.99244	0.38885	0.00036	176	0.99202	0.27399	0.00037
132	0.99244	0.38591	0.00036	177	0.99201	0.27180	0.00037
133	0.99243	0.38299	0.00036	178	0.99200	0.26963	0.00037

t	$p_{x,t}^{\tau}$	$_t p_x^{\tau}$	$_{t|1} q_x^d$	t	$p_{x,t}^{\tau}$	$_t p_x^{\tau}$	$_{t|1} q_x^d$
179	0.99199	0.26747	0.00037	224	0.99137	0.18385	0.00037
180	0.99198	0.26533	0.00037	225	0.99135	0.18226	0.00037
181	0.99196	0.26320	0.00037	226	0.99134	0.18069	0.00037
182	0.99195	0.26109	0.00037	227	0.99132	0.17912	0.00037
183	0.99194	0.25898	0.00037	228	0.99131	0.17757	0.00037
184	0.99193	0.25690	0.00037	229	0.99129	0.17602	0.00036
185	0.99192	0.25482	0.00037	230	0.99127	0.17449	0.00036
186	0.99190	0.25276	0.00037	231	0.99125	0.17297	0.00036
187	0.99189	0.25072	0.00037	232	0.99124	0.17146	0.00036
188	0.99188	0.24868	0.00037	233	0.99122	0.16995	0.00036
189	0.99187	0.24666	0.00037	234	0.99120	0.16846	0.00036
190	0.99186	0.24466	0.00037	235	0.99118	0.16698	0.00036
191	0.99184	0.24267	0.00037	236	0.99117	0.16551	0.00036
192	0.99183	0.24069	0.00037	237	0.99115	0.16404	0.00036
193	0.99182	0.23872	0.00037	238	0.99113	0.16259	0.00036
194	0.99181	0.23677	0.00037	239	0.99111	0.16115	0.00036
195	0.99179	0.23483	0.00037	240	0.99110	0.15972	0.00036
196	0.99178	0.23290	0.00037	241	0.99108	0.15830	0.00036
197	0.99177	0.23099	0.00037	242	0.99106	0.15688	0.00036
198	0.99175	0.22908	0.00037	243	0.99104	0.15548	0.00036
199	0.99174	0.22719	0.00037	244	0.99102	0.15409	0.00036
200	0.99173	0.22532	0.00037	245	0.99100	0.15270	0.00036
201	0.99171	0.22345	0.00037	246	0.99098	0.15133	0.00036
202	0.99170	0.22160	0.00037	247	0.99096	0.14996	0.00036
203	0.99169	0.21976	0.00037	248	0.99094	0.14861	0.00036
204	0.99167	0.21793	0.00037	249	0.99092	0.14726	0.00036
205	0.99166	0.21612	0.00037	250	0.99090	0.14593	0.00036
206	0.99164	0.21432	0.00037	251	0.99089	0.14460	0.00036
207	0.99163	0.21253	0.00037	252	0.99087	0.14328	0.00036
208	0.99161	0.21075	0.00037	253	0.99085	0.14197	0.00036
209	0.99160	0.20898	0.00037	254	0.99082	0.14067	0.00036
210	0.99159	0.20722	0.00037	255	0.99080	0.13938	0.00036
211	0.99157	0.20548	0.00037	256	0.99078	0.13810	0.00036
212	0.99156	0.20375	0.00037	257	0.99076	0.13683	0.00036
213	0.99154	0.20203	0.00037	258	0.99074	0.13556	0.00036
214	0.99153	0.20032	0.00037	259	0.99072	0.13431	0.00036
215	0.99151	0.19862	0.00037	260	0.99070	0.13306	0.00035
216	0.99150	0.19694	0.00037	261	0.99068	0.13182	0.00035
217	0.99148	0.19526	0.00037	262	0.99066	0.13060	0.00035
218	0.99147	0.19360	0.00037	263	0.99064	0.12938	0.00035
219	0.99145	0.19195	0.00037	264	0.99061	0.12816	0.00035
220	0.99143	0.19030	0.00037	265	0.99059	0.12696	0.00035
221	0.99142	0.18867	0.00037	266	0.99057	0.12577	0.00035
222	0.99140	0.18706	0.00037	267	0.99055	0.12458	0.00035
223	0.99139	0.18545	0.00037	268	0.99052	0.12340	0.00035

t	$p^\tau_{x,t}$	$_tp^\tau_x$	$_{t|1}q^d_x$	t	$p^\tau_{x,t}$	$_tp^\tau_x$	$_{t|1}q^d_x$
269	0.99050	0.12223	0.00035	315	0.98925	0.07672	0.00032
270	0.99048	0.12107	0.00035	316	0.98922	0.07589	0.00032
271	0.99045	0.11992	0.00035	317	0.98919	0.07508	0.00031
272	0.99043	0.11877	0.00035	318	0.98915	0.07426	0.00031
273	0.99041	0.11764	0.00035	319	0.98912	0.07346	0.00031
274	0.99039	0.11651	0.00035	320	0.98909	0.07266	0.00031
275	0.99036	0.11539	0.00035	321	0.98905	0.07187	0.00031
276	0.99034	0.11428	0.00035	322	0.98902	0.07108	0.00031
277	0.99031	0.11317	0.00035	323	0.98899	0.07030	0.00031
278	0.99029	0.11208	0.00034	324	0.98896	0.06953	0.00031
279	0.99026	0.11099	0.00034	325	0.98892	0.06876	0.00031
280	0.99024	0.10991	0.00034	326	0.98889	0.06800	0.00030
281	0.99021	0.10884	0.00034	327	0.98885	0.06724	0.00030
282	0.99019	0.10777	0.00034	328	0.98881	0.06649	0.00030
283	0.99016	0.10671	0.00034	329	0.98878	0.06575	0.00030
284	0.99014	0.10566	0.00034	330	0.98874	0.06501	0.00030
285	0.99011	0.10462	0.00034	331	0.98871	0.06428	0.00030
286	0.99009	0.10359	0.00034	332	0.98867	0.06355	0.00030
287	0.99006	0.10256	0.00034	333	0.98864	0.06283	0.00030
288	0.99004	0.10154	0.00034	334	0.98860	0.06212	0.00030
289	0.99001	0.10053	0.00034	335	0.98856	0.06141	0.00030
290	0.98998	0.09953	0.00034	336	0.98853	0.06071	0.00029
291	0.98996	0.09853	0.00034	337	0.98849	0.06001	0.00029
292	0.98993	0.09754	0.00034	338	0.98845	0.05932	0.00029
293	0.98990	0.09656	0.00033	339	0.98841	0.05863	0.00029
294	0.98987	0.09558	0.00033	340	0.98837	0.05796	0.00029
295	0.98985	0.09461	0.00033	341	0.98833	0.05728	0.00029
296	0.98982	0.09365	0.00033	342	0.98829	0.05661	0.00029
297	0.98979	0.09270	0.00033	343	0.98826	0.05595	0.00029
298	0.98976	0.09175	0.00033	344	0.98822	0.05529	0.00029
299	0.98974	0.09081	0.00033	345	0.98818	0.05464	0.00028
300	0.98971	0.08988	0.00033	346	0.98814	0.05400	0.00028
301	0.98968	0.08896	0.00033	347	0.98810	0.05336	0.00028
302	0.98965	0.08804	0.00033	348	0.98806	0.05272	0.00028
303	0.98962	0.08713	0.00033	349	0.98802	0.05209	0.00028
304	0.98959	0.08622	0.00033	350	0.98798	0.05147	0.00028
305	0.98956	0.08533	0.00032	351	0.98793	0.05085	0.00028
306	0.98953	0.08443	0.00032	352	0.98789	0.05023	0.00028
307	0.98950	0.08355	0.00032	353	0.98785	0.04963	0.00027
308	0.98947	0.08267	0.00032	354	0.98781	0.04902	0.00027
309	0.98944	0.08180	0.00032	355	0.98776	0.04843	0.00027
310	0.98941	0.08094	0.00032	356	0.98772	0.04783	0.00027
311	0.98938	0.08008	0.00032	357	0.98768	0.04725	0.00027
312	0.98935	0.07923	0.00032	358	0.98764	0.04666	0.00027
313	0.98932	0.07839	0.00032	359	0.98759	0.04609	0.00027
314	0.98928	0.07755	0.00032	360	0.98755	0.04551	0.00027

The GMAB Option Price

L et H_{t_k} denote the random payout at t_k under the guaranteed minimum accumulation benefit (GMAB) option; t_k are the renewal dates. We assume two renewals at t_1 and t_2 and maturity at t_3, though clearly this can be adapted to more renewals. The start date is $t_0 = 0$.

The segregated fund at t is F_t; the underlying stock price process is S_t. F_t and S_t differ because of the management charge and because of any injections of cash into the segregated fund required at renewal dates. The annual charge is $100m$ percent compounded continuously. At the renewal and maturity dates, if the fund has fallen below the previous renewal date value, the fund is increased to that value. $F_{t_k^-}$ represents the value of the segregated fund immediately before renewal and $F_{t_k^+}$ immediately after renewal. That is, let H_{t_k} denote the payout under the GMAB at time t_k, then

$$F_{t_k^-} = F_{t_{k-1}^+} \frac{S_{t_k}}{S_{t_{k-1}}} e^{-m(t_k - t_{k-1})}$$

$$F_{t_k^+} = F_{t_k^-} + H_{t_k}$$

$P(S, K, n)$ denotes the price for a European put option, with stock price S, strike K and remaining term n years. K_0 is the initial guarantee; F_0 is the initial segregated fund. Using the notation of Chapter 8, we let

$$P(t) = P(e^{-mt}, 1, t)$$

and

$$P_{S_0}(t) = P(S_0 e^{-mt}, K_0, t)$$

The option price for the GMAB option is:

$$E_Q[H_{t_1} e^{-rt_1} + H_{t_2} e^{-rt_2} + H_{t_3} e^{-rt_3}]$$

271

Clearly

$$E_Q[H_{t_1} e^{-rt_1}] = P_{S_0}(t_1)$$

Also

$$
\begin{aligned}
E_Q[H_{t_2} e^{-rt_2}] &= E_Q[E_Q[H_{t_2} e^{-rt_2} | F_{t_1^+}]] \\
&= E_Q[F_{t_1^+} e^{-rt_1} P(t_2 - t_1)] \\
&= E_Q[(F_{t_1^-} + H_{t_1}) e^{-rt_1}] P(t_2 - t_1) \\
&= (S_0 e^{-mt_1} + P_{S_0}(t_1)) P(t_2 - t_1)
\end{aligned}
$$

And, similarly,

$$
\begin{aligned}
E_Q[H_{t_3} e^{-rt_3}] &= E_Q[E_Q[H_{t_3} e^{-rt_3} | F_{t_2^+}]] \\
&= E_Q[F_{t_2^+} e^{-rt_2}] P(t_3 - t_2) \\
&= E_Q[(F_{t_2^-} + H_{t_2}) e^{-rt_2}] P(t_3 - t_2) \\
&= \{E_Q[F_{t_1^+} e^{-m(t_2 - t_1) - rt_1}] + E_Q[H_{t_2} e^{-rt_2}]\} P(t_3 - t_2) \\
&= \{E_Q[(F_{t_1^-} + H_{t_1}) e^{-rt_1}] e^{-m(t_2 - t_1)} + E_Q[H_{t_2} e^{-rt_2}]\} P(t_3 - t_2) \\
&= \{S_0 e^{-mt_2} + E_Q[H_{t_1} e^{-rt_1}] e^{-m(t_2 - t_1)} + E_Q[H_{t_2} e^{-rt_2}]\} P(t_3 - t_2) \\
&= \{S_0 e^{-mt_2} + e^{-m(t_2 - t_1)} P_{S_0}(t_1) \\
&\quad + (S_0 e^{-mt_1} + P_{S_0}(t_1)) P(t_2 - t_1))\} P(t_3 - t_2)
\end{aligned}
$$

This gives a total option price of

$$
P_{S_0}(t_1) + (S_0 e^{-mt_1} + P_{S_0}(t_1))(1 + P(t_3 - t_2))P(t_2 - t_1)
$$
$$
+ P(t_3 - t_2)(S_0 e^{-mt_2} + e^{-m(t_2 - t_1)} P_{S_0}(t_1))
$$

Actuarial Notation

We have generally used standard actuarial notation in this book, with the exception that we are generally measuring term and duration in months. Standard actuarial notation uses the following conventions:

$_tp_x$ is the probability that a life currently aged x survives to age $x + t$.

$_tq_x$ is the probability that a life currently aged x dies before age $x + t$.

$\mu_{x,t}$ is the force of mortality at age $x + t$ for a life currently age x. The force of mortality is also known as the mortality transition intensity or hazard rate. It is defined as

$$-\frac{1}{_tp_x}\frac{d}{dt}\,_tp_x$$

$\ddot{a}_{x:\overline{n}|}$ is the expected present value of an annuity of 1 per time unit, paid at the start of each time unit until the life age x dies, or until n time units expire, whichever is sooner. For an interest rate of r, continuously compounded, the equation for the annuity is

$$\ddot{a}_{x:\overline{n}|} = \sum_{t=0}^{n-1} {_tp_x}\, e^{-rt}$$

The force of interest is the continuously compounded interest rate.

v is the annual discount factor; for a force of interest r, $v = e^{-r}$.

T_x is the random future lifetime of a life currently aged x years.

In this book we have used these symbols adapted to allow for the two decrements, death and withdrawal. The superscript τ indicates that both decrements are allowed for; d indicates decrement by death and w indicates decrements by withdrawal. The specific notation used is
it is assumed to take the value $t = 1.0$.

$_tp_{x,u}^{\tau}$ is the probability that a policyholder currently aged x years and u months survives and does not withdraw for a further t months.

$_tq_{x,u}^{\tau}$ is $1 - {_tp_{x,u}^{\tau}}$.

$_tq_x^{w}$ is the probability that a policyholder currently aged x years withdraws before t months expire.

$_tq_x^{d}$ is the probability that a policyholder currently aged x years dies in force before t months expire.

$_{u|t}q_x^{d}$ is the probability that a policyholder aged x years is still in force after u months, but dies in force before the expiry of a further t months. If the t is omitted, it is assumed to take the value $t = 1.0$.

$_tq_x^{\tau}$ is the probability that a policyholder aged x years dies or lapses the policy before t months expire.

$\mu_{x,t}^{(d)}$ is the force of mortality experienced by a life aged x years and t months.

$\ddot{a}_{x:\overline{n}|i'}^{\tau}$ is the value of an annuity of 1 per month paid monthly in advance for n months, contingent on the survival, in force (the τ indicates the double decrement function), of a life age x. The rate of interest is i' per month, which means that the discount factor for the payment due at t is $(1 + i')^{-t}$.

References

Akaike, H. (1974). A new look at statistical model identification. *IEEE Trans Aut Control,* **19,** 716–723.

Annuity Guarantee Working Party (AGWP). (1997). *Reserving for Annuity Guarantees.* Published by the Faculty of Actuaries and Institute of Actuaries.

Artzner, P., Delbaen, F., Eber, J.-M., & Heath, D. (1997, November). Thinking coherently. *RISK,* **10,** 68–71.

Artzner, P., Delbaen, F., Eber, J.-M., & Heath, D. (1999). Coherent measures of risk. *Mathematical Finance,* **9**(3), 203–228.

Bacinello, G., & Ortu, F. (1993). Pricing equity-linked life insurance with endogenous minimum guarantees. *Insurance: Mathematics and Economics,* **12,** 245–257.

Bakshi G., Cao, C., & Chen, Z. (1999). Pricing and hedging long-term options. *Journal of Econometrics,* **94,** 277–183.

Black, F., & Scholes, M., (1973). The pricing of options and corporate liabilities. *Journal of Political Economy,* **81,** 637–654.

Bollen, N. P. B. (1998). Valuing options in regime switching models. *Journal of Derivatives,* **6,** 38–49.

Bollerslev, T. (1986). Generalized autoregressive conditional heteroskedasticity. *Journal of Econometrics,* **31,** 307–327.

Boyle, P. P. (1977). Options: A Monte Carlo approach. *Journal of Financial Economics,* **4**(4), 323–338.

Boyle, P. P., & Boyle, F. P. (2001). *Derivatives: The tools that changed finance.* United Kingdom: Risk Books.

Boyle, P. P., Broadie, M., & Glasserman, P. (1997). Monte Carlo methods for security pricing. *Journal of Economic Dynamics and Control,* **21,** 1267–1321.

Boyle, P. P., Cox, S., Dufresne, D., Gerber, H., Mueller, H., Pedersen, H., Pliska, S., Sherris, M., Shiu, E., Tan, K. S. (1998). *Financial economics.* Chicago: The Actuarial Foundation.

Boyle, P. P. & Emmanuel, D. (1980). Discretely adjusted option hedges. *Journal of Financial Economics,* **8,** 259–282.

Boyle, P. P., & Hardy, M. R. (1996). Reserving for maturity guarantees (96-18). Ontario, Canada: University of Waterloo, Institute for Insurance and Pensions Research.

Boyle, P. P., & Hardy, M. R. (1998). Reserving for maturity guarantees: Two approaches. *Insurance: Mathematics and Economics, 21*, 113–127.

Boyle, P. P., & Schwartz, E. S. (1977). Equilibrium prices of guarantees under equity-linked contracts. *Journal of Risk and Insurance, 44*(4), 639–660.

Boyle, P. P., Siu, T. K., & Yang, H. (2002). A two level binomial tree for risk measurement. *Research Report 325*. University of Hong Kong, Dept. of Statistics and Actuarial Science.

Boyle, P. P., & Tan, K. S. (2002). Valuation of ratchet options (02). Ontario, Canada: University of Waterloo, Institute for Insurance and Pensions Research.

Boyle P. P., & Tan, K. S. (2003). *Quasi Monte Carlo methods with applications to actuarial science.* Monograph sponsored by Actuarial Education and Research Fund; Forthcoming.

Boyle, P. P., & Vorst, T. (1992). Option replication in discrete time with transaction costs. *Journal of Finance, 47*(1), 271–294.

Brennan, M. J., & Schwartz, E. S., (1976). The pricing of equity-linked life insurance policies with an asset value guarantee. *Journal of Financial Economics, 3*, 195–213.

Cairns, A. J. G., (2000). A discussion of parameter and model uncertainty in insurance. *Insurance: Mathematics and Economics, 27*, 313–330.

Campbell, J. Y., Lo, A. W., & MacKinlay, A. C. (1996). *The econometrics of financial markets.* Princeton, NJ: Princeton University Press.

Canadian Institute of Actuaries. (1999). Call for papers. Symposium on stochastic modelling for variable annuity/segregated fund investment guarantees. Canadian Institute of Actuaries.

Chambers, J. M., Mallows, C. L., & Stuck, B. W. (1976). A method for simulating stable random variables. *Journal of the American Statistical Association, 71*, 340–344.

Chan, T. (1998). Some applications of Levy processes to stochastic investment models for actuarial use. *ASTIN Bulletin, 28*, 77–93.

Cox, J., Ingersoll, J., and Ross, S. (1985). A theory of the term structure of interest rates. *Econometrica, 53*, 385–487.

David, H. A. (1981). *Order statistics* (2nd ed.) New York: Wiley.

Engle, R. F. (1982). Autoregressive conditional heteroscedasticity with estimates of the variance of united kingdom inflation. *Econometrica, 50*, 987–1006.

Exley, J., & Mehta, S. (2000, March). Asset models and the Ballard-Mehta stochastic investment model. Presented to the Conference in Honour of David Wilkie, Heriot-Watt University.

Faculty of Actuaries Solvency Working Party. (1986). The solvency of life insurance companies. *Transactions of the Faculty of Actuaries, 39,* 251.

Finkelstein, G. (1995). Maturity guarantees revisited. *British Actuarial Journal,* 3(2), 411–482.

French, K. R., Schwert, G. W., & Stambaugh, R. F. (1987). *Journal of Financial Economics,* 19, 3–29.

Gerber, H. U. (1979). *An introduction to mathematical risk theory.* Huebner Foundation Monograph No. 8. Philadelphia: University of Pennsylvania, Wharton School.

Gilks, W. R., Richardson, S., & Spiegelhalter, D. J. (Eds.). (1996). *Markov chain Monte Carlo in practice.* London: Chapman and Hall/CRC.

Hamilton, J. D. (1989). A new approach to the economic analysis of non-stationary time series. *Econometrica,* 57, 357–384.

Hamilton, J. D., & Susmel, R. (1994). Autoregressive conditional heteroskedasticity and changes in regime. *Journal of Econometrics,* 64, 307–333.

Hancock, G. H. (2001). Policy liabilities using stochastic valuation methods. Canadian Institute of Actuaries Segregated Fund Symposium.

Hancock, G. H. (2002). Private communication.

Hardy, M. R. (1998). Maturity guarantees for segregated fund contracts; hedging and reserving (98-07). Ontario, Canada: University of Waterloo, Institute for Insurance and Pensions Research.

Hardy, M. R. (1999). Stock return models for segregated fund investment guarantees (99-12). Ontario, Canada: University of Waterloo, Institute for Insurance and Pensions Research.

Hardy, M. R. (2001). A regime switching model of long term stock returns. *North American Actuarial Journal,* 5(2), 41–53.

Hardy, M. R. (2002). Bayesian risk management for equity-linked insurance. *Scandinavian Actuarial Journal,* 3, 185–211.

Hardy, M. R., & Hardy, P. G. (2002). Regime switching lognormal model (rsln.xls). Excel workbook available from www.soa.org.

Harris, G. R. (1999). Markov chain Monte Carlo estimation of regime switching vector autoregressions. *ASTIN Bulletin,* 29, 47–80.

Huber, P. P. (1997). A review of Wilkie's stochastic asset model. *British Actuarial Journal,* 3, 181–210.

Hull, J. C. (1989). *Options futures and other derivative securities.* New Jersey: Prentice Hall.

Klugman, S. A., Panjer, H. H., & Willmot, G. E. (1998). *Loss models; From data to decisions.* New York: Wiley.

Kolkiewicz, W. A., & Tan, K. S. (1999). Unit linked life insurance contracts with lapse rates depending on economic factors (99-09). Ontario, Canada: University of Waterloo, Institute for Insurance and Pensions Research.

Lee, H. (2002). Pricing equity-indexed annuities embedded with exotic options. *Contingencies,* Jan/Feb 2002, 34–38.

Leland, H. (1995). Option pricing and replication with transactions costs. *Journal of Finance,* 40, 1283–1301.

Lin, X. S., & Tan, K. S. (2002). Valuation of equity-indexed annuities under stochastic interest rates (02). Ontario, Canada: University of Waterloo, Institute for Insurance and Pensions Research.

Manistre, B. J., & Hancock, G. H. (2002). Variance of the CTE estimator. Working paper, MMC Enterprise Risk Consulting, Toronto.

Maturity Guarantees Working Party (MGWP). (1980). *Journal of the Institute of Actuaries,* 107, 103–209.

McCulloch, J. H. (1996). Financial applications of stable distributions. *Handbook of Statistics,* 14, 393–425.

Merton, R. C. (1973). Theory of rational option pricing. *Bell Journal of Economics and Management Science,* 4, 141–183.

Morgan, M. S. (1990). *The history of econometric ideas.* Cambridge: Cambridge University Press.

Nolan, J. P. (1998). Parameterization and modes of stable distributions. *Statistics and Probability Letters,* 38, 187–195.

Nolan, J. P. (2000). Information on stable distributions. [On-line]. Available: http://www.cas.american.edu/jpnolan/stable.html.

Nonnemacher, D. J. F., & Russ, J. (1997). Equity linked life insurance in Germany: Quantifying the risk of additional policy reserves. *Proceedings of the 7th AFIR conference, Cairns,* 719–738.

Pagan, A. R., & Schwert, G. W. (1990). Alternative models for conditional stock volatility. *Journal of Econometrics,* 45, 267–290.

Panjer, H. H., & Sharp, K. P. (1998). Report on Canadian Economic Statistics. Canadian Institute of Actuaries.

Panjer, H. H., & Tan, K. S. (1995). Graduation of Canadian individual insurance mortality experience: 1986–1992. Canadian Institute of Actuaries.

Panneton, C.-M.(1999). The impact of the distribution of stock market returns on the cost of the segregated fund long term guarantees. *Segregated Funds Symposium Proceedings.* Canadian Institute of Actuaries.

Pelsser, A. (2002). Pricing and hedging guaranteed annuity options via static option replication. Working Paper, Erasmus University at Rotterdam, Netherlands. [On-line]. Available: http://www.few.eur.nl/few/people/pelsser.

Persson, S.-A., & Aase, K. (1994). Valuation of the minimum guaranteed return embedded in life insurance products. *Journal of Risk and Insurance,* 64(4), 599–617.

Press, W. H., Teukolsky, S. A., Vetterling, W. T., & Flannery, B. P. (1992). *Numerical recipes in C.* Cambridge: Cambridge University Press.

Roberts, G. O. (1996). Markov chain concepts related to sampling algorithms. In Gilks, W. R., Richardson, S., & Spiegelhalter, D. J. (Eds.). *Markov chain Monte carlo in practice* (pp. 45–57). London: Chapman and Hall/CRC.

Ross, S. M. (1996). *Simulation.* San Francisco: Morgan Kaufmann Publishers.

Schwartz, G. (1978). Estimating the dimension of a model. *Annals of Statistics*, 6, 461–464.

Segregated Funds Task Force (SFTF). (2002). *Report of the Task Force on Segregated Fund Investment Guarantees.* Canadian Institute of Actuaries. [On-line]. Available: http://www.actuaries.ca/publications/2002/202012e.pdf

Streiff, T. F., & DiBiase, C. A. (1999). *Equity indexed annuities.* Dearborn Financial Publishing, USA.

Tiong, S. (2001). Valuing equity-indexed annuities. *North American Actuarial Journal*, 4(4), 149–170.

Wang, S. X. (1995). Insurance pricing and increased limits ratemaking by proportional hazard transforms. *Insurance: Mathematics and Economics*, 17, 43–54.

Webber, N., & James, J. (2000). *Interest rate modelling: Financial engineering.* London: Wiley.

Wilkie, A. D. (1986). A stochastic investment model for actuarial use. *Transactions of the Faculty of Actuaries*, 39, 341–381.

Wilkie, A. D. (1995). More on a stochastic asset model for actuarial use. *British Actuarial Journal*, 1 (V), 777–964.

Windcliffe, H., Le Roux, M., Forsythe, P., Vetzal, K. (2002). Understanding the behavior and hedging of segregated funds offering the reset feature. *North American Actuarial Journal*, 6(2), 107–124.

Windcliffe, H., Forsythe, P., Vetzal, K. (2001). Valuation of segregated funds shout options with maturity extensions. *Insurance: Mathematics and Economics*, 29, 1–21.

Wirch, J. L., & Hardy, M. R. (1999). A synthesis of risk measures for capital adequacy. *Insurance: Mathematics and Economics*, 25, 337–347.

Wright, I. D. (1997). *A stochastic approach to pension scheme funding and asset allocation.* Ph.D. thesis, Heriot-Watt University, Edinburgh, Scotland.

Yang, S. (2001). *Reserving, pricing and hedging for guaranteed annuity options.* Ph.D. thesis, Heriot-Watt University, Edinburgh, Scotland.

Zhang, P. G. (1998). *Exotic options: A guide to second generation options* (2nd Ed.). River Edge, NJ: World Scientific Publishing Company.

Index

CPSIA information can be obtained at www.ICGtesting.com
Printed in the USA
LVOW07*0034071213

364256LV00001B/1/A